Signs of the Heart

CHRISTOPHER HOPE was born in Johannesburg. He has published seven novels: *A Separate Development* (winner of the 1981 David Higham Prize for Fiction), *Kruger's Alp* (winner of the 1985 Whitbread Prize for Fiction), *The Hottentot Room* (1986), *My Chocolate Redeemer* (1989), *Serenity House* (shortlisted for the 1992 Booker Prize), *Darkest England* (1996) and *Me, the Moon and Elvis Presley* (1997). He has written two other works of non-fiction: *White Boy Running* (winner of the 1998 CNA Literary Award in South Africa) and *Moscow! Moscow!* (1990).

ALSO BY CHRISTOPHER HOPE

Novels

A Separate Development
Kruger's Alp
The Hottentot Room
My Chocolate Redeemer
Serenity House
Darkest England
Me, the Moon and Elvis Presley

Shorter Fiction

Learning to Fly and Other Tales (Stories)
Black Swan (Novella)
The Love Songs of Nathan J. Swirsky (Stories)

Non-fiction

White Boy Running
Moscow! Moscow!

Poetry

Cape Drives
In the Country of the Black Pig
Englishmen

For Children

The King, the Cat and the Fiddle
The Dragon Wore Pink

CHRISTOPHER HOPE

Signs of the Heart

Love and Death in Languedoc

PICADOR

First published 1999 by Macmillan

This edition published 2000 by Picador
an imprint of Macmillan Publishers Ltd
25 Eccleston Place, London SW1W 9NF
Basingstoke and Oxford
Associated companies throughout the world
www.macmillan.co.uk

ISBN 0 330 36704 8

1 3 5 7 9 8 6 4 2

A CIP catalogue record for this book is available from
the British Library.

Phototypeset by Intype London Ltd
Printed and bound in Great Britain by
Mackays of Chatham plc, Chatham, Kent

Les grandes pensées viennent du coeur.
Marquis de Vauvenargues

For Carmen, Liz
&
the King of the Clocks

Acknowledgements

Material from Chapters 5, 6, 10, 16, in revised form, was first broadcast on BBC Radio 4, in 1996, as 'Love and Death in Languedoc'. 'Death in the Midi' was published in the *Independent* in 1997. The account of 'God, My Neighbour' first appeared in the *Daily Telegraph* in 1997. An adaption of Chapter 20 was published in BBC Music in 1998 as 'La Fanfare'.

This is not a guidebook. Kissac is not simply a place, it's a heartland. Kissac is a mixture of villages I know and love in Languedoc. And from the people I know I have taken a cast and peopled Kissac. I have changed the names of the living and the dead – except in the case of God. She is, was, will be – Sophie Magdalena, and I remember her with awe.

CHAPTER I

I CAN THINK of many reasons why I came to the Midi, to this stretch of Languedoc between the Black Mountains and the sea. Good reasons, convincing reasons – and they are all wrong.

There is no rationality to be discerned. How could there be? No careful reconstruction of motive will do because it does not go to the heart of the matter. I landed here because I got lost. It was an accident, a rush of blood to the head.

Or maybe it was luck. The King of the Clocks says you make your luck. Lizzie from Lézignan says luck is a British thing; and childless Madame de la Pipe, who plies her trade along the canal, says luck is what a mother gives the child she loves. Thierry believes luck is nonsense, what you have is genius, or nothing – but that's Thierry for you.

So let's say that luck and sadness carried me here, together with some vague gravitational urge to attach myself, like an errant moon, to some larger, better body.

At about this time I fell in love. Colette says somewhere that she always spent her wars in Paris. In some way, I seem always to go to France to have my love affairs. Somehow it serves, it suits; there I go to put things, and myself, to rights. In my book, France does well by lovers on the run

– and exiles. And they sometimes amount to the same thing. It is a heartland – a country without borders, it offers travel without papers, asylum without questions.

Now there will be those who point out that this is absurd, and France, far from being a haven for the homeless, is a fiercely policed hexagon, determined to keep strangers out. And they would be right. But they should read no further – this book is not for them. I do not care what France is 'really' like, any more than I care what life is 'really' like – that is a matter for the police or book-keepers. What intrigues me is why some places should serve; ideal heartlands, where one is well, whose gift is to receive and cherish, for reasons unknown, lovers and exiles and, it should be said, the sad and demented. No doubt we invent these heartlands: that is why we are at home in them – even if we cannot say exactly how we got there. Even if we've never been there. I was on what I might call kissing terms with France years before I set foot in the place.

When I was about thirteen I spent a lot of time kissing a girl called Mary, and we liked it. But one Saturday morning her mother invited me for a drive in her seal-grey Opel Record and gave me a little talk about 'French kissing'.

She said the words with such force that she seemed quite shocked by her own daring and never used the phrase again. She skirted around it – part of an entire universe of undesirable things that you 'gave way to' and 'indulged in' and 'bitterly regretted'. The exploring tongue, germs, passion. Everything was against it – hygiene, morals, even semantics . . .

It was the first I'd heard of it. I wanted to know more

but it didn't seem the time to ask her. Instead I asked about love.

She made it clear she had nothing against love. 'I'm a Christian Scientist. We believe God is love.'

Mary's mother was a big woman, wearing a lot of face powder – and she spoke clearly. There is something frightening about careful enunciation in sharp sunlight in the middle of the morning. I had the sinking feeling that if God was love then I was in deep trouble because, like Mary's mother, He considered the sort of kissing Mary and I liked to be part of some wider wickedness, a foreign conspiracy.

'It's the French form,' said Mary's mother. 'You never know what it leads to.'

It was the sort of thing you saw in gangster movies, someone got taken for a little ride and warned off. Except Mary's mother didn't hire a hit man, she was the heavy. She had a way of leaning forward so that her talcum powder floated off her upper lip in little clouds. I remember the smell of sunlight on vinyl seats. I remember feeling beaten up. What a gang! God and the Opel, vinyl and sunlight, Mary's mother – and love. It's odd to be roughed up in a theology class, in the front seat of an Opel. I didn't have a clue what she meant. But I knew this. I was not at home in the air she breathed.

Then she made me promise never to see her daughter again – and dropped me miles from anywhere and I had to walk home. It's hard to walk anywhere with a broken heart. I swore a vow then: if the French did it – kissing, cheese, leave, letters or mustard – then it was fine by me.

And when my uncle Basil swore loudly and said,

'Excuse my French,' I thought to myself: 'What's to excuse?'
And took off, if you see what I mean, for France.

* * *

South Africa was my other great love affair – messy, painful
and full of people ready to take you for a little ride, if you
didn't get the message.

Some years after losing to Mary's mother, I had a run-
in with the Minister of Internal Affairs. An avuncular brute
– who refused to issue me with a passport: then a standard
way of bullying people. I wrote him an angry letter pointing
out that I would, like so many South Africans, get another.
The Minister told me he was revoking my citizenship. I
was almost thirty; I'd never never set foot out of Africa.
I was granted an exit visa and I flew to Paris, never expecting
to return.

I might have been on the moon. Gravity decreased
dizzyingly, Paris seemed weightless; I had trouble keeping
my feet on the ground. It wasn't a trip, it was a space walk.
Anyone who has lived under autocrats will know what I
mean; they have the weight of mountains, and use it to
sit on you. They are in love with rationalities, proofs,
mechanisms; they possess the adiposity of elephants, and
the mean minds of cultists, pragmatists, bookkeepers; they
are cheerful sadists addicted to facts, figures, conclusions,
systems – and that terrible thing called 'good sense'. They
will kill to make a point; so fat, so gorged on their own
convictions, so reasonable, so horribly 'sound', so sincere
that the religious fanatic in all his willingness to fry you
alive to save your soul is a child beside them.

I checked into a small hotel on the Left Bank, called

the At Home – nothing could have been further from it – and I wandered along the Seine like a man drugged. It was summer and the crowds flowed like water down the rue de Seine and through the Luxembourg Gardens. I had just one address, that of a fellow called Donald, a teacher at the Sorbonne. I got a taxi and went to see him.

Somewhere in the city, the door of a posh apartment opened to my knock, all honeyed panels and shining parquet, and a sharp-eyed, quizzical woman looked at me as if I had just climbed out of a tree. In a sense, exactly what I had done.

I asked for Donald. She said he wasn't there. I asked where he was and she said she very much hoped he was dead.

Only later, when I found him camped in a garret in the rue de Seine, did I realize that Donald was going through one of his divorces. Bourgeois life had got to him, and so, very much in the spirit of the times, he absconded to a garret on the Left Bank. He was in the wars, his wife was magnificent in attack, but he was entirely charming about it. He took me off to buy lunch. A handful of olives, a tomato or two, bread, wine, cheese; then he laid the table under the skylight and we ate.

The lunch remains with me still; the light from the murky skylight fell on the table, modest and perfect, it had all the glow of a good painting, all the solidity of a still life; the tomatoes throbbed, the olives took on that strangely secretive look of good black olives, the cheese melted, the bread scattered crumbs.

I must have eaten that lunch. I am not among those who believe art comes first. Meat first, then dreams, I say.

And yet – that meal lasts better in my heart, is more interesting, looking back, than it could have been, in what we must laughingly call 'real life'. I have always remembered its healing powers. In Paris, on that first brief visit, I began listening to the stories the way a child listens; certainly I knew as little as a child. I watched the old fencing master, in his skullcap, so thin he slid around the corner like a bannister; Les Halles and its noise and its whores; and the last surviving mistress of Raymond Duncan, her clogs pattering in the courtyard, a plump druid in her long white woven tunic.

Like French kissing it brought on a state of receptive desire, in a good, secret place. How Mary's mother would have hated it. I got that sense of physical well-being – arousal might be the word – which I began to feel in my early life as a listener, sitting in a warm room with my grandfather, listening to story after story. Love and stories? Or is it that love *is* stories – certainly, they make for a kind of love life – with this difference: stories are fictions we tell others. Love is a story we tell ourselves.

* * *

Six years ago, I landed in Toulouse with a scrap of paper in my pocket. On the paper was the name of a village about an hour away: 'Kissac'. But the directions on my piece of paper were terse: 'Follow Barcelona' . . .

I rented a car and hit the autoroute.

Toulouse was old pink brick and pretty squares, and lots of unapologetic hustle. There was no diminuendo about Toulouse. This wasn't fancy France; this was high-tech country; the new road curving out of the airport absolutely swanked of it. This place was in a hurry and it enjoyed the rush.

I passed a motorway museum dedicated to rugby – and memory began to trouble me like a bad knee, or an old wound; somehow this place, plus rugby, looked like the French equivalent of that fabled wild west of South Africa, the mad remote country of the Karoo, where real men spent time kicking around the rugby-ball, or the staff, when they weren't shooting animals, their wives, and each other.

In the tatty motorway shop on the Autoroute Entre Deux Mers, watching clients shoving their plastic cups into the coffee dispenser, like punters in some dead-end casino, I got the feeling this was France, only in a manner of speaking: sans *haute couture* or *grande cuisine*; this place preferred shell suits; it ate *steak-frites*; it thought the *haute* and *grande* of Paris a pain in the backside. This was take-it-or-leave-it France, less chic than this you could not find in France – and if you didn't like it, this was to-hell-with-you France.

The green country ran from Castelnaudary to Bram; then the vineyards rushed up like infantry and swarmed over everything. Over to my right the icy heads of the Pyrenees made a nice line.

'Turn south,' they said, 'you can be in Barcelona for lunch.'

After Bram the country got drier, chalkier, and vines ran all the way to the horizon. The little villages I was passing through, with houses of stone the colour of caramel, and naked bells on the church roof and bleak cement walls, were islands in a vast wine-lake.

I overshot Carcassonne. Across the fields, there rose up

shimmering turrets, battlements and steeples, a medieval fortress on a hill – the storeyed outlines of La Cité. When I swung off the autoroute the mirage vanished and I was lost among the blurred and bleary suburbs of modern Carcassonne, scored with the allotments and billboards. And again came that curious feeling of relief; the tacky suburbs of the real Carcassonne, after the shining city on the hill.

I got lost briefly in Trèbes, a warty little place on a beautiful stretch of river, and some half an hour later, I stumbled on Kissac by accident, going in the wrong direction, something I have done ever since. I headed downhill and was decanted – that is what happens, the road rolls you down and plunges you – into the medieval village which hugs the hollow, where the old Priory rises above every roof.

The stone was golden, the look Tuscan; the little *ruelles* were so narrow the house corners shaved my fenders, and only up by the Port de Narbonne, where the public wash-house stood, did I squeeze my way to the main road, and popped out of the village, like a cork from a bottle.

I found signs to the chapel and I knew the farm stood nearby. Down a rutted track, which I chose equally blindly, I bumped between cherry orchards and came to a stretch of grass, a stream at the bottom of the garden, an orchard of apples, and a stone house in a valley, surrounded by woods of pine on the mountain slopes. It was a shock to realize I'd found it.

The bedroom floated at the top of the house; it held a big square bed, old and yellowed; muslin was draped across the window and filtered the light rather as one might do milk. On the window ledge sat a small brass sign inscribed: INSPECTOR OF WEIGHTS AND MEASURES.

Inspector of what? Weights, truffles, caviare, flesh? And of whose measures? I never did discover. But the joke was good because precisely nothing weighed in that room; on the contrary it was always bumping against the rafters like a balloon; so likely to float away that it had been anchored to a solid bathroom of old terracotta tiles, dark blue candles, chipped gilt mirrors, a bead curtain across the lavatory, and a heavy cast-iron bath on four fat paws.

CHAPTER 2

I STAYED IN the farmhouse for about a month.

Walking to the Chapel of Our Lady Under the Mountain, I followed the path up the hill to the old quarry on the peak, a big hole gouged in the hill's head. Achingly empty. Its sheer, squared-off sides make it a natural amphitheatre. Steel cables stretched across the rock face in some lilliputian effort to tie down the mountain: here and there the cables had snapped, and dangled like frayed nerves.

Pink marble had been quarried here for centuries. The colour was ruddy, like streaky bacon. Or it could look like measles; like strawberries and cream. Or rump steak marbled with fat. It was often buffed to a high gleam, and used for altar rails and baptismal fonts. I like it unpolished – fingernail pink. When it weathered it flaked and crumbled like rosy cheese.

Pine, dwarf oak and brambles, and muddy vineyards that October; a crouched silence on the higher, wooded slopes and at almost every second step, red or green brass and plastic casings of shotgun shells. Shooting country.

The Lady Chapel under the mountain had been restored several times; there was a fading *Madonna* in a niche at the chapel door: the sculptor had fixed on proportions that are rudimentary – and perfect; the plump peasant mother is as round as a loaf, and cradles her baby with a wonderfully natural affection. She's been placed behind a grille for her own protection; her cult is long gone in these hills.

I was not alone on the farm; there was sad-eyed Cyrille, the *gardien*, dark, sallow as old wax, and as grasping a man as you could ever meet. The face of a martyr and the greed of a leech. The stream in the garden muttering and Cyrille sighing. Standing watch, as certain the world was crooked as only a crooked man can be. Convinced the house was under siege by thieves of every stripe. He'd surprised a tramp asleep in the bedroom; little boys who fished the stream without permission; strangers who stole cherries.

No one knew where he lived; no one knew how he knew. Did he have a tree house, a mountain-top hide? Spies, scouts, tripwires? Infra-red detectors among the vines, closed-circuit cameras in the cherry orchard? Where did he watch from? No hut or house or dwelling overlooked the farm. But let anyone set foot in the place and five minutes later Cyrille was bouncing down the rocky, dangerous driveway in his tinny old Peugeot, the fan belt shrieking – hooting to scatter the nervous intruders.

He took a dismal view of the house: it was full of pictures of parrots, and angels and books, and he really didn't see the point. Besides, it was liable to flood and in the rain the electricity supply was uncertain; he muttered and complained and overcharged; foreigners were mad but they were rich and one was forced to work for them. He kept in the garage (the only part of the house he really liked because it was new and did not leak) his garden tools, and a *remorque*, a little wooden handcart that rode on skinny pram wheels, rather beautiful in its spidery grace, like an old penny-farthing.

Cyrille said, 'It belonged to my great-grandfather.'

He stared at the *remorque* sadly, as if unsure what to do with it. Loyal, unrecompensed, sad, beautiful, rare, lost, overlooked, inimitable, irreplaceable, undervalued.

'No one makes things like this any more.' And he jabbed his thumb into his chest.

I'd meet him as I walked through the fields. He looked at the mud thick on my boots. 'If you go on like that, the weight will wear you down and you'll come to a stop.'

I saw myself with boots the size of boulders, so heavy with mud from the vineyards that I stuck fast for ever.

Then I began to understand; it was Cyrille who was weighed down. Heavy with watching, waiting, fearing.

One night an entire detachment of the paratroop regiment from Carcassonne pitched up in the garden, and Cyrille stayed away. Trainee killers with blackened faces on autumn manoeuvres. They went splashing through the stream at the bottom of the garden in the small hours of the morning, and yet he didn't show himself.

It puzzled me – until I began to understand his genius: Cyrille was always there – when you wished he wasn't. Cyrille, I think, was not really alive: he was a doleful sprite who haunted the farmhouse by the river. He was the ragged ghost of the extinguished Languedoc; kicked about and gone at the seams, always looking like he was about to burst into tears. But sorrow had its price, whatever buried grief gnawed away at Cyrille, it never cancelled out business – whenever he got really distressed you knew he was about to put the bite on you. Sorrow cost. Sadness paid. Suffering scored. You found yourself giving Cyrille money to make him go away.

The rains fell in sheets that October, the garden became a water-meadow and then a pond, lapping at my back door. The power failed regularly. Cyrille showed me how to rummage in the outside fusebox, set into an old wall under a fig tree. He didn't see the point of this; it would only fail again; but foreigners and fools expected him to go through the motions. He examined the flooded yard outside the kitchen door and warned that the stream sometimes rose a metre. I'd wake one morning – to find myself drowned.

I knew what really worried him – he couldn't swim.

* * *

I walked into the village once or twice a day: the morning walk for bread from the bad-tempered baker in the High Street; in the evenings for supper, *chez* Nicolas. I drank beer in the café, the Lapin Fou. The walk took about an hour either way through vineyards, their leaves rusting into autumn. The last few grapes, missed in the harvest, had an extraordinary sweetness.

Kissac hugs its hollow below the Black Mountains, keeping its head out of the wind: three winds blow – the *tramontane*, bringing clear weather; the *marin* wafting grey dullness from the sea when the air hangs heavy; and the *circe* from the east – bringing trouble.

The old Priory sits on the village ramparts, its twin towers rising above the red-tiled roofs and the skinny lanes – the Street of the Washerwomen, Street of the Martyrs,

Olive Press Alley – dart to and fro, rather like the starving cats that haunt the village.

When first I arrived in Kissac the loudspeakers still broadcast daily news to the village: they hung in dark clusters under the eaves like wasps' nests. Twice a day, at 10 and 5, the speakers cleared their throats and buttonholed passers-by, like drunks at a party: '*Allô! Allô!*' A slightly wheedling, insinuating tone from an office in the *Mairie*, meant to be value-free, a public service, informative, but it was also the secular substitute for the sermon. The *fonctionnaire* simply replaced the *curé*, and got up in his electronic pulpit and gave us the works:

' . . . The travelling *fromagerie* arrives tomorrow, and the *poissonnière* is in the place de la Liberté today . . . next week's tournament against Brissac at the *boulodrome* is, alas, cancelled . . . A *femme de ménage* is sought in the *Mairie* . . . To Monsieur and Madame Laurencin, our friends the butchers, is given a lovely little girl – Elsabelle . . . The Circus of Dreams joins us next week . . . On the bridge this morning, we welcome the Paella- and Pizza-man, and his pan of yellow rice stuffed with prawns . . . On Saturday night, in the Foyer, the Club of the Third Age invites friends to an evening of old-time dancing . . .'

Death got a couple of bars of a funeral march, fuzzy in the low registers; painfully squeezed on the top notes: then the greeting, slower – the *a-ll-ô*'s drawn out, in a word, grave – and even more unconvincing:

' . . . We announce, with sadness, the death of Patrice Pujols, this morning, at 2 a.m. . . .'

In life, in death, the official crackle; shop talk. Spurious good cheer and formalized grief. Intimate and alienating. Like the first day at school when all the old hands gang up on the newcomer in the playground, and talk in code. But they spoke to me, worried me, called to me, the loudspeakers... I began to think of moving into the village; I wanted to be nearer – to what, I did not know.

I had met a few people: like Sad Bob, the English drifter with ruined eyes who did a bit of roof-repair, made a few francs shifting rocks in gardens, and sat over a beer a long time in the Lapin.

Sad Bob lived with Pascal's sister. She was beautiful – black hair and grey eyes, olive and ash. Her last boyfriend had, as they say, 'done a suitcase' and she moved Sad Bob into her bed. The idea was that he would mind the kids while she was at work: she was his mistress; he was her home help. But her kids scorned him. He didn't speak a word of French.

So she kicked him out and he camped in a cold, deserted house a friend owned at the end of the town, and there he shivered away.

'I must foresee things better,' he told me. 'I must lay in a stock of tinned stuff – for – for next time.'

Sad Bob sat in the café, rolling cigarettes; he was thinking of doing a suitcase himself. His girl sat at the other end of the bar and they ignored each other. After a week of this, Pascal's sister took him back because, she said, opening wide her rain-grey eyes, he was as thick as pig-shit but staff were hard to find.

Pascal, her brother, was dark and difficult, with a passion for Dutch women – and there were a couple of Dutch colonies between villages, or by the Canal du Midi

– twenty neat northern Dutch bungalows, a garden gnome or two, and a caravan in the drive. New Amsterdam in the vineyards . . . Pascal swore that he visited these women and played gin rummy; but husbands or boyfriends were certain he was sleeping with them, and they reacted by going on the most colossal blinders; boozing it up all night in the Lapin and then wandering into the mountains in the dark – the gendarmes had to be called out, with dogs. The villagers looked at each other and muttered that there was more to this than met the eye; Pascal's legendary Dutch lovemaking rivalled, in oddness, his dad's hopeless passion for death. Maybe the two things were related?

Pascal's dad kept trying to kill himself; he had been trying for ages. He tried pistols, poison, carbon monoxide; but he never got it right. Pascal felt the pressure of it. He was in business with Sad Bob, they planned to restore houses and fix gardens and make some money. Except Pascal's sister kept kicking Bob out and then family honour demanded that Pascal refuse to work with him. It was tough. Though Pascal's dad's hopeless career as a suicide certainly drew brother and sister together.

Bob sat in the Lapin, a bit like a spaniel, so fuzzy and soft, rolling his cigarette, sipping his draught beer and licking his lips. 'I'm in France, right? So I eat well.'

He was quite wrong; the food, by and large, around Kissac and the region was pretty awful; mostly it came out of the freezer and the wine came from the village co-op. That was precisely its charm, the place had no pretensions and the relief was enormous.

Mind you, it was all relative. Bob was living out of tins in the periods he was banished from his girlfriend's bed;

but he was eating pizza and paella when allowed back into the family hell-hole, with her impossible sons . . . So I understood why he sat there on the bar stool, licking his lips and telling me how well he ate in France; he even rubbed his stomach – like a cannibal. Mention French food and certain switches turned on in his head. I sympathized with that.

When Pascal got a job as the waiter at the bistro in the High Street, Le Poet Perdu, Bob was in heaven; he was round there every night, rubbing his belly and feasting on the microwaved *daube*, which Pascal sold him at half price. The following week his girlfriend gave Bob the boot, and he was back on tinned food.

* * *

Only at the little restaurant in the Hotel des Cathares was cooking taken seriously. The Cathars were medieval heretics – true children of Languedoc, who were hunted down by Church and Crusaders and wiped out, every last one.

The Cathars were Puritans who did not touch alcohol, or meat, and shunned the pleasures of the flesh. But what began, long ago, in heresy, ended in tourism – and the Cathars have given their name to everything from restaurants to wine routes. It's tough being a heretic. First, the authorities burn you alive, then they name the *menu gastronomique* after you.

The name of the hotel in Kissac was pretty misleading. A pretty place on the village square, opposite the *Mairie*, built of stone the colour of butterscotch, with leaded Renaissance windows and a medieval well in the courtyard where tiers of galleries mounted to a circle of pale sky.

The restaurant was most misleading of all – in its careful observance of appearances; menus under glass outside the front door, tables with pink cloths, black and white Provençal floortiles, walk-in fireplace: it felt, looked, smelt like a restaurant – and sometimes it *was* a restaurant.

But it wasn't easy. People turned up, found a table and sat for long minutes, as solitary as the clock in the corner, as untended as the fire in the grate. Conversation sagged and died. They got nervous.

That was the idea. When the guests began to hum and sweat Nicolas came padding through the stone arch that leads from the kitchen, and upon which hung a photograph of a string quartet, taken in the Priory garden. Nicolas was short and solid and faintly ursine – his bushy eyebrows busily signalling his astonishment: 'What's this? Unidentified life forms in my dining room? And – oh, my God! – they wish to be fed!'

The effect was deadening; old friends, lovers, families fell to furtive whispering; or faced each other in blushing silence, like strangers in lifts. The only other person I knew who could so numb a room was Thierry, and he came later. Besides, Thierry was an intellectual.

Nicolas was a living fossil, and a shape-shifter.

At the start of summer, when people began to crowd into his restaurant calling for food and wine, and he had not yet hit his stride, he was a bear with a sore head, muttering his mantra, 'I'm the only Frenchman in the place.'

As the seasons changed, so did Nicolas. He was a woolly mammoth, a giant sloth. But his great trick was for being nothing. As the year wore on he dwindled. Each time you saw him, there was less of Nicolas. I had had some training in vanishing acts in my time with Cyrille; but Nicolas was a virtuoso absentee. He wasn't there even when he showed up; he inhabited the void, the world of not-to-be. And the fact that other things, and other people, existed exasperated him.

He was the master of the flounce; not a movement natural to a stocky man with a centre of gravity well below the waistline, but Nicolas flounced to perfection. He didn't simply walk, he wafted. When taking an order even his eyebrows joined in the general deportment – conveying in their fluting derision Nicolas's ineffable scorn. For you – but not for you only – also for his destiny, his job – himself – for this closed circle in which he was trapped; for his parents who had given him the hotel and so sentenced him to suffer the terrible ennui of serving table. Nicolas injected even into the recitation of the dessert menu a despairing, mocking note; so that you knew, whether you chose the *crème caramel* or the *tarte aux pommes*, it was hopeless, you were wrong, you should have known better.

If his majestic contempt had been expressed in scornful silence, one might have ignored it. But Nicolas talked – to himself admittedly, but it carried; he transmitted a static of squeaks, groans, growls as he padded between tables. Asked for something simple – the pepper grinder, or a jug of water – he gave this incredulous giggle and went away shaking his head. It shocked strangers. I saw hardened diners, who believed they could take care of themselves in the South of France, reduced to pale disbelief as Nicolas took their orders, raised his eyes to the rafters, sighed, whistled and flounced off.

If Nicolas was difficult when the short season opened, he was impossible when it wound down. As summer gave way to autumn, you needed to get to the Cathar earlier and earlier, because the shrinking days and the early evenings triggered his hibernatory instinct. If you gave him half a chance, Nicolas sent the chef home, doused the lights, and battened down the hatches. Many a time I arrived around 7 to find the lights off, the door locked. Inside, Nicolas sat in the dark, waiting for the knocking on the big oak door to die away.

By late October I was often the only diner in the silent room with its empty tables, its loud clock, its muttering fire. Latecomers got short shrift: opening the door a fraction Nicolas gave them the works, singing out the bad news: the veal was finished; the lamb cold; the kitchen closing; the cook ill . . .

As the hungry visitors turned away – he would toss after the lost ones, like a forgotten hat, his triumphant parting shot:

'*Bonne soirée!*'

* * *

One night in November, I sat over my coffee at my usual table; the Mozart Concertante was playing. Nicolas liked music. He told me he went to Italy in winter for the opera. I did not believe him. I believed he went to sleep in winter.

Nicolas had his foot on the fender, smoking quietly by the fire, his eyes closed, dreaming.

Traditionally, the Cathar closed at the end of December and did not reopen until Easter. But Nicolas had a dream

– why not shut in November, maybe even October? Earlier and earlier, longer and longer, was his dream.

He paced around the empty tables like the Captain of the *Titanic* past caring if she's sinking; dammit – he had seen the passengers into the lifeboats; now he was preparing to go down with the ship. Like the Cheshire cat, he would one day fade away, leaving behind nothing but his flounce.

But first he had to dispose of extraneous goods, not wanted on voyage. The question was – how to dispose of me? I was a fixture, like the corner cupboard where he kept the menus, or the photograph of the string quartet – which he told me was faked; just four friends in evening dress, holding fiddles.

I remember how the brilliance of the solution hit him. I saw him lifting his foot off the fender, blinking sleep out of his eyes.

'It is a long walk through the vines to the village.'

I agreed it was.

'Christopher, if you had a place in the village, you'd find it easier.'

'Find what easier?' I wondered.

'Cooking. Meeting people. I know a place.'

From the cupboard beside the fake string quartet he took a big green folder. He found a leaflet; a little brochure. *The Cherry Orchard*, colour snaps of clocks on a bedroom wall, a swimming pool, and a round-faced fellow holding a billiard cue, wearing a bowler and grinning like a lunatic.

Nicolas scribbled a name and address and saw me to the door.

'Tell him I sent you.' And, as if this clarified matters, 'He's a Dutchman.'

And then he pitched me overboard, like some unwanted item of deck furniture. The door closed behind me, and when I looked back the lights were going out and the dark bulk of the Hotel des Cathares sailed on into the night.

That was how I met the King of the Clocks; he came out of a catalogue.

CHAPTER 3

THE NEXT MORNING I set off, following Nicolas's directions.

When I look back, every moment of that walk, every item – the curving line of terraced houses, painted shutters, uneven kerbstone, the cidery rush of last year's apples escaping from the forester's barn – rises crisp and clear. I was aiming for the Avenue de la Montagne Noire. Many villages have one; often it's just the road out of town and into the mountains. But in Kissac it's a broad and curvaceous thoroughfare, and wears its plane trees like decorations; it is an avenue aspiring to be a boulevard.

To this day I can't walk along it without being somehow cut in two, like a centaur; half of me feels the solid ground under my hooves; the other half of me is awash in emotion and memory; out of whose messy imprecisions comes – and this is the strangest thing – a picture so real that the real thing pales beside it. And that, I suppose, is the key; I make that first walk again and each time the details are painted into place. And manufactured, of course – I know that. Made up. The model improved on. It is always overtime in the memory factory. But, like Mary's French kisses, or that long-ago lunch in the rue de

Seine, the results are real, as *factual* in all the boring, question-begging ferocity of the word as any in arithmetic. It's just that these facts are drawn from feelings, which give them the kind of accuracy only memories from the heart can have.

I pass the Lapin Fou which stands beside the public fountain, an old king's gift to a grateful village; it has a warning chiselled into its base: 'Life flows faster than the waters of this good, clean spring, and does not return.' This is where Little Anna Half-a-face would bleed so profusely that the water ran red: the plastic café tables are set out beneath the gigantic plane tree where thousands of *hirondelles* roost on summer evenings.

Opposite the Lapin a line of old men in blue shirts, chins on their sticks, sit all day long on the wall; six black berets like crows on a telephone line. They watch the cars go by with a concentration that is really very sad. Now and then jobless young men join them; the *chômeurs*; they have never worked, they never expect to work. Tomàs the ex-blacksmith sometimes turns up, in a new black T-shirt, and flexes his muscles on warm summer nights; he is banned from the Lapin for getting mad drunk and eating glass and bleeding.

To my left a hidden alley runs down to the *urinoir* beside the stream. Further to my left is the bank; a dismal, backward place full of scowls and rubber stamps. Next, the public phone box, the bus stop, and the bridge over the stream, where Lionel fell last Christmas.

Across the road is the Bar à Go-Go; a slab of pink marble serves as a pavement table. It has blue shutters, and steady drinkers, it is the rougher of the two watering-holes, and often better patronized than the Lapin. It was in the Go-Go that Lionel had been drinking the night he made the fatal mistake of resting on the bridge, and fell five metres onto the concrete buffer that banks the stream. On Christmas Eve. What a time for it!

Another few steps and you come to the baker; she has the face of an indignant mussel, smooth and hard. Next is a big crumbling house; a single rose pulls itself up over the front door with the muscular grip mountain roses have; and a pail rusts on its rope, above the old well in the yard. Here the lovers live. Both in their late sixties, they walk out each afternoon, arm in arm. He looks like a rain cloud, in dark grey flannels. She wears old beige trousers and has a withered hand. They are never apart. They even share a limp, they are a blessing. Who knows what will happen when one of them dies! It doesn't bear thinking about.

The memory of Lionel is still fresh – three *pastis* and oblivion.

People smile and spit. Death. The bony jester, what tricks he pulls! And a neighbour one sees too much of. Like many a village, Kissac is full of the old and the dying; the young and healthy head for the towns. Funerals are frequent. Death is a coming fellow.

* * *

On that first walk, six years ago, I passed a shuttered *horlogerie*; the painted name was flaking: the elaborate 'o's lifted sepia eyelashes. Next, a row of small terraced houses with blue shutters and then, just before the Avenue de la Montagne Noire turned on its heel and headed up into hills, I came to a broad, double-fronted, nineteenth-century *maison de maître*.

And here I met a man crossing the road carrying a silver jug. He wore an olive-green apron and half-moon glasses, his hair was grey; he had red cheeks in a round face. And a curious way of walking; he stuck out his elbows stiffly, swung his hips somewhere between a strut and waddle, and quick marched – as if he were on parade. He seemed very pleased to see me.

'Best water in the world, free as air and sweet. From the spring.'

He used the French word *source*.

He thrust the jug at me. 'Here, taste.' Then he darted into the field and began digging with a screwdriver. He came back carrying what I thought was a root.

'Wild leek. Wonderful! Good water, red wine, radishes, wild leeks . . . my favourites. And mushrooms, of course.' He wiped a hand on his corduroy trousers and thrust it at me. 'Call me Siggie. Come and have a drink.'

He looked like Hans Christian Andersen on speed; a troll on the run; a cross between Rumpelstiltskin and Al Capone; he was the fat boy in the sweetshop, and the terror of the class.

He took me into his large, dishevelled house. In the sitting room, a Dalmatian called Fred was tearing up a pillow; a nude torso of a girl, cast in bronze, stood on a table; a line of pewter beer mugs topped the oaken cupboard. 'What a mess!' he said happily. 'Let's go outside.'

He led the way upstairs and out to what he called his 'summer kitchen' – a raised gravelled square under a lime tree. A flight of steps climbed to the top of the summer-kitchen wall, and the big garden, with its cherry trees, a swimming pool and scatterings of pots and jars – laid in clusters like painted eggs, navy, electric blue or mustard yellow. Painted or glazed, they were everywhere; it was a plain of jars; and most had some injury, they were cracked, crazed, chipped.

'All seconds,' said Siggie proudly.

Bought from his friend Armand, a hunchback, over towards Mazamet; Armand had found a hoard, two hundred pots. Not since Armand found five thousand glass chimneys for old oil lamps had there been such a bargain. He simply could not afford *not* to buy.

'It was for nothing!'

We sat at a table covered in green plastic stamped with pink roses, a table made, he told me, of old coffin lids. So cheap – 'They were given!' Did I know, Siggie wondered, that the cheapest door knockers one could buy were medieval cast-iron coffin hinges? Absolutely perfect for the job – if you ignored the skull and crossbones traditionally moulded on the surface.

It was my first taste of Siggie's strange fix on death: a mixture of loathing, respect, and commercial excitement.

He poured me a glass of red wine from a jug which he filled from a plastic jerrycan he kept in the roots of the lime tree. Two grey angels, with clasped hands and that air of mourning that speaks of graveyards, watched us. Bought, he told me, from a defrocked priest turned hawker of slightly chipped church property.

It was a mistake, I found, to empty your glass when Siggie was pouring; he thought like a Russian in these matters, an empty glass was an insult, a provocation, a horrid vacuum it was his duty to fill.

There was a brown donkey tethered to a cherry tree and he poured it a glass. 'Only one,' he said fondly. 'She is a treasure, she keeps the grass down. Better than any lawnmower, and cheaper.'

But she drank too much.

'She has a love problem. Poor Plusbelle. It's sad, sad, sad! So many people have these problems. Take this wine: and the man who makes it . . . *Sad.*'

He bought twenty litres a week from M. Villeneuve, over towards Olonzac; a cheap clean red. But twenty litres went nowhere – when one was pouring for oneself, a lovelorn donkey and the visitors who dropped in. He held up the half-empty container, sloshed it about and looked gleeful – time to restock. He was heading over to Olonzac later, for more supplies – would I like to come?

'At six francs a litre it's a bargain. It's for nothing, really.'

When I asked if he had an apartment to rent he didn't know what to say. His eyes bulged a little and across his face there moved a look of slightly sulky defiance: he was hurt, disappointed, like a boy told to tie his shoe laces or finish his homework.

'You'll have to ask Ria. That's her side of the world, nothing to do with me. My business is clocks. They call me the King of the Clocks: *Le Roi du tic-tac.*'

There were a lot of things Siggie didn't do but they got done because he left them to Ria. She was pert, pretty, with that slightly abstracted air of someone rushed off her feet. He believed that a king with a competent consort does nothing but reign – and bask in her competence. She was the motor of their marriage. She cleaned, fixed and rented the small apartments that sat like chubby wings on either side of their tall house: she was mother, manager, cherry picker, gardener, bookkeeper.

Young Gretel, a girl of about sixteen, wandered into the garden, stared dreamily at her father and blew a kiss to the donkey. The King of the Clocks was a linguist – he spoke Dutch to Ria, or German, or English, simultaneously; and French to his daughter because, like him, she was native now; so they spoke the furious patois of the countryside.

Gretel kept watching her father, she seemed to be expecting something. Siggie grinned: a mixture of schoolboy cunning and bubbling delight.

'Did you hear the story about the bishop, the penguin and the choirboy?'

'Oh Pappi – not *again*!' said Gretel and went away.

'Gretel is in love,' said Siggie. 'More's the pity. She'll be sorry. And who is to blame? We are! We give our children too much and then they do nothing.'

'Gretel may be in love,' said Ria, throwing a loving, sympathetic glance after her daughter, 'but *she* is not the child who gives me most trouble. That's a terrible joke, Sigismund. Gretel is not the one who has a problem.'

He was nonplussed. 'Who has a problem? Me? Never!'

Ria ignored him and talked to me about rents and rubbish removal and it sent Siggie batty. He got a hurt, frantic look – he was bored with all this *stuff*!

'Christopher and I are off to see old Villeneuve. To buy some wine. After that we may see the woman in Olonzac; the one who sells her body. If we need cheering up. Poor Villeneuve – what love has done to that man!'

Ria stared at the ceiling: she turned simmering pink. She let out her breath slowly. Sex, I was to discover, like business, was something else Siggie did not do – though he talked about it a lot. And Ria – one might have thought she had found a very effective weapon – publically questioned his competence.

'And – with this woman – will you know what to do? Not you!'

But Siggie didn't mind having his competence questioned.

'Don't worry. Dogs that bark seldom bite!'

As I was to find out, he was always willing to concede, to give way; he hated fuss, hostile questioning, so he made a point of agreeing about things that didn't really rate: what Ria said about his sex life didn't trouble him; in the important matters – luck, bargains, clocks – he knew he was always right. Just as he always had a good day. This made it difficult for Ria to fight him.

* * *

We drove over to the vintner's house, in a small damp green village in the mountains. On the washing line in the yard hung an old bra and a pair of bloomers; grey and baggy as elephants' knees.

M. Villeneuve had a handlebar moustache, side-whiskers, bright eyes; he wore a crisp green shirt, yellow braces and immaculate petrol-blue trousers; his manner was jaunty; he looked like an old sea captain. He was hugely, naturally debonair, he had all the flash of a gold tooth in a mouthful of porcelain. He looked quite monstrously out of place in that hamlet in the hills.

'Long ago,' said my guide, 'M. Villeneuve was married but he fell in love with a local girl and they had a child together. But she was not of his class and in those days that was the end of it. They parted and never met again and he went on being married to Mme Villeneuve, whose items you have just seen floating in the wind and he is an old man now and his wife has sad breasts.'

Siggie looked at the vintner as a case specimen, like Plusbelle. Love had done for him. M. Villeneuve looked at Siggie and something about that look suggested that he thought Siggie was interesting, odd, alarming – a kind of splendid misfit wandering the hills and valleys of the Black Mountains, like some gifted and enchanted idiot.

When I'd got to know Siggie better, I reckoned M. Villeneuve got it just about right.

He sowed confusion, he puzzled people. To some in Kissac he was The Flying Dutchman, never at rest. The closest he came was hopping on the spot, he'd bury his hands in his pockets, rattling his change in his fists, elbows flapping like chicken wings, in his urgent need to be off and away.

People said, 'The King of the Clocks? He hasn't got a heart, he's got workings. Press an ear to his chest and hear him tick.'

Even his wife protested. Ria would not shop with him, travel with him or sleep in the same bed with him.

'Why? It's only two minutes he gives to anything . . .'

She paused significantly 'and then it's over and on to the next thing.'

Then there was his nationality – Emile, who ran a flea market in the old cinema, over towards Homps, a big fellow with belly slung like a hammock, gave Siggie a Hitler salute every time they met at the dealers' fair, the *déballage*, in Beziers, on the first Tuesday of each month. That Emile was a happy collector of Nazi regalia, and meant well, made it worse.

Siggie was so angry he told his friend the gendarme, who sold antiques too, that he planned to lay a charge of defamation.

The gendarme, who was of an ironic turn of mind, said Emile was being affectionate. Some French people liked Germans so much that half the country went around giving Nazi salutes throughout the Occupation.

But it hurt because Siggie had never felt German. He had been a child in vanished Koenigsberg, that Prussian enclave on the Baltic, taken by the Russians and renamed Kalingrad after the war. His family left everything and fled to East Berlin, only to find the Russians there too. So they kept going and made it to the West and freedom. But they stayed poor refugees; there was never enough food, and it marked Siggie with a hunger that never left him.

At eighteen he did military service and trained as an aircraft-technician. And he loved it. For the first time in his life he was eating; he got paid, he slept in a real room, and when he was posted to Holland he was in heaven – the girls were wonderful – and, in the little town of Wirt, he met Ria.

Of course, there was the usual suspicion of Germans – who only a few years before had retreated from Holland, taking with them anything they could carry. But the Dutch were a tolerant lot; when Holland played Germany in the 1966 World Cup, the crowd held up signs reading 'Can we have our bicycles back?'

Siggie never went home. When he was discharged he stayed on in Wirt, opened a little shop and began buying, fixing and selling clocks. Ria already ran her own shop: selling leather handbags and coats. They got married, they made some money.

It was a perfect arrangement.

Perhaps that was the trouble. Things began to bother Siggie. Little things, but they added up. His childhood haunted him; the world was ruled by fat, lazy, crooked stupid bullies with rank, the right papers, and height. I came to see, as I got to know him better, that Siggie's great enemy was, simply, the grown-up world: that tall, terrible race made up of fathers, stepmothers, mayors, police officers, gypsies, cardinals, bank managers, *fonctionnaires* – and Death in all his disguises.

When Gretel was born he made a big concession; for the first time in his life he presented himself in a govern-ment office to register her birth. But the clerk in the Registry Office sent him home because it was his lunch-break. Siggie yelled at him and walked out, refused to return, ever. The authorities threatened to prosecute, said they could lock him up, but he would not go back to that office.

He began brooding: shop, marriage, fatherhood. He was trapped in a gauzy, easy, fatal mesh. He'd forgotten his rules – always make your own luck, go in hard, get out fast, remember, the Russians are coming.

He sold his shop, told Ria she could follow him if she liked, and headed south.

CHAPTER 4

My APARTMENT WAS at the top of the house, high in the wing above the old barn: three small rooms under low, sloping ceilings, carved out of the roof beams like crow's-nests. I had a view of the cherry orchard and a little terrace lined with weeping angels, in green cast-iron, marching nose to wing; the booty, I always thought, of some plundered graveyard.

I was very happy there; Ria had painted the place white and Siggie had donated a series of pieces found on his Wednesday buying raids on the *brocanteurs* and bric-à-brac shops in the Black Mountains: wooden goblins; many clocks (all dead); much-darned tapestries of threadbare lovers stealing kisses from country wenches; low leather settees which looked as if they had come from brothels or banks; *fin de siècle* posters for boot polish; and, on the landing, was a 50s peep-show.

Siggie would arrive with a pocketful of francs, and insist on playing the machine: a parade of what were once known as all-American lovelies, with smooth armpits and dimples, and red pouting lips rolled round – regular as cherries in a fruit machine – showing what used to be called their curves, bolted into those metal bathing suits Hollywood once found so sexy.

This was typical of the man. Siggie enjoyed sharing his treasures. Games were for playing. Afterwards, he'd reclaim his francs.

I think the peep-show was as good a picture of his sexual habits as I was likely to get; it rang all the bells – it served those arousal centres that most delighted him; a minimal outlay bought a harem of inflatables he didn't have to talk to – and Siggie had incredible trouble talking to women. But put a franc in the slot and he could turn them on and off at will; he could see them but he really didn't have to *do* anything; and that was a relief – because women terrified him. Best of all – this was the really sexy part – he got his money back! So it was better than a bargain; it was for nothing!

He was astonished to find that I wrote books and had no car, that I walked to fetch my bread. He hadn't read anything for years, and that included newspapers. Though from time to time he would consult two cherished works on silver hallmarks and old clocks, but that was reference – not reading.

He was appalled to learn that I travelled. He took the view that if one strayed one might never come home and why should anyone wish to leave this paradise? He never did. He worried about my 'gypsy' ways. Gypsies haunted Siggie – he was sure they watched his house, ready to make off with his treasures. They'd staked him out – it was only a matter of time.

Over in the second little apartment, above the old stables on the other side of the house, lived his other tenant.

The first days I was in the house I never spotted her. Her name, said Siggie, was Sophie and she spent much time indoors – 'praying' said Siggie and he giggled.

Siggie's giggle was the wildest thing; it broke cover like a startled pheasant. On evenings when he was entertaining guests in his summer kitchen, I'd lie in bed, hearing his startled squawk; it tore up the night and scraps of noisy darkness rained down for hours. Yet I never heard him laugh aloud in public, he was too aware of himself, too uneasy off his home ground; but in his back garden under the cherry trees his wild cackle rang like a fire alarm.

Sophie had paid a month's rent and become invisible. Siggie waited for her to show herself.

'If you see her in the garden – please, have a talk. Find out what she does. I think she's mad. She's from New Zealand.'

But the new tenant kept to her room.

Then one morning, Siggie knocked on my door and asked me to come to his workshop.

He was wearing his green butler's apron, and his hair was up in wisps. We stood in his workshop, always a wondrous place: he'd been buffing old brass candlesticks on the lathe. Scattered about like scalps were pale clock-faces, stone angels, and painted ceramic oil lamps swinging from the ceiling. His workshop was directly beneath her little apartment.

Someone was pacing in the room above.

'That's Sophie,' said Siggie. 'She'll start singing soon.'

And so she did. A few paces this way, then that, and then this quavery voice: '*I am God, I am the De-v-il!*'

'Both!' said Siggie, impressed, this was two for the price

of one. 'Every morning, every night – she walks and sings. Why do you think she does it? Because she's from New Zealand?'

Siggie believed that we were all prisoners of our national characteristics: all gypsies were thieves, all Italians in the Mafia, all Americans were racists, all Indians were mean, all the Dutch were sex-starved. All New Zealanders, he decided on the basis of Sophie, were religious freaks.

Once he had made up his mind, he never changed it. If he came up against contrary evidence, he never let it worry him. He simply rearranged reality to suit his decisions. He felt sorry for Sophie. But he was unsettled as he always was when God was mentioned. Behind God was organized religion and behind that the Vatican, and the Mafia. Someone was always on the take.

'She gets letters, from the States. It's some cult. For sure. They send her books. I'm sure they make her pay. Soon she'll be broke.'

That worried him – when her money was gone, how would she pay her rent?

'Will you talk to her?'

'Why me?'

He couldn't answer that – but I think it was because I wrote books and Sophie was, he felt, in some vague way, also 'intellectual' – a term which meant you were no earthly good at anything. To Siggie it ranked even lower than 'dreamer'.

'What shall I say?'

'You could say you've come to get your books back?'

'Which books?'

'I lent her some of your books, while you were away.'

I'd been travelling and when Sophie asked him if he had anything to read he'd given her the run of my books. He was not in the least abashed. He probably thought it backed up his thesis; turn your back and someone takes your stuff. He might have thought he was doing all of us a favour.

She'd taken an odd selection: a *Social History of the Third Reich*, and a *Life of Christ*, a study of cults, and a manual on the care of the aged and infirm.

I knocked on her door and offered her a cup of coffee.

Sophie was a solid, good-looking woman of about fifty, her shoulders broad, her hair auburn. The most extraordinary thing about her was her eyes: they were grey-blue, wide, blind. Later I realized contact lenses gave her some of the gravity; but it was also a deep fixation inside herself. She was proud of her eyes which she made up elaborately with duck-egg-blue eyeshadow; and her lashes were stiffened and spiky. She had an odd way of fluttering them, like sails over thin, frozen waters.

She wouldn't come in for coffee – 'I'm giving it up' – so we sat on the small terrace with the weeping angels. Siggie had been sure she'd tell me very little. But Sophie settled back in the white plastic chair and did not stop talking for almost an hour. She talked with conviction; she talked till I ached: she did not slacken or hesitate or doubt. She told me, in a number of ways, one thing: She was God Almighty.

Her theology had that wild confusion that baffles the listener but is always so very clear to the believer. Her true name was Sophie Magdalena. When Sophie talked of herself it was as 'The Magdalene'. She was, she told me, 'an Ascended Master'; she was also the sacred link between the Inner World Government and Luminous Masters from distant galaxies. Her gift was immense; she fused in her person the powers of angelic beings and wise spirits from West and East.

Her mother had been a Rosicrucian, her father was an American fighter pilot who came to New Zealand during the Korean War. He got her mother pregnant and then vanished. Mother and daughter were forced to live with her grandparents, both Presbyterians.

That hurt the child terribly. She longed for her father, hated her grandparents; and they were all condemned to living unhappily together in a house called Harmony Lodge, in suburban Christchurch. Caught between Rosicrucianism and Presbyterianism, America became increasingly the great good place, the religion of her childhood. Her father had given her his nationality. Sophie was half-American and she clung to it like a vocation. Her vanished daddy began appearing to the little girl in nightly visions: he sat on the girl's bed and talked to her. He told her she was special.

And these visions came back in middle age. She woke one night dreaming of stones and blood. 'Minervois, Minervois!' said her voices. They told her to seek God's country. She looked up Minervois in the encyclopedia and found it in France.

She still showed traces of her shock. It was so sudden – one moment she was a middle-aged woman, with grown children, living in suburban Christchurch, and the next she was expected to run the Universe. And getting anywhere from New Zealand was very expensive. Where would she find the money?

That is when the miracle happened – Sophie flashed that curious blank glassy stare and the faint, dreamy, merciless smile – her mother died, and left her a small bequest.

'It was the happiest day of my life.'

She wasted no time. Sophie, who had never left home and spoke no French, bought a plane ticket to Paris, and there she rented a car and headed south.

When she reached Castelnaudary, she had another vision: 'Minervois! Minervois!' said her spirit guides. 'Find the stones washed in blood.'

And so to Cathar country she came. Cathars combined in their beings good and evil, God and Satan. Sophie came to Kissac and found the pink marble common in these parts; and she found stories of blood; in the destruction of the Cathars' priests, male and female; these 'Perfects', as they were known, who were tortured and fed to the flames. True martyrs in a cruel, uncomprehending world.

Sophie Magdalena knew she had come into her kingdom.

* * *

I saw quite a bit of her. It felt odd to have God as a neighbour. But you get used to it. And she was not just any god, she was every god that ever had been: she was Jesus and Buddha and Shiva and Satan; and she was also lots of other people, like Cleopatra and Ron Hubbard and Mary Magdalene.

Sophie said, 'My body is divine. It's also a very firm, good body.'

It is curious how youth and divinity and firm flesh mingle. She reminded me of Barbara Cartland in this radiant love affair with her own body and the easy way she talked to strangers about it. A few years ago, when she was in her nineties, Barbara Cartland told me, with a sincerity that confirmed this came with as much superb surprise to her as it would to me, had I been lucky enough to share the vision, 'If *only* you could see me without my clothes. I have the body of a young girl.'

Sophie was smitten, deeply loving of that cherished and splendid thing – her divine self; she was a lovely envelope containing heavenly truths: 'They're inside me, like beans in a pod, Christopher. It takes a bit of getting used to.'

That was the endearing side of Sophie – at least in the beginning – a streak of modesty amid the blaze of divine glory. She was willing to learn. This explained those letters from the States. She was taking a correspondence course in things a Deity must know if She is to do Her job. Tips from Ascended Masters on how to deal with omnipotence.

I asked, tactfully, about sects. There was something in this that reminded me of the Raelians, who believed gods rode in spaceships.

Tactful, perhaps, I was, but it was a mistake as I soon realized because Sophie gave me a sideways glance with her glassy eyes; a chill look that said she'd seen my books, too – and that the Deity really should not be so patronized. One did not consort with cults when one was Mistress of the Cosmos.

'I didn't just wake up one day and decide all these

things. I was a very ordinary person. But the visions started and the voices. I can't believe I have been chosen to do this work, me – Sophie Magdalena. But I'm trying to accept what I have been told. I know things that will amaze you, change the world. I have to care for the world.'

Again Sophie turned her frozen blue stare on me.

Her days were spent in prayer and meditation, pacing and praying, in the apartment over Siggie's workshop. Sometimes Sophie walked in the cherry orchard, and called it her paradise. When the days were warm, she braved the water and entered the pool with majestic assurance, in a blue costume that matched her eyes.

Siggie was schoolboyishly rude about this, calling her a blue whale – but that was just because she scared him. Sophie pulled herself through the water and watching her one could not help feeling that if God swam, She would do the breaststroke.

* * *

Below my apartment was a barn which Siggie had made his billiard room. The door carried a blue ceramic sign, MONSIEURS. It was a generous, private space which reflected his passions. Perhaps two dozen clocks hung side by side on the walls around the table, and each clock wore a hat. Small carriage clocks wore yarmulkas or fezzes; bigger fellows – the grandfather clocks, station clocks, church clocks – wore toppers or trilbies; tall thin clocks that the King thought of as 'military' were dressed in legionnaires' kepis – Prussian brass Picklepiercers; he was pretty nationalistic: English clocks wore bowlers, or bobbies' helmets; and French clocks wore berets, or Napoleonic tricorns.

They mooned over his nightly games.

And the young Ronald Reagan and Simone Signoret watched too, from the old movie posters Siggie collected and stuck between the clocks.

Siggie loved company, yet he was the most unsociable man one could imagine – he had no social skills. In his billiard room he solved the problem, he had the ideal audience, always ready to play, to listen, to clown. And never talk back. On a slab of pink marble, possibly the base of some church altar, a jazz trio was playing. The trio wore black ties and toppers and not much else. Siggie had formed the band from three shop-window mannequins: two blondes – one on drums, one on sax – and a bloke in a top hat on piano. The women wore low-cut, see-through blouses. If you looked carefully you noticed that a squirrel's head peeped from the pianist's unzipped fly. As things turned out, exposure to Siggie's trio had a most unhappy effect on the local doctor.

In the corner was the crimson chaise longue where the King took his lunchtime siesta; and beside the bed stood the massive iron safe he swore had once belonged to the Duke of Wellington.

Siggie liked billiards. And he was good. When he played himself, as he often did, this moon-faced crew around the walls were a perfect audience. I think the delight lay in the way the game knitted together all the elements close to his heart. On the one hand, brutal simplicity: black or white, right or wrong. Then the calculation of angles.

Putting your opponent in an impossible position – which Siggie called 'making an offer'; followed by the sudden ruthless conclusion, or 'making a kill'.

And the joy of slipping out of tight corners. He liked that too. Billiards is about trapping your opponent – Siggie would push Siggie towards certain doom and then – with a swerve, a fine angle, a fancy calculation – *voilà!* – he was free. And the clocks he'd saved from the cellars of death looked on, the band played, Ronald Reagan doffed his stetson and Siggie hugged himself with joy.

In those days, Siggie often spent nights playing du Toit, the new doctor; a small violent, milky-pale man from Alsace. He was nice enough, Siggie said, if rather 'too easily inflamed'. When inflamed the doctor ran after women like a puppy chasing a ball; he did animal impersonations, usually of poultry, late at night. His wife had left him and gone back to Alsace, and because French law is what it is, the doctor had custody of their two small boys, Peter and Tomi, who trailed after him like ducklings.

He often forgot to feed them and Ria gave them bread and butter and cheese because they looked half-starved. And put them to sleep on the sofa, on either side of Fred, the Dalmatian.

In the barn, their father lost steadily to Siggie and began to imitate a chicken, hopping about and crowing. Out in the orchard, Plusbelle joined in. With Siggie's wild cackle ringing out, it was like a farmyard down there, some nights.

The doctor could not handle the home-made hooch Siggie pressed on him. Siggie had flasks of the stuff which he kept in decanters in the Duke of Wellington's safe and it was worryingly, nakedly colourless.

'It's pure brandy. As good as anything you could buy. If I added a few oak chips, to colour it, who could tell the difference! It's 45 degrees of alcohol. That's maybe one thousand francs worth. And I had it for nothing!'

But he never drank anything but red wine.

The doctor went on hitting the stuff, then he stole the hats from the clocks and around midnight he went over to the jazz trio and began fondling their breasts.

Siggie wheeled the doctor next door where his lost boys, Tomi and Peter, slept on the sofa. Ria covered them with a duvet and Siggie fetched his torch and led the way; with the doctor staggering and his two sons tagging sleepily behind him, Siggie steered them up the hill to their house.

'He's a lot of fun,' Siggie said.

* * *

When Sophie began accosting guests in the orchard, and preaching to them, Ria decided she had had enough. She gave Sophie notice, she would have to go . . . But Ria was a kind woman and wanted to help so she turned to her friends, Hervé and Marie-Jo. They owned a little cottage in the woods, near Villardonelle, a hamlet in the hills above Carcassonne. A plain little cement box of a place in a damp hollow, but Sophie took to it. The rent was low and she would not be there for long – she was expecting a visit from an angel who would announce her divine mission to the world. Besides, she did not care where she lived; she was her own cathedral.

The apartment above his head was strangely silent, no God, no Devil – and Siggie, down in his workshop, missed Sophie. He thought of her from time to time and shook his head and repeated to himself the expression he used only to express true wonder: 'Oi, yoi, yoi, yoi, yoi.'

CHAPTER 5

———◆———

WHEN SIGGIE FIRST came south, to Languedoc, he settled in the hamlet of Les Martyrs, on the slopes above Carcassonne. Ria followed with little Gretel who was then about five years old, and she still shivered when she remembered.

'I lived in a castle, once,' Siggie always recalled happily, 'but that was before the War.'

He had gone into partnership with a Dutchman, afterwards only ever referred to as 'Him the Horrible'. In Les Martyrs, they bought a ruined chateau; a noble pile with park and woods and battlements, in the centre of the tiny village. Next door was the house of the Mayor. And on the other side lay the fields of old Maurice, an asparagus grower.

The partners planned an hotel: added a kitchen, refurbished the rooms and settled back to dream of cheap red wine and rich visitors; they even printed a brochure which made the usual promises – 'pleasant ambience, companionable surroundings, decent table'. They put in a pool and they dreamed of reeling in profits like fat silver fish on sunny days, and endless games of cards.

Within a few years the partners were at war. It had to do with the usual things: money, sex, and electricity bills; they were struck blind by the light; bamboozled by the dream, the wine, laid low by the peculiar follies of visitors from the North – born to be sensible, they became fancy-free.

There is no rage more violent than that between foreigners who fall out in the Midi. Soon the partners were not speaking to each other; soon their wives fought in the laundry and the attics; and the men began shouldering each other aside in the long, carpeted corridors beneath portraits of the vanished noble owners. They staked out separate territories and patrolled with shotguns. Siggie had spent his life escaping the authorities, and now he had landed among the Russians, again.

Siggie keeps a couple of snaps of those days. He is thin, his eyes feverish; he clowns wildly in the pool; he perches on the tops of cupboards like some demented gibbon, his dark hair falling over his eyes like palm fronds. He looks quite mad.

'I wanted to shoot Him the Horrible,' says Ria. 'The only time in my life I wanted to kill a man. I still hate him. I'd shoot him today.'

Siggie's daughter, Gretel, frightened by oaths and screams among the increasingly homicidal former friends, took to spending more and more time next door in the garden of old Maurice, the asparagus grower.

Maurice was pleased to have company. He owned a little chocolate donkey with melting eyes, called Plusbelle; and as Gretel rode around the paddock, holding gently to Plusbelle's strong ears, Maurice talked to her of love and desertion. Of his wife who ran off with the idiot from Narbonne. Imagine that! A grown man pretending to be a toy. And Maurice would take from his pocket a tin soldier in a blue coat and black busby and spit on it (the soldier was rusty from all the spitting Maurice had done) and then he'd give a loud wail; but it was nothing compared with the screams and swearing in the cellar on winter nights. She rather liked old Maurice's despairing hoot.

Gretel learnt the meaning of love from Maurice and Plusbelle, gentle in her meadow. Plusbelle moved under her knees like a magic rug, hard, warm, bristly and smelling strongly of happiness.

One night, under a pale crisp moon, Siggie and Him the Horrible fought hand to hand on the great balcony with its fine view of the park. The balcony was normally used as garden shed, laundry room and greenhouse and was open to the elements. And so the war was a domestic one. A homes and gardens war. They fought with hosepipes, tomato canes, bits of old deckchairs, picket fencing, laundry lines and boxes of washing powder which had long ago turned to rock.

Siggie and Him the Horrible were cut and bruised and streaked with Persil when the police arrived, summoned by the Mayor, M. Rochas, whose house sat by the wall of the chateau, and whose wife, Madelaine, had woken him in the small hours with the complaint that the foreigners next door were behaving badly.

Half the hamlet of Les Martyrs was tuned in to the big fight. Some people, listening to the grunts, thudding fleshy blows and hissing intakes of breath, thought some orgy was in progress. If anything, the discovery that it was murder, and not sex, the foreigners were up to, disappointed the neighbours. Once again the Germans had displayed a lack of originality. Those who remembered the Occupation, the tank emplacements near Lézignan; the Resistance active in the woods and valleys of the Col de Salette, repeated the old and comforting boast:

'When the Germans first came, we were working for them. But after a few servings of cassoulet – *voilà!* – they were working for us.'

Siggie fled the chateau that very night and came to live in Kissac and never once returned to the battlefield.

* * *

There was a long court case and, in the end, the chateau was auctioned and the proceeds split between the enemies. The buyer was Happy Harry's, a Paris casino and strip joint, which wanted the place as holiday quarters for its faithful girls and loyal croupiers.

Siggie was terribly proud.

'Imagine! It's like the *Story of O*. Fine girls, chains, whips and rich lovers.'

For an utterly unsentimental man, he is given to strange, romantic flights.

Ria was impatient with these ravings. 'Bring me whips and chains and we'll see if you're up to it.'

We were sitting in the King's summer kitchen. Plusbelle the donkey was tethered to a stake under the cherry tree, looking around for the bottle and licking her lips.

'I'm not giving that donkey another drop,' said Siggie, 'she's worse than the Colonel's Lady. Maurice bought Plusbelle when his wife left him. It was his idea of a bargain. Lose a wife, replace her with a donkey.'

This with a look at Ria.

'Try it,' she said, pursing her lips the way she did when she was dangerous.

But Siggie told me instead the story of how Maurice came by the little donkey.

A few years before he arrived in Les Martyrs, Maurice Pradelle married Claire Depot, a girl of eighteen, over forty years his junior.

Her parents were very worried and tried to talk her out of it; they argued that the man was not just old, he was badly connected. Yes, he might have some money, very well – for Maurice sold wonderful asparagus, the tips swollen to a purple globe that made the lips pucker – and must have put a fair bit away, but his brother, René, was . . . a goatherd. So familiar with his animals that he would sleep and eat with them, wore the same filthy coat all year round, black with mud and manure, held together with nails twisted through the buttonholes. A man who dossed down in a stone byre in the Black Mountains, ankle-deep in goat droppings.

It did no good – Claire said she would marry him anyway.

I never knew Maurice but Siggie gave me a photograph of the goatherd. He wears an old grey – not black – jacket over his one item of extravagance, a black zippered shirt; his beret is the same grey as his jacket which is indeed fastened with pins where the buttons are missing. He is standing in the doorway of the goat pen, holding a large bearded nanny goat; he holds her firmly by the tail and the neck, while under her belly a kid suckles. He has a firm broad face with crisp black hair. He looks far younger than his sixty years.

Maybe here is the reason for Claire's determination. If Maurice looked anything like his brother, he was a dashing man.

On his marriage to Claire, Maurice told anyone who raised an eyebrow: 'I don't say that my asparagus is the best – all I will say is that nobody else's comes close.'

It was not clear if he was talking about his crop or his acquisition of the blonde with pretty ankles and a love of very short skirts. The precedents were there and almost uniformly bad. There had been that friend of Humph-Humph, the dealer in prints. Humph's friend had taken himself off to Morocco, and he was sixty if he was a day, and bought himself a seventeen-year-old wife. For a month things had been animated. Very well. But then she started looking at boys and going to discos and he beat her and she ran away. Well, what did he expect – laying wet wood on a new fire?

Down at the Lapin Fou, and among the watchers on the wall across the road from the café, or in the rich patchwork of delectable vegetable gardens by the river, over *pastis* in the Bar à Go-Go, there was talk.

Maurice was all bubbles but no champagne. All air and no pump. Who should know better than he that late asparagus is of no interest? The vegetable turns woody, it wilts if it is not tasted early, if not dipped in warm butter, and all the boasting in the world would not save an asparagus grower who was all shaft and no tip.

Maurice knew about the talk. He told Tomàs, the ex-blacksmith, that he was as good as any man Claire might have married.

Tomàs said, 'Fine. But how do you prove it?'

Difficult one, that, everyone agreed.

Maurice gave it some thought and he came up with an answer so daring a lot of people were so impressed they wouldn't hear another word against him.

On the first Friday of each month he showed his little book with its intimate calculations to Bertin, proprietor at the Lapin Fou. What he did was to keep a tally, in a little green notebook with a picture of Rheims Cathedral on the cover. On the café table, in a space cleaned of spilt *pastis* and cigarette ash, in the circle of honour, as it were, rested the notebook for public examination. And very neat it was; as good as a cellarmaster's calculations.

Below each day's date were pencilled three arrows; the first, up with the morning sun; then horizontal at noon; and downward after dark.

* * *

If Maurice saw marriage as a challenge, Claire saw it as a game, and she loved to play. And she wanted to beat him – maybe she wanted to hurt him. Perhaps the rigour of the timetable upset her; the clockwork regularity of it all. The business of being written up. So she began changing the rules.

Maurice would arrive home at noon, after a morning among his asparagus, to find a note from Claire: she was hiding. If he could find her he could have her.

A good game, he thought.

At first she hid under the bed or in the cupboard. He took to coming home unexpectedly, but she kept a sharp watch and slipped from the house, just as he arrived, leaving an empty room smelling of the jasmine-scented soap she had used in her freshly run bath. She'd hide in the stone huts in the corners of vineyards. Often she made him give chase and he would cover a kilometre, boots sticking in the clayey soil between the vines, before running her down.

Maurice stopped going out to his asparagus under its huge horseshoe of creamy plastic and would sit in the kitchen all day playing solitaire on an old board with polished ball-bearings as counters. Ready and waiting.

Claire upped the stakes. Started taking the bus to Carcassonne and the movies, arrived home and told him the plot, and it terrified him. Tales of beddings and shootings and things young people do.

Over at the Lapin Fou, Bertin said it made him want to weep to see how the arrows began to change; there were days when the morning shaft was a horrid shadow of its former sharp self; increasingly, the afternoon horizontal failed to appear. Perhaps Claire had outrun him in the orchard or had remained undiscovered in the barn. The nightly record, once so proud and strong, began to wither; cupid's dart wore a clumsy, crumpled tip, arrows designed never to fly.

After three months, Maurice still dropped in at the Lapin on the first Friday of the month, but he no longer took out his notebook. He sat there frowning into his *pastis* – 'and we knew,' said Siggie, 'that even the first arrow of the day had failed.'

Because her husband, as she put it, no longer showed her attention, Claire sat watching the early morning *téléshopping* programme and buying on a large scale: multitudinous casserole dishes sufficient to feed a family of twelve; cunning freezing moulds which would allow her to construct entire banquets embedded in ice; innumerable revolutionary dicers, scrapers, shredders, peelers and a wide variety of fitness videos.

Evidently, before she killed her husband, Claire planned to bankrupt him.

Love is odd, as Siggie liked to say. Meaning it was dangerous where it wasn't fatal. He regarded what happened next as a miracle. Maurice probably owed his life to the visit his wife paid to the market in Narbonne, one Saturday morning . . .

* * *

Siggie took me to the market in Narbonne and pointed out the fatal place.

The market hall is turn of the century, all bolted girders and glass. It has aisles running at right angles, and stalls selling flowers and honey at the front door. Somewhere in between are fruit, bread, wine – and lining the edges are the butchers' stalls. At the back door is the fish cathedral; rainbows, enamels, entire rose windows of sardines' eyes, astonished prawns, and usually half a hunk of tuna, hacked like a sea cow to a bloody stump. At the front door, the chicken brothers grill their birds. Rough-plucked chickens, freshly killed, lie in heaps. I last saw bright eyes and sharp beaks like these among the masters of a minor English public school. And like the chickens, they didn't know they were dead. A blowtorch vaporizes the last few forgotten feathers and a chicken brother threads the birds on a spit, like beads.

You begin to sense how odd and strange and far from the world this is; how much of it is forbidden: this is the house of religions other people have abolished or preached against. Here is foie gras, naked; overstuffed goose liver, and proud of it. Come Christmas every town has its Fat Fair – its *Foire au Gras* – where the best examples of the goose-stuffers' art are on show. The geese lie on trestle-tables, their long necks dangle like bus-straps, their stomachs are carefully slit and beside them lie their round yellow livers to be prodded, sniffed, traded, venerated; and jars of duck's fat; and bowls of duck's hearts for spearing on a brochette.

'Fat is to be eaten; this is the Midi,' Siggie reminds me. '*On mange gras.*'

Perhaps this place of sacrifice was a fine setting for the salvation of old Maurice, burnt to ashes in the fiery play of love. Siggie quailed before the plenitude of the market. If you had it – fine, but what if you lost it? For the same reason love terrified him. Its hugeness, its riches. Its mad unpredictability. And he shivered. He remembered the hungry people on the road from Kalingrad. He gave compulsively to the beggars who rattled tin cups on the market steps. 'Imagine how terrible it must be to have your belly groaning for food – in the middle of all this!' And he'd point to chunks of veal, with the milk-calf look still fresh on them; horsemeat dark as roses, snails, frogs' legs. And swags of dried sausage on silver hooks.

And he points out an automaton, white-faced and frozen, who performs on an upturned pail.

'The boy who went with Claire was better looking, and had red hair.'

We slide onto stools at Armand Poitrine's coffee stall.

Dour, nodding, Armand wipes his hands on his blue

apron – and bangs home the cork in a bottle of dry light Narbonnaise, breakfast tipple for those who take just a glass. Armand does not serve food. He will grill you a steak, if you buy your own from the butcher next door and slap it on the counter as if you brooked no argument. He will also make you an omelette, if you ask politely, or a sandwich of *saucisse* de Toulouse, grilled, and pushed into half a baguette.

A group of men are finishing huge steaks, they've sunk a bottle of rosé and now they're wiping their plates with bread.

To the left of the bar is a patch of open floor. Ahead is the glass counter and melting cheeses of the *fromagerie*, and the food counter of the *traiteur*; a huge paella rice mountain rising to a peak of prawns occupies the third side of this triangle, this fighting floor.

A couple of years ago this space was worked by an automaton, dressed like a cross between the Tin Man and a circus clown, Charlie Chaplin and the character who promotes hamburgers. He wore red skintight pants, a large cherry nose and orange hair under a bowler hat and he carried a skinny cane. Placing on the ground before him a paper cup, he hopped onto an upturned pail and froze. For maybe half an hour he did not flicker, until someone dropped a coin into the cup. Then, like a man receiving an electric shock, his limbs would shiver, his eyes would roll, his cane would twirl and for a few moments you watched a statue turn into a mechanical toy. It was droll.

The automaton earned anything up to a hundred francs a stint. Enough to feed himself until the winter migration of his travelling tribe who lived in the old red London bus, parked on Narbonne *plage*. Enough to feed a dog on a string and a harmless habit, or two. Good enough for a beer, now and then. He was a happy automaton.

Then one morning Claire, blonde as honey, says Armand, the crazy girl with a *'beau châssis'*, squeezed into a white micro-skirt and cerise halter, hair tied up in a golden jungle, sat down at the bar and fixed the automaton with adder-green eyes.

Armand lifts his chin, closes his eyes, stops breathing. We forget his paunch, worn well down under his blue apron – he has become the boy with the *'cheveux carotte'*, frozen on his upended pail.

Armand points to the stool – there she sat in her skinny little skirt.

'She fiddles with the top button of her blouse, and up and down in the V between her breasts she plunges her finger, while she sips her coffee. She fixes her eyes on the automaton; him, burning, burning!'

But she never spoke, not a word.

Armand says it is only normal. 'One does not talk to an automaton.'

The automaton's red pants were pulled tightly across his thighs, red nose shining in the electric light, one foot behind him, still as stone. When the girl put the hex on him, the boy fought back. His eyes glazed. He was, says Armand, focusing on things far away, neutral, icebergs perhaps, and interstellar vacuums. Willing his body to obey.

Armand turns reflective. He reaches for metaphors to give the true sense of what happened next.

'But the sterner the government on high, the more apparent is the revolution below stairs.'

'It was bizarre.' Armand opens his thumb and forefinger and twists his wrist. 'She could turn him on and off like a spigot. So what does the boy do? He begins flapping away like a landed fish, even though no one has put a centime in his cup. Moving. To hide that bit that won't obey. But it's no way to run a career. Not if one wants to eat. You understand? She played with him. He never had a hope.'

In time, the automaton understood what she wanted. She would ruin him. There was only one way back to the pleasant time when he was a frozen man who turned into a clockwork toy at the clink of a coin – to pay, and her price was high.

One day, an automaton wearing a yellow crash helmet, which sat oddly on his orange wig, with a girl in a very short skirt, mounted a motorcycle, and took the road to Perpignan.

Chapter 6

———•———

According to Siggie, old Maurice had been lucky. Claire would have killed him, sure as shooting.

'Lucky? When his wife ran off?' Ria asked sweetly.

Siggie looked hurt. 'Ria – try to understand. He got Plusbelle. Maurice and she were happy. They spent hours turning about in the meadow, talking.'

'And drinking,' said Ria. 'He gave her brandy.'

'Animals are true friends. You can depend on them. You come into the house and straight away they love you. Like Fred, here.' He patted the Dalmatian who raced around the room tearing up the cushions. Siggie watched the spotted destroyer with dazed affection. 'Your family can hate you but your dog always loves you. Hundred per cent. Maurice had his donkey and she kept him going. Or he might have—'

'He did,' Ria reminded him.

'But only later.'

The King of the Clocks hardly ever used the word 'death' – it gave too much to the enemy. But no busy undertaker, greedy heir or eager pathologist could have taken more professional interest. He watched grimly, sceptically, crossly. But the effect of his close study was not to remind him of extinction – it made him think of business. The two things were closely linked in his mind and his strange philosophy.

What it came down to was this: he hated death with a child's fury and saw it as monstrous and unfair and stupid. It was crooked, a cheat. Why should he respect it? In a better world it would be arrested – run in. Since that was not going to happen – the officials were all asleep at their desks – his way was to use a sliver of luck and a dash of magic.

He never forgot his childhood and the refugees on the road west; when he saw big strong grown-ups lying down and giving up the ghost. He gritted his teeth, and took a vow: 'Not me; not ever!' Meaning, I suspect, that he would not grow up – or lie down.

In the War, when the family was starving, his father fed him stories about talking geese and uppity trolls and magic springs, and he went to sleep on an empty belly 'dreaming of soup and gold'. Siggie went to business school in fairyland. He began dividing the world into the lucky, and the dead. And if anything infuriated him, it was the thought of the rich dead and the living poor: that was why he did his best to liberate the possessions of the dead. He really didn't care about money. The emphasis was on salvation. Saving something from a dead man's cellar; keeping it moving, even when the owner wasn't. This was not just business; Death was in business, Siggie was in the rescue services.

Graveyards appalled and fascinated him. He called them caravan sites where the dead spent eternal holidays – 'cold camping'. And when they were not cold campers, they'd 'given up smoking'.

Once he asked Humph-Humph, the print dealer, to meet him in the graveyard; Siggie lay down on about half a dozen graves, his eyes closed, his hands on his breast, wearing a red sweater and a mad smile and had Humph snap him with his Nikon. No one, since John Donne made a habit of regularly dressing in his shroud and running rehearsals for the long silence, has so enjoyed stealing a march. He was getting the full treatment – for nothing! Why does a cold camper need a marble headstone, wrought-iron railings or weeping angels?

To drive past a cemetery always had the same effect, mourning: grave-goods made him wince and say, 'Christopher, do you know what I could *get* for those?'

Now clocks! That was different. If there was a God, and Siggie did not believe there was, then it is only so that clocks might be created. Having created clocks, God created Siggie so that he might find them, fix them and sell them for a good profit at the Horologists' Fair in Dusseldorf. It was very lucky. It was the Divine Plan. Siggie's was a mad but orderly universe, where things always went his way – and that was not surprising, since it was entirely of his own arranging. Siggie was part of the masterplan. Sometimes I had the feeling he believed he *was* the masterplan. Even Plusbelle was part of the plan – hadn't he acquired her by a stroke of luck?

'No, you did not,' said Ria. 'Gretel saved Plusbelle. You fought and fought not to buy her.'

But when Siggie told me the story of how Maurice

had died, it was a commercial parable, filled with divine intervention and blessed good luck.

* * *

Siggie had been working in his den one morning, using nitric acid to clean the swags ornamenting the ends of a rather nice eighteenth-century brass fender, when the loudspeakers broke in with the Death March:

'It is with sadness that we announce the passing, on Wednesday morning at 2 p.m., of Maurice Pradelle, at the age of seventy-five . . .'

From time to time Siggie had news of Maurice from his brother, René, who still kept goats, and sold their succulent kids to the restaurant near La Bastide, where they were grilled with rosemary.

Now Maurice was dead. Duty required that the dead should be relieved of their possessions as soon as possible. And Maurice, he remembered, had one or two nice eighteenth-century clocks. But Siggie had other, deeper principles, because they concerned luck. Or fate. He had almost died in the war against Him the Horrible, and Siggie believed that when something was gone, it was gone, you moved on, you never went back.

I saw him take this attitude again and again. Extraordinary in a tolerant man who hated emotional wrangling: when he was crossed he never made the slightest effort to patch things up. Behind him lay bad luck – so the wise man put it where it belonged, out of his mind. It was over, finished, dead.

But this time he struggled. He totted up the value of the clocks he would miss and, typically, he said nothing, knowing that when Maurice's house was cleared, other dealers would be quick to tell him about the prices. Siggie grieved, briefly, for the lost clocks, and then did what he does so well – he forgot.

And he was getting along fine, he said, when he hit trouble.

When I moved into the apartment over the barn, Gretel was madly in love. Siggie regarded his daughter as a slightly less dangerous version of her mother. Gretel was then about sixteen; round and soft and creamy, and a lot of boys at the Lapin were crazy about her – and this, according to Siggie, triggered her memory. She was in love and so she was bound to cause trouble. When Maurice died, Gretel suddenly remembered something she hadn't thought about for years.

'But what has happened to poor little Plusbelle?'

A decade had passed since old Maurice let her ride Plusbelle around the paddock and talked to her of love and betrayal and mechanical men; now the thought of Plusbelle, alone, perhaps starving, made her cry.

She begged her father to find out what had happened. Siggie said she was mad. The Mayor had enjoyed the collapse of the chateau, the town-clerk had celebrated; he certainly was not going back there. Never had, never would.

But Gretel went on crying and he couldn't stand the tears so he phoned the Mayor, who turned out to be helpful. It seemed there was nothing to be done and Siggie felt, as a reasonable girl, she'd see that. And he told Gretel what the Mayor said – with great relief.

The donkey had been sold, to a butcher over in Carcassonne. A horse butcher.

Gretel wouldn't leave her room, she wouldn't eat.

'Do something, Pappi,' she kept saying.

Siggie's grey eyes took on a baffled, glassy gleam when he recalled his quandary. He had argued with her. But how do I know which butcher it is? Carcassonne is full of them. The donkey's gone – weeks ago. She's probably *saucisson* by now!'

This was the start of an extraordinary sequence of events. Siggie detested the phone – I never saw him make a phone call – and if ever he picks up the receiver to take a call, he always disguises his voice, just in case someone wants him for something. Yet Siggie phoned every horse butcher in Carcassonne until he found one who could answer his questions.

'Did you buy a small brown donkey at the Pradelle place, in Les Martyrs?'

'Certainly I did. What of it?'

'Have you killed it?'

'What a question!'

'Yes or no?'

'I am a master of my trade. I sell the very best. That donkey is too old for my purposes. I took him as a favour to René, old Maurice's brother. He keeps goats, you know. And I took the beast off his hands as a favour. He mentioned a small sum to defray my expenses. He was grateful. The sum I have not seen. One waits. Gratitude is a prickly fruit. I'll sell her on soon – to someone who will find use for the extremities.'

'Make me a price.'

'For you, 1,800 francs.'

It was too much. For a clock, he would have bargained. But there was Gretel to think of.

The horse butcher arrived at Siggie's door in a blue van pulling a horsebox. Plusbelle was led into the cherry orchard and tethered to a tree with a length of washing line, a relic of the laundry wars against Him the Horrible in the big chateau. Gretel fed her cherries and rubbed her forehead against Plusbelle's muzzle.

Sigismund paid over the money. The horse butcher accepted a glass of *grenache* and admired three bronze sculptures of young nude female torsos, left in lieu of rent by Wolfgang, an artist from Dusseldorf who arrived from time to time without warning in his red Lamborghini, partnered, as usual, by another teenage mistress who'd been his model.

Siggie took the butcher into his barn for a game of billiards, and there the horse butcher saw the grandfather clocks, standing like sentries around the living room, each wearing a different hat: bowler, topee, kepi, panama and even tasselled nightcap. He admired the walls adorned with yellowed, worm-bored maps of sixteenth-century Amsterdam; and posters from B-grade movies of the 50s; Ronald Reagan in a red cowboy bandanna, his hair swept back like black cream; and Simone Signoret clinging to a beefy man with a gun . . . And he made a memorable pronouncement:

'I see you like old things.'

It turned out that the horse butcher had a friend with a house in Carcassonne, stuffed with old things. His friend planned to move to a village in the mountains. What was he to do with his treasures?

The next day the horse butcher led the King into a house on the rue de la Liberté and there he beheld, crammed into three rooms, old wooden stereoscopic viewers, with thousands of photographs of Lourdes, Cathar castles, and Montpellier's principal fountains, circa 1910; and handpainted studies of nude women disguising their parts with ostrich feathers; he also found walnut headboards; brass bedsteads and brass engines for pumping grapejuice; antique sets of boules, slightly rusty, in elderly leather carrying-cases; dozens of straw Provençal chairs, gilt mirrors, three billiard tables, naked shop-window mannequins, silk toppers, musty furs, demijohns of distilled alcohol, paraffin lamps, painted angels, plaster Madonnas, cowboy film posters, clocks, cases, pendulums and movements.

And for all of it – why the owner wanted next to nothing at all. It was a gift. Pure magic.

Once upon a time, when they were starving, said Siggie, his dad told him stories about the donkey whose dung turned to gold. Did I know it?

He seemed amazed that I did not. He seemed even more amazed that I did not see the divine intervention, of which this treasure was a sign, manifest in the sacred movements of luck and destiny that combined to make the miracle. The pattern went like this: Maurice's death brought Plusbelle, who brought the horse butcher, who brought treasure to the coffers of the King of the Clocks. The dung of death was changed into the gold of good luck. As it had done in the story his father used to tell him in far-away, long-ago Koenigsberg where there was never enough to eat.

'And now, Sigismund likes Plusbelle,' said Ria with faint irony. 'And he thinks he did it all himself.'

'But I did,' Siggie agreed, and he looked tenderly at the donkey who was grazing in the grass by the pool. 'What good luck! She eats grass all day; I don't need to buy a lawnmower.'

He took huge delight in the way she followed him when he walked outside late at night to take a pee in the garden.

'She watches me and, as soon as I've finished, she goes over and takes one herself. In exactly the same spot as me. And a donkey's doing it is not like a man's doing it. It lasts for ages! And when she's finished, she lifts her head – and makes like so.' Siggie lifts his head and brays at the sky.

Siggie used the worst to innoculate himself against worse to come. He was frightened of dirt because it is something you get among the poor; of women because they put a jinx on men. Kindness was never its own reward. Too often it is a mistake. He was a generous man. But it was not charity that made him generous: it was self-protection. Superstition took him in its iron grip and squeezed him till he gave, and he gave freely – cash to beggars, kindness to strangers; he loved animals with a pagan love that spoke of very ancient belief, primitive magic, of times when frogs turned into princes and trolls promised gold to honest boys. He avoided babies. They were something women did – for their own reasons. Bad omens. But he was very kind to terrified children.

'*My father murdered me*,' the children of the Black Mountains once used to sing, ' – *and my mother ate me . . .*'

A gruesome, funny, fending-off-of-demons song. An

old wisdom that knows in its marrow you're more likely to be harmed by your nearest and dearest, than by a nomad of the forest, gypsy, witch or wandering charcoal-burner.

Siggie's wisdom – his magic.

Naturally, this led to misunderstandings. A number of people in and around the village felt Siggie was not to be trusted, either for his morbidities, or his bargaining dementia. In short, some people, and this included old friends of his, called him a liar; in much the same way, I suppose, that long ago, people complained about the tribe's teller of tales; and then said, *sensibly*, that the old boy was a fraud, made it all up, and they didn't believe a word of it!

Certainly, a residue of suspicion weighed in all private discussion of my friend – he was too sharp, or too silly, or combed his hair too often, or struck it lucky more than any honest man should – with another chipped mustard-yellow Provençal jar, once used for storing goose fat and now added to the plain of jars in his back garden. Or because he insisted so fiercely on having fun, and nothing but fun – it wasn't right or fair, and certainly not grown-up. People preferred a bit of seriousness, at least now and then. And watching Siggie wore them out.

* * *

I had not been very long in Kissac when I began to realize it was the very opposite of picturesque. Despite old stone walls and red tiles and humpback bridges over the river, this was not some polished village that won awards for beauty; there was nothing of central casting in Kissac. The sullen young men on the wall were seriously jobless; and there was beauty, unexpectedly, on summer evenings – three old ladies pulled a bench into the narrow street and sat knitting in the sun. But they were lonely, summer was short and life not easy.

The old men on the wall opposite the Lapin watching the cars go by were lonely. Some had gone strange. A bunch of them sometimes congregated for reasons of their own – magnetic attraction, or warmth or maybe some secret, masonic urge? – at the crossroads where the Avenue de la Montagne Noire met the road out of town and a confusion of street signs plastered the wall of the *notaire's* office. And there they changed shape in much the way the gardeners do in Alice in Wonderland. This is a Kissaquienne talent – Nicolas has it, he turns from waiter into sloth and back again, between the soup and the dessert. These men turned into living street signs; they'd pose at the cross-roads, one rose up on his toes, another flung back his arm – they'd freeze into human fingerposts.

The place sorted out, pretty quickly, the sentimentalists from the sons-of-bitches. Kissac was poor, times were hard, so were people.

Silvie, the new young doctor, only a couple of years out of medical school at Montpellier, put it this way: 'When I first arrived, I really thought people were very sympathetic. Then, after a while, I thought they were a bit rough. But kind underneath. Now I know they're awful, even underneath.'

The GP's unsparing view of her patients was strangely encouraging. A little loathing made for a healthy sense of order. Small wine-farmers thought the respectable classes stupidly stuck-up; anyone with pretensions to status claimed to come from Paris and looked down on rustics and small traders who believed that to come from Paris was a calamity. And everyone had a low opinion of foreigners – barbarians with loaded wallets from unspeakable parts of Europe.

Kissac was brimming with jealous, suspicious, small-minded souls – it wasn't pretty, it was poor, and only misdirected blokes like Sad Bob thought differently. Where was the gloss of French village life, as popularly pictured? Nowhere. Kissac had none and the villagers would have been appalled to think it had.

They found Siggie's enthusiasm for the village, their world, worrying. He was a mean, scheming bastard with a clockwork heart. Up to something. He infuriated people, there was his relentless good humour, his mad cheerfulness. His urge to screw them for every centime he could get.

And he returned this – creative animosity? – in his own peculiar, exasperating way. Siggie was cheerful, helpful, full of camaraderie – would not live anywhere else on earth, the best patriot Languedoc could have. Running on the spot like a tin toy, people laughed at him; while he rated everyone, more or less, so low they'd barely show up under a microscope. His superiority ran through his veins like liquid rocket fuel and when he got hot, it blasted him into orbit above their heads from whence he conducted graceful raids, picking up a clock, lamp, angel, wine-press – smiling, affable, ruthless.

Siggie's way was *Jack and the Beanstalk*'s way, when the Giant died and all his money was up for grabs: or the Princess's way when Rumpelstiltskin spun eighteen-carat straw; he did not say, I'm sure someone needs this more than me. He did not take the magical donkey aside and warn it to be very careful what it did with its miraculous dung. Not at all – he grabbed the loot with both hands and ran for the hills.

Chapter 7

When I remember my first days in Kissac, my thoughts are always autumnal. This was how I counted my time, it began when the vines turned, leaves fell. I counted my time from the October clock, the calendar the farmers hold.

* * *

That first November, I walked the vineyards; the vines purple, freckled with gold, and furry as pelts hung out to dry on sticks. The last black grapes, those the pickers missed, lasted sometimes right into December, sweeter each day. When they fell they dried so fast all I found was the corner of a path splashed with purple. The last almonds were even more stubborn; the nuts blackened and the branches put out whiskery, old men's stubble. Unlike the grapes that let go, there was a fierceness to the almonds; stripped of their soft pouches, burnt by the cold, they still hung on like grim death.

The line between life and death was hard to draw. The stalky skeletons of last summer's cherries, beside the fattening buds of next year's fruit. The terrible rush to get going again. In what was, after all, dead midwinter. The sureness that, on this Mediterranean plain, the sun was just around the corner.

The farmers were pruning. A rusty Citroën by the culvert; and deep in the vineyards, an old man and woman in khaki anoraks, bending in the icy wind off the high snows, cutting back the vine shoots to a fist of stiff fingers and dropping the cuttings in neat piles. The clippings lay for a few weeks to dry and then, across the plain that stretches to the Pyrenees, dozens of small fires burned.

This was the time when the walls began collapsing. The drystone walls may have stood for centuries, but winter seepage and frost shifted the balance. The bigger topstones tumbled along with the fill of small stuff that backs up the wall: a mess of pebbles, and chunks of pink marble, flaking, cheesy spewed into the ditch.

The stone walls needed no mortar and, even more useful, no dressing, if you knew what you were doing. Stone has always been friendly here: it stood against the slow slippage of topsoil down to the sea; and built the corbelled cabins in the corners of the vineyards, where a farmer could get out of the midday sun. Stone igloos. Some were grand, with a couple of rooms, shelves and windows; others were no more than big bread ovens.

For most people money ran away. Into the pockets of the rich, or the Church. What you got, if you were lucky, was a patch of mean land, high in the hills – room enough for a goat or a couple of olive trees. But topsoil washed off the mountains to the sea. The terracing locked precious scraps of land into place, sometimes up slopes so steep I could barely stand.

The feeling everywhere in the empty hills was of

busyness, of tilling, terracing, hoeing, grazing, building. In the most impossible, rough places I found ruins of houses, hovels, castles, moats, ditches, ramparts often centuries – even thousands of years – old. The places of charcoal-burners, ice-makers, woodcutters, goatherds; all long gone – jumbled stones on a windy hillside. Stones, and ghosts.

I had the feeling that people had always made their own calendars; it was a tradition that went back to the invaders, to the Romans, Goths, Moors, Crusaders, Cathars, and the French Revolution.

In the churchyard, under a plain headstone, ornamented with a sober revolutionary star, rests Citizen Boulade. So faithful to the French Revolution that he kept to the New World Calendar long after it had been abolished by Napoleon. So reliably anticlerical that when the Corpus Christi procession wound past his house, noisy with hosts and priests and choir, he pushed his harmonium to the window and counter-attacked with the *Marseillaise*. And death did nothing to dim his faith. He died, his tombstone records, on the eleventh day of Thermidor, in the year 100 (or, 1 August 1892).

In Kissac, official Christian feasts were observed, but there was still an uneasy feel to them. When Christmas came round I noticed the small tree, a tiny triangle of lights, and a skinny clog dangling from the overhead power lines, in the main road through the village. And the long curves of the Avenue de la Montagne Noire showed a single red star with a yellow forked tail, strung up like an electrocuted prawn.

On the other hand, in the village of Peyriac was the

Bar Au Coin. So nondescript, with its birdcage, its smoke, its single mad and toothless pensioner for lunch, and its fanatical chess games. But on the bar mirror – to the left of an ancient photograph of the founding family, staring into the camera on some fine afternoon earlier this century, with something approaching quiet horror, as if they've seen the future and it will be fatal – is a scrawl of green tinsel spelt out as *Bon Noël* – which I saw, still there, in June.

Timekeeping, then, was an individual thing. Some went by the Priory clock which struck a flurry of notes, exactly six minutes before the hour. Some went by the loud-speakers. Others relied on the bread van; twice daily: at 9 sharp, and 1.30, hooting like a wedding cavalcade, fresh baguettes bouncing on the steel floor; or the meals-on-wheels lady in her unmarked Renault van, from 11.25 until noon; planting creamy plastic lunch boxes on the doorsteps of her elderly customers. She left her engine running, and its diesel vibration was felt whole streets away, as if the village pressed an electric razor to its cheek. Then there was the *fromagerie* from Carcassonne, at 10 on Tuesday; the *poissonnière* from Conques, at 9 on Friday . . .

* * *

Siggie, with dozens of clocks all around him, never wound them. He believed time, like death, was an enemy to be disdained. He did not wear a watch or use an alarm clock and claimed he woke 'when I'm thirsty'. He got up and skipped across the road for a jug of fresh spring water; he drank five or six glasses for breakfast and took a piece of bread – which he ate on the lavatory.

'It's not nice, I know – but it's convenient.'

His working day was divided by the broadcasts from the *Mairie*; at 10 he paused; and at 4.30 he wound up in his workshop. Radio Marseillete pumped out non-stop *bal musette* accordion classics. Because he had very few clothes – 'a terrible waste of money' – he took great care of them and always wore his green butler's apron over old dark corduroys. His half-moon glasses were dusty with polishing powder or diamond paste, and his workshop bench a jumble of keys, cogs, pendulums, nitric acid, buffing machines, silver paint, gold leaf and beeswax. Light from two diamond-shaped panes, cut into the barn doors, was stamped on his chest and he looked like a playing card.

He knew when it was midday because Ria marked it with a full lunch; he drank a litre of M. Villeneuve's red and followed it with a siesta on his chaise longue, in the billiard room, dozing under his silent clocks – until his internal alarm woke him and he ate half a dozen radishes – 'They settle the stomach' – and returned to his workshop.

When the *Mairie* broadcast funeral music, Siggie moved fast.

'It's not nice,' he said, 'or kind, but a raid must be quick – or things go off. In these matters, delay is fatal.'

It was vital to get in there before Death did any more damage. As if things left behind might catch the terrible mortality of their dead owners. His raids on the houses of the dead were a joyful duty. He rode to the relief of the recently bereft. He saw himself as a service, somewhere between an ambulance brigade and the cavalry.

And there was so much to be saved. People let things go for a song. Clocks, of course, also cast-iron firedogs, brass candlesticks, flat-irons, earthenware pots once good for storing cassoulet, duck fat or blood pudding and now much sought after in the shops of the *brocanteurs*. He loved finding home-made schnapps, or *marque* – better still, flasks of pure alcohol which people laid by in the old days, for distilling illegal high-octane hooch. Sometimes he came across bottles of vintage champagne. It was so exciting, relieving the ghosts of what they left behind. And a kindness. He was doing the poor souls a favour.

It also accorded with deep urgings. Scraping a living, getting by in a tight corner; this need was still sharp in Siggie, and still a reality in Kissac. The past was too close for comfort and the past was poor. The customs of the place recalled how it had been. I often saw scavengers on the municipal rubbish dump outside the village; yet people weren't that poor, they didn't really need to do it but – it was merely being sensible, recalling the hungry times.

It was still legal to glean any grapes the pickers had missed, and the most unlikely people saw to it that their winter supplies were in the cellar: cherries were bottled, they pickled their vegetables, and they gathered chestnuts, wild leeks, truffles. Even if most shopped at the *hyper-marché*.

There lingered in Siggie, in perverted form, the old true meanness of the hungry man who knows in his belly the knife-edge between not-enough and nothing-at-all. He believed that no one ever did anything that was not a way of storing up provision: hoarding against the cold, the dark, the lean years to come.

When I went walking he asked, puzzled, 'But what are you walking *for*?'

Simply to walk was a waste of time; he walked only

when after mushrooms, and he always carried in his car boot a plastic shopping bag – and a kitchen knife.

'Everyone does; just in case they find something.'

'What sort of thing?'

'After rain you sometimes get good fat snails beside the road. Imagine not having anywhere to put them!'

When he drove up over the Pic de Nore and the Col de Salette, he was on the lookout; a few days of rain and mist, a burst of sunshine and he'd brake sharply near the peak and with a whoop, like a boy hunting Red Indians, he vanished into the thick pine forests, wearing city shoes and grey flannels, brandishing his knife. And, when beneath an oak he found what he was looking for, he fell to the ground and began hacking away with a fury that made me look in the other direction.

He had found a patch of orange *pied-de-mouton*; or sheep's foot; and he was cutting off their yellow heads and stuffing them into his *Intermarché* bag like a man who expected the gamekeeper to show up at any moment. Thirty-two, at least!

Back home, he threw open his arms and, like the little tailor, embraced his luck and daring, which grew on each telling: he announced to the neighbours, 'I have mushrooms – dozens!'

He'd have paraded them through town on an open-top bus, like a football trophy.

But when Ria cooked them in omelettes Siggie groaned, 'More mushrooms!'

The truth is he didn't really care for mushrooms; he liked the hunt, the find, the gift, the luck!

Autumn was the time of the hunters and everyone in

Kissac seemed to hunt. Taciturn men in fatigues popped up in the vineyards and copses, looking for rabbit, pheasant, quail, duck, wild boar. In real life they were farmers, bakers, plumbers – now they were transformed into deadly serious marksmen, huntsmen, stalkers, hardy outdoorsmen licensed to kill. They drew up their Renaults in circles, like covered wagons, and sighted down the barrels of their shotguns; they creaked impressively in their waxy new camouflage jackets, and they ran into the copses, hissing and whispering.

Their dogs did the same. Their dogs were just house dogs in real life but now they were pointers and retrievers, real gun dogs. But they were as clueless as their masters who shot each other, and passers-by, with frightening frequency; the more sensible hunters tied bells to their dogs' collars because the dumb mutts ran loose, sheer amateurs that they were.

And if something moved, the hunters blasted away; all day long the thud of guns and, sometimes, the strangled cry of the little hunting horn, when a posse of hunters ran after the wild pigs that roamed the Black Mountains. And among the purple of fallen grapes in the vineyards, were the brass and plastic casings of shotgun shells.

Siggie hated the hunters. 'What's the point?' he demanded. 'They've shot just about everything by Christmas.'

But, again, his principles clashed.

He hated them because they got in the way of his mushrooming. A mixed emotion, I suspected, because he felt bad about the animals. But part of him approved of the principle; hunting was what you did if you were hungry.

Then one day he was stopped and reprimanded by a group of hunters, after wild boar that ran in the mountains.

'They told me as I went by, "you're not allowed here. You'll scare the game." They told me this – on the open road. Christopher, I got so mad when they told me. It's not true – they have no right to stop me. I got back in the car and drove very slowly down the road and every time I saw some hunters in the bushes I tooted my klaxon and waved my hand and greeted them loudly, so every rabbit in the world must have heard me coming!'

A week later, as we passed through the steep little hamlet of Citou, a bunch of hunters was dividing its spoils: they were butchering five large black wild boars in the road. It swam like a lake of blood, and its islands were heads and legs. The hunting dogs, locked in car boots, bayed and scrabbled; villagers arrived with plates and walked away with steaming trophies; it was carnage; there was blood on our tyres.

'Oy, yoi, yoi,' said the King.

I knew what he was thinking. Horrible, but natural. Meat on the hoof – it's for nothing; you don't let it go . . .

For me the lost dogs were the worst thing. Neck-bells chinking in the middle of some remote road, frantically sniffing; panic-stricken mongrels miles from home, and running I felt sure, in the wrong direction.

And the rabbit.

Once, I was walking from Kissac, taking the path through the vineyards that ran beside the thirteenth-century chateau whose cellar walls were crimson – made of cement, mixed with wine because water was always short – and I met a rabbit. When I say we met, the animal simply walked up to me and sat down, shaking.

We looked at each other. It was a small, thin rabbit. Chased to a standstill; run ragged by the dogs. There were hunters in the fields all around us. I knew if it stayed out in the open it was a target. I shooed it as you do a cat. The rabbit sat there, staring at me, shaking. It was past caring.

* * *

Siggie showed an instinctive sympathy with the hunted, even when he knew it was bad for business.

In that first autumn, when Sophie Magdalena left the house, and retreated to the cottage over Carcassonne way; a party of northerners came south to take the sun, four teenage Dutch girls rented Sophie's old rooms over the clock workshop. Autumn weather is often the finest in the year. Though too cold to swim, the days were powder blue with a high bright intense sun, and the pool made a fine suntrap. The girls removed the tops of their swimming costumes, and aimed their breasts, like oiled and shining hillocks, at the sun.

Then Doctor du Toit began sneaking into the garden, coming in quietly through the top gate, where the cherry trees screened him. Soon he wasn't bothering to hide; he showed himself openly, licking his lips and shouting suggestions. The girls did not speak French but du Toit did his rooster imitation – the cock on the dunghill – and his meaning was clear.

At first the King took a kindly line: saying that, after

all, his wife had left him, and a man badly treated by love deserved help.

But when the doctor took to appearing in the orchard, whistling tunelessly, his trouser zip undone, Siggie banned him from the house.

'I don't mind his desires,' said the King. 'But I draw the line at encouraging girls – in my garden. It's indecent. Giving women the idea that men are an easy touch. If they just unleash a nipple, we'll come running . . . our tongues hanging out.'

The doctor went up onto a small hill that climbs above the house and lusted from there.

'Not much good – blowing kisses from the far side of Elysium,' Siggie said.

He had a point. It must have been peculiarly painful for a professional exhibitionist to expose himself to nothing more exciting than the elements. The dimensions were wrong. Display requires proximity.

The doctor withered, he vanished. I never did find out what happened to him. One day he was gone, and his two small sad boys with him. But he remained a tiny figure in my autumn calendar; glimpsed when least expected, like one of those little men in a weather station, who pops into view carrying a brolly to warn of rain. A distant figure on a stony hillside, unzipped among the olive trees.

CHAPTER 8

———◆———

MY FRENCH WAS elementary and so I went looking for a teacher.

As with so many of my introductions to the curious spirit of Kissac – at once unexceptional and bizarre – Siggie put me on to him. Had I seen the Stranger who had come amongst us? The Man in the Mac?

I think Siggie had more in common with Sophie than he knew: she awaited the coming of the angel of the Lord who would trumpet her divinity to the world. Siggie expected the Enchanted One who would turn glass into diamonds.

Just the week before, a mysterious rider had trotted into town, in cape and sombrero. Siggie got terribly excited. A cowboy in the village! On a cold evening as rain sluiced out of the sky, a hero on a tall horse slouching down the avenue was a strange sight. But next morning, the horse was penned in the meadow by the river, and the rider proved to be just another misfit on the make . . . selling rides to tourists. Siggie sighed; even the sly scepticism he wore on his sleeve as a kind of talisman against imposters didn't lessen his craving for magic.

Each time his hopes were dashed, he staggered to his feet again, he always beat the bell.

He told me about The Man in the Mac; I couldn't miss him, said Siggie. He walked along the avenue, in the late afternoons.

'He has a swagger.'

I didn't have to wait long before I saw him. He wore a belted raincoat, collar and tie, and carried a briefcase. This was enough to set him apart in Kissac where no one wore a tie except for funerals and military remembrances. More strangely still, he was walking.

No one walked; no one local, or respectable, at any rate.

Watching him from my high window it seemed he was too short to swagger. Small, bald and pale, darkly dressed, sober – like an undertaker or a debt collector, or like Lenin, off to an execution. At a dogged trudge . . . that was odder still – you might walk along the Avenue de la Montagne Noire, or sail along its lovely big bends, swinging left and right as it flowed – but you did not trudge. Trudging was a lost skill; it required blindness and stoicism, a professional disinterest in any world but the one you had made yourself.

Yet Siggie was right – in the trudge was the hint of a swagger.

At the end of the village the avenue turned sharp right and vanished into the mountains; on that corner a yellow house on the hillside waved its palm tree like a flag. The trudger turned too, and vanished.

Siggie was very taken – at last, the Enchanted One! In no time at all he had asked him over for a glass of wine. And again the vision failed and he came to see me gloomily.

'I gave him M. Villeneuve's best. D'you know what he tells me? He doesn't usually drink the "little" wines of the Minervois. He prefers the big reds – from Bordeaux. And he likes Picasso!'

I don't know which caused Siggie to feel more bitter. The big wines of Bordeaux or Picasso.

Then a small handwritten notice went up in the bakery: FRENCH LESSONS BY REAL TEACHER. ALSO GERMAN OR GREEK.

* * *

I met him a few days later. I was walking in the foothills behind Kissac. A small path known as Anastasia's Chemin cuts along the side of the hill through dwarf oak and lavender. Its spectacular surprise comes unexpectedly, when it bursts out of the scrub, and you find yourself high above a plunging valley.

He was coming towards me, his mac unbelted, hands in pockets, talking quietly to himself and looking like a lawyer's clerk in his suit and his ragged but tight white collar and black tie. His bald head was smaller than I'd realized, and paler, and very delicate, polished like the portraits the Japanese carve on tiny scraps of ivory.

The path is so narrow walkers must slow down as they pass: we stopped and chatted. He had a booming voice, a heartiness I found unconvincing, and a crushing handshake, surprising for so small a man. He spoke French with the spacious precision of the Parisian, so odd in the Midi – where wine was '*du veng*' and bread '*du pang*' – that it sounded stuck-up, or put on. I asked him about lessons. He seemed pleased I'd seen his notice but he warned that he spoke not a word of English. This was promising and we agreed on an hour and a half twice a week.

His name was Thierry. Through the spring he came over to my apartment twice a week and, for one hundred francs a time, he read the novels of Phillipe Solars with me.

'Pronounce the "S",' said Thierry, 'because Solars is Spanish by origin. Like Degas!'

Soon we stopped reading Solars and he talked about genius.

It was like receiving visits from a monk, an ascetic who belonged to an enclosed and very strict order; Thierry was a Trappist of Art. He was not really interested in improving my French; he had a more important mission: he preached the religion of Art. He worshipped at the altar of the Greatly Bright: his Holy Trinity was Heraclitus, whom he was translating; Hölderlin, whose poems he had recently recited in live performance in Toulouse (there were plans for a CD); and Arthur, his friend, the painter poet. A few others were admitted to the Pantheon: Dante, Shakespeare, Rimbaud.

His beliefs, like his clothes, were impressive and sternly old-fashioned. He was very devout and shy and confessed his faith in the reverent tones of a young girl contemplating her First Holy Communion; or Sophie, discussing the beauties of her body. Urgently, even violently. And, like all crusades to save souls at the point of a sword, the determination to spread the faith went hand in hand with an even greater hunger – the urgent need for cash.

I have an idea that those who flee south, in search of a freer life, carry with them a list of things they will not do. For freedom-seekers, they are curiously stubborn. Siggie would never answer the telephone or take orders. Sad Bob would accept only 'French food'; and I was soon struck by the number of things Thierry did not do.

He did not listen to the radio, or watch TV, he never read newspapers because all journalism was lies. And he did not drink the little wines of the country. Thierry also had a list of things he wouldn't do for money; yet I've seldom met anyone so short of the stuff, so needy, so determined to lay hands on it.

I did not know what Thierry was in flight from; all he would say was that Paris had become impossible and so he headed south. Just another refugee. He had a frayed look, a kind of debtors'-prison pallor. He had eyes I can only describe as round drops of light blue milk. I should also say that he was so odd that if he did not exist I could not have invented him.

He'd moved first to a mountain village in the Ariège, where he lived with his friend, Arthur.

'The neighbours looked, and thought, "Two men – they *must* be homosexuals." '

They had been shunned. The memory caused him weary pain, Parisian pain; he felt all the disdain of the metropolitan for these hicks who could not tell the difference between sexual attraction, which was not the case, and something much more powerful, more vital, to Thierry – the blazing fire of Arthur's genius. Thierry's feeling for his friend went well beyond love; it was adoration.

He brought me a catalogue of Arthur's recent work. The artist had taken photographs of himself to illustrate his paintings; and he looked a bit like Epstein, dark and tousled; then there were his paintings: a series of heads of John the Baptist, all himself . . .

Arthur, said Thierry, was a genius as great as Rimbaud. Sometimes he seemed to think Arthur *was* Rimbaud. And being a genius, Arthur went off after the Ariège incident and was doing fine. But then Arthur was among the gods of Art. Thierry was a servant. Acolytes, temple virgins, lesser priests who merely ministered at the altar of greatness had best look to themselves.

Thierry came to Kissac alone, broke, as *gardien* of a house outside the village. He lived rent-free and in return he cared for the garden. Or, to be more accurate, he did not care for the garden. And not being a hypocrite he could not pretend to care. Now and then he went into the great field of vegetables and fruit trees and he tinkered; moved stones, pulled a few weeds and left it looking – smudged.

Not since du Toit had tried to expose himself on the hillside, did a man so fail to impress himself on the landscape.

Thierry was a driven soul; Hölderlin and Heraclitus called. It took more and more effort even to venture into the wilderness, and check the tomato canes and pull the weeds.

It got harder to come to me and read Solars. After all, I was slow and he was only coming because I paid him the hundred francs. He wanted to get back to Hölderlin, back to Art. That was also on his list: *not* hiding his impatience with anything that was not Great Art; Great Genius; Great Thought.

Thierry was dead broke, but even being broke wasted

his time. It pained him to need my hundred francs. Stupid! Like the pettiness of life. Thierry knew some of the money I paid him was earned by writing for the papers and that grieved him too: he would have preferred me not to do it. He only took my money because he had to; but it did nothing to lessen his pain, or his disapproval; it was not to his taste – like the little wines of the Minervois. He drank only big red-blooded genius.

Thierry's French was beautiful; he liked good writers; and his reverence for Art brought a religious intensity to our lessons – but there was a problem. Dirt. Or the lack of it. I wanted the basics, the hard facts of French, and he really couldn't get his hands dirty, messing about in rocky grammar, and pulling up the weeds that blighted my poor patch of French garden.

Then Thierry was fired. He told me as we were walking at Lastours, the five ruined Cathar castles in the mountains near Salsigne. There were cold flurries of rain. Everybody else was scrambling up the trails to the ruined towers in anoraks, jeans, trainers; Thierry was in his tie and collar and black city shoes and looked vaguely sinister, like the undertaker, or a child molester on a day out.

'The Midi, the South, Languedoc especially,' said Thierry, 'was abandoned. Ruined. First by history. The King, the Crusaders, the Church. Then by politicians. It's nowhere, it's not serious, it doesn't rate.'

Every so often the sun came out and his domed head flashed like a hand-mirror. Thierry mentioned he would not be giving me lessons any longer: the owner of the house had thrown him out.

In the next days, Thierry showed a strange adaptability,

based on inefficiency, poverty, disapproval. How curious that something so flawed may be so strong; Thierry was quite unable to do anything. And he showed all the eerie resourcefulness of a helpless man for getting others to do what he cannot and will not do himself . . . It was fascinating, even a little frightening to see the ability fully deployed. In short order Thierry got his angry landlord to drive all his possessions to my place and he talked Siggie into letting him store them in his barn.

Then he vanished.

Siggie was appalled. He was left with Thierry's possessions in his barn, covered with an old army blanket. Like a corpse, he said, lying there among his wrought-iron altar railings, drinking fountains, clocks, mantelpieces. Contaminating his treasures! He lifted the blanket with a careful toe, as if he might uncover the horrid broken victim of some terrible road smash.

And the stuff was perplexing: three large sticks, rough cudgels, of oak or cherrywood; a lot of cardboard boxes filled with paper; an electric kettle; a couple of rusted lidless pots, a frying pan without a handle; an Olivetti electric typewriter that seemed to have been struck by lightning; several empty sacks, a groundsheet, a broken radio, a rock carved like a loaf. Siggie was scandalized. It was like spitting in church! Nothing worked, it had no value! No beauty! No point! Why did Thierry keep them, with his big talk, his Bordeaux reds, and his Picasso!

Thierry phoned from a public box, somewhere over the mountains. He'd found a place – would I load his stuff and bring it?

His new place, a cottage in the Tarn, was damp, the

roof leaked, icy mist rose out of the grass in waves. His job was to fix the roof. His raincoat was a little more grubby, his handshake firmer, his greeting boomier. It was June. When I got the heavy stuff out of my car he laid it out in the hall and covered it with the blanket. It could wait – his new place was great; he planned on staying for quite some time.

All his real treasures he had taken with him when he left Kissac, and they were in place: his Hölderlin poems on the table; his German and Greek dictionaries, and his most precious belongings, a couple of tiny framed drawings – the sacred heads of and by his favourite artist, on the wall.

'If this house caught fire, that is all I would save.'

He took me outside and amazed me by picking tomatoes in his suit and his city shoes, tenderly weighing the fruit in his dead-white tiny hands. Next he lit a smoky fire in the tiny grate; he had picked fresh thyme from the field, he had a parcel of fresh sardines (he must have walked miles to buy them); he had a bottle of rosé chilling in the bathroom basin – no big Bordeaux red, which would have been his choice, but then I was drinking this wine and not Thierry. He had one knife, fresh bread, no butter, and a twist of salt in a piece of newspaper. Along the mantelpiece he had pinned his Great Sayings – true but unexceptional *pensées*: 'Art Is Eternal' and 'Genius Will Sing!'.

He turned the sardines on the grill in the fireplace and sprinkled them with thyme, he poured the wine; and he served that day a lunch I can only compare with that feast all those years ago under the skylight, in the garret in the rue de Seine.

Thierry's sardines, grilled to a turn, are now words on

a page; not poetry or painting. I know better than to claim such memories, such lunches, in all their sparse perfection, should mean something to anyone else simply because they meant so much to me; but I resist the notion that because they meant so much to me they cannot mean anything to anyone else.

These moments have been a kind of consolation; but they have also given me something more helpful – ammunition. Flags to fly in the faces of pragmatists, the accountants of souls, the sensible, the logical, the utilitarians who say that France is merely a country and the heart is only a pump and lunch is, well, simply lunch – though even as I unfurl my flag I feel a twinge of something like guilt – after all, one should not tease the blind.

* * *

A few months later, Thierry phoned – from a callbox. A neighbour had offered him a lift to Carcassonne. And he needed to see me.

We met at Chez Jim's, on the square. Another of those places I owed to Siggie, though he never went inside; he liked to raid and leave.

Thierry was reading at a pavement table. His collar was frayed down to the cotton fibres. He closed his book – the *Collected Works of Georges Bataille* – gripped my hand and his greeting was as madly, boomingly, hearty as ever.

'*Cher Christopher: Comment allez vous?*'

The waiters shied away when they saw Thierry. They seemed to sense trouble, like dogs dive for cover before thunderstorms; or birds alarmed by prowlers; they swooped and twittered warnings, they sent out silent alarms as trees are said to do when attacked by pests.

We sat at a table on the square; he was wearing his (one and only?) grey suit. Just as Jehovah's Witnesses wear dark unobtrusive suits, which you sense are cut from steel and sold by a secret supplier known only to members of the cult, Thierry's outfit was a uniform masquerading as civilian dress: the white shirt, the mourner's tie, the prep-schoolboy charcoal suit.

But something puzzled me; he wasn't a priest, though he preached, and he wasn't a terrorist, though he gave himself over to a form of fanaticism. So what was he?

And then it struck me – Thierry was the artist *and* the show, he was performance art. The suit, the careful shirt – Thierry was togged out in 'philo-couture' – he was the 50s, the Left Bank. Retro-Sartre, perhaps? Except he would have hated Sartre who succumbed to politics and journalism and money and women, and even philosophy.

He didn't care for the *stuff* of any of them; he didn't even really care, I think, for the stuff of art; no, it was the gear, the attitude, the style; it was the romance – no, not even that – it was the anti-glamour that got him going.

Thierry's great exhibitionism lay in his downplaying, down-grading glamour until it became all but invisible yet very powerful. He was like a black hole: get near him and nothing escaped, not even light. He was so deadpan it was positively exotic, and that was where the swagger came from. If you saw just a man in a grey flannel suit, an old mac, you missed the truth of it. Because in fact, he dressed to kill, he made office-wear gamey, cheesy, wildly, darkly flamboyant – at heart, Thierry was a dandy. An actor-beggar. And all his effects were achieved by the tension between the little bald man in the mac and the stuff he wrote or carried.

Like the big book of Bataille's erotic writing he put on the table.

Bataille's big best work painted, in some detail, unusual couplings with human eyeballs and a good deal of blood about.

And then there was Thierry. In a grey suit – plus three rusty pots, three cudgels and a dead typewriter in Siggie's barn. It took a lot to imagine Thierry having sex with anyone. If he spent 120 days in Sodom, he'd be doing the audit.

But that was to miss the point. His point was *not* doing it. In style!

I asked him if he thought of writing anything himself.

'If I can't write as well as Shakespeare, what's the point?'

Then he got on to me. He'd just read one of my novels, in French, and there was a lot wrong with it. It was tainted by politics, infected by current events, missing all the vital signs of Great Art. He hoped, politely, that his opinion did not bother me and asked if I could let him have some cash. The cottage in the Tarn was not working out. Did I see his problem?

I did, I did. The roof still leaked; things were 'complicated'. Hölderlin called. And Art. Genius. He didn't have a sou to his name – yes, I saw the problem. I wanted to say that, as a rule of thumb, if you're going to touch a writer for cash, be careful what you say about his books.

But Thierry was too far gone for telling.

I gave him some money and we drained our coffee.

Then he disappeared into the crowds in the pedestrian *piéton*, a tiny figure in his mac, his polished dome winking like a warning light, Bataille under his arm, the mild-mannered philosopher in a grey suit who changed in a twinkling into a superman of sexual prowess . . .

CHAPTER 9

THE CIRCUS WAS a sign of early summer.

Hercule, the little collector from across the Black
Mountains, introduced me to the Circus of Dreams. Hercule's hump so entranced the audience and the performers
that there were times the clowns, trapeze artists, and even
the dromedary forgot what they were doing, and stared;
and the ringmaster cast a longing look, as though to say –
if only *we* had a hunchback like that!

The Circus of Dreams played every village between
Kissac and the Pyrenees and the strain was telling. The
troupe was small, the trailers in the station parking lot were
poor, the acrobats' spangles tarnished. Siggie suggested it
was the fault of the respectable classes, who didn't go to
the circus any longer. The fat *notaire*, the new lady
doctor, the prim little chemist and his wife and his two
children, all of them asparagus-pale and timid as bats, but
undeniably modern, of this era, and the smart photographer
and the woman from Paris – none of them ever set foot in
the Circus of Dreams.

Siggie was wrong when he blamed 'the respectable
classes' for the death of the circus. Wrong because, for a
start, the phrase was contradictory – there were no classes

which could be called respectable. Wrong, too, because the people he blamed never did go to the circus. They did not destroy the troupe in the Little Top camped in the old station yard, opposite the municipal camping site. They had no feelings about the circus, they simply didn't see it.

What was killing the Circus of Dreams was the new religion, the need to pull apart and dissect. What modern sensible people did with animals was to eat them or study them; either way this meant killing them, and cutting them up. Animals were a meal – or an experiment. They served the appetite or science. The Circus of Dreams did neither.

* * *

The Circus of Dreams arrived without warning. Like the *marin*, blowing from the sea. You got up one morning and the posters were roped to the lamp-posts beside the bridge and across the road from the *maternelle*. Tied in neat bows – the rope was used again and again. Posters red and blue as blood and bruises, touting trapeze artists, clowns . . . hours of fun for all the family! See the Dromedary; the Wonder of the Desert! The Beautiful Boy Clown!

Promises dizzying in their lies.

Siggie wouldn't come – the circus was for dreamers, kids, gypsies.

I think he was frightened of the dancing monkey and the prancing camel and the Beautiful Boy Clown – he had a superstitious horror of charms, omens, tricks – they seemed to him the other faces of Death. Anyway, the circus was on its last legs and he didn't want to get too close to a losing outfit, full of sad relics of the old days.

Unless he knew where he was going, unless he was

bound to some iron routine that guaranteed a good time, profit and – this was vital – prompt return home, he was uneasy. He hated leaving home; and when he did so, on his Wednesday tours, there was huge excitement. It was *Hansel and Gretel* all over again. Well, Hansel, yes. Siggie would have had trouble with Gretel. Females were folly. Women, wives, witches. Be warned, turn your back and she'll push you into her cauldron.

These mountains were called Black not because of their colour but because, once, they were home to wandering charcoal-burners, nomads of the forest. Just the sort of people likely to kidnap a small, round, blue-eyed boy and sell him, or eat him, or change him into a pig for hunting truffles! Oh, the horrid, magical, marvellous danger of it all!

I wouldn't have been surprised if, before setting out on his Wednesday raids – on the junk shops and *brocanteurs* and flea markets of the Black Mountains, searching for clocks, commodes, stone angels – he'd hidden a handful of breadcrumbs in his pocket, just in case he got lost.

* * *

The old days were exactly what Hercule enjoyed remembering. When country was country; and conmen came to town and took everyone for a ride – when everyone wanted to be taken for a ride. When there were still rides to be taken. Shooting galleries, tombola: country boys on the tear; girls greedy for ribbons. When bravado rang the bell and things were shining. And there were enough wonder-workers around to do the business: which was to get your heart out of your boots and into your mouth.

'Country folks were stupid. Lots of them – and things were fine.'

Hercule began to glow, his eyes watered, his shoulders heaved, he loved every second of this memory – how he'd been working the sideshows with his sister: and how clever Pujols, the gypsy, did the business.

His French got so thick, so quick, the *patois* so heavy that it was very difficult to follow. But I heard what he said. Because Hercule shaped the objects, the wooden booth, even the flow of air, with his hands; and made the sounds, the smack of the ball against skittles, cracking his elastic cheeks, banging his big hollow chest which echoed right through to his hump – when he wanted to remember how the skittles had their legs knocked out from under them by the wooden ball swinging from the roof of Pujols' wooden booth.

'Three skittles down wins a goose; five a pair of clogs; knock over the lot and triple your stake!' Hercule called long-dead punters to play.

The young man lifted the ball and let fly. Everything depended on Pujols; so casually lolling against the door jamb, leaning left or right, tilting the entire wooden booth on its axis, Pujols, god of the box. Playing the punter like a fish.

'Prizes get suckers, and suckers bring faith. Faith gets wonders,' said Hercule. 'With faith there is love and money and magic.'

But that was then. This was now. The Circus of Dreams was so small and so threadbare it took a special effort to stay loyal. Those who turned up seldom rose above thirteen or so. It was a good house when the audience outnumbered the artistes and animals.

We were not an audience, we were a support group.

The guy who brought his tiny daughter for the lucky dip, a fat funnel of red paper with a rattle, a doll, a bracelet inside which they sold the kids in the interval. Six boys, young teens, in the front row; so modern they didn't even believe what they saw on television. They came because they couldn't believe their eyes – people doing tricks, in a circus ring, in the flesh, in costume, in public. Three fat young friends of the girl who sold candyfloss – 'Father's Beard' – under a hand-lettered sign: WE ALL LOVE BARBE À PAPA! And the Colonel's Lady; she came to look at the dromedary who trotted round the ring with his shaggy pelt, balding knees, appalling odour, bobbing head, and a look of sweet dignity. We did not know then why she was so keen on the beast but I had heard the whispers about the Colonel's Lady, and what happened down in the municipal picnic area beside the river.

* * *

Traditionally, the Circus of Dreams unbundled in the parking lot on the edge of the village, once the yard of the old train station. It has been decades since the last train stopped here – when Kissac had four hotels and four cafés and a brothel. The station is a gym now. We have one hotel and two cafés, and no one knows what happened to the brothel.

But it has to be said, against the odds, the Circus of Dreams kept coming, it kept faith.

A groundsheet of scuffed plastic, in red, white and blue

stripes, was unrolled, and stuck like a rather greasy giant postage stamp to the tarmac. The struts went up next, then the guys, then the thin patched skin of the Not Very Big Top.

The wooden tiger cage was wheeled into position. I never could see how that cage held two big cats. One good smack with those paws would smash the flimsy green box; and then, like a nightmare gone mad, they'd burst out of the dark and eat up the world.

But it was not going to happen: the tigers were flimsy, too, a shade quivery on their pins, stripes fading. A small handwritten notice, all curlicues in purple ink, was wired to the bars, above an enamel cash box: 'WE NEED TO FEED OUR MASTERS: YOUR FIVE FRANCS WILL HELP'.

What would happen, I sometimes wondered, to the artistes in the Circus of Dreams, as earnings dropped and hunger increased?

In Mozambique, when civil war brought famine, starving soldiers raided the zoo and feasted on the remaining cheetahs. Normal behaviour in a mean, pinched, murderous age. Once upon a time, the jungle was dangerous; it was full of tigers who ate people. Now it's worse: the jungles are going and people think nothing of eating tigers.

The loudspeakers next. They belted out cover versions of heavy metal numbers by scratch bands – then choked and died – hanging from the lamp-posts like strangled dictators.

Thirty francs bought a seat in the gallery (a line of trestle benches); forty a plastic garden chair at the ringside. The usherette led the way into the strange yellow light of the tent. Short and compact, long blonde hair tied tightly in a green ribbon, she walked with a tripping motion you see in ponies.

Hercule and I sat in the gallery – you got a better view. Besides, the clowns picked on the ringside audience and my French was not good enough to swap banter with a clown.

The usherette did not return our tickets. Tickets were recycled, like the posters.

The band was a man in a red beret, playing drums, trumpet, cymbals; he blew a little fanfare, like a bullfighter's salute. The band was over sixty, I reckoned. He gave a big riff on the cymbals: the ringmaster ignored him, so the band played it again – hitting the drum hard and low.

The ringmaster told the band he'd lost his whip. Then he walked about the ring, kicking at the plastic flashing.

When the band offered to look for the whip the ringmaster ordered him back to his post. We waited. The light through the canvas turned buttery. The tent smelt of camel and plastic. The old men quarrelled gently like two slowly boiling kettles.

The Boy Clown, blond hair and red cheeks and a sassy bow tie and floppy shoes, marched on and handed his grandad the missing whip. All the family were in the wings, applauding, you'd think the kid had walked on water. The ringmaster flicked the whip crossly, like a man trying to start a car with a cold engine; it backfired feebly; and the band played a riff, by way of congratulation.

The show was running.

The Circus of Dreams had one trapeze artist, she was also the usherette, married to the strongman who was the father of the Boy Clown; a pretty young fellow of about six. Like, say, a family of giant pandas who have succeeded in breeding in captivity, the Flying Fortunas had given up living in the wild; now they wanted to be applauded for simply surviving – and they had pinned their future on this wonder child. They all looked on horrified when he climbed into the ring; on the trapeze the boy smiled and swung; the strongman stood below, anxiously twanging the safety net. The family closed its eyes – one child between them and extinction.

The ringmaster lifted his mike. 'Welcome, friends, to the Circus of Dreams!' He had another go at the whip but this time it would not work.

'Merde!' he said, with that Midi beat on the last syllable.

* * *

After the show, Hercule and I gave ten francs to the tiger fund in the station yard; ahead of us was the Colonel's Lady, in her old fox-fur and her cloche hat – she was in no hurry, and who would blame her? I thought it difficult to square the gentle gaze of the village on the tall thin lady, given the stories told of beatings – perhaps the Colonel might that very night, as he did sometimes, take her to that special spot down by the river, where he thought no one heard her cries . . .

It made Hercule moist-eyed; he wept often and he hated cruelty of any sort. Because his hump served to emphasize his round strong chest, when he cried he spouted like a leaky barrel.

We found Siggie in his living room eating radishes and watching *Question pour un champion!* He revered the quiz, it expanded the mind. His friend, Marie-Jo, had once made the final round on the show – her subject: 'The travels of Rimbaud'.

He grinned when he heard where we'd been. Dreamers were disabled people – where had it got us – Hercule and his hump, me with my books? He ran through the Great Dreamers: Thierry; Rimbaud – he'd died in Africa; Ria's father – he'd wanted to be a cowboy in America. He was very pleased that there was no dreaming in him.

In fact, there was a lot of dreaming in Siggie, but it was of a primitive, elemental, god-struck kind, the sort of thing I imagine found in very early human beings, like Cro-Magnon man; the continual edgy awareness of powers which demanded to be placated. Siggie was a throwback – a living fossil, in him there was perfectly preserved that time when man, bold and brutish, began thinking of death and gods and prevention, began painting his prayers on his cave wall, crossing himself for luck.

Siggie embodied that point in human history when the clever, opportunistic hominid somehow meshed his talents as scavenger, hunter, scrounger and tomb-robber, and came up with a combination that made modern homo so successful – the manners of the killer ape and the heart of a commercial salesman.

That was the thing about Siggie: his intense and godless piety: his atheism – so much did it mean to him he had turned it into a religion. Siggie was noisily, defiantly anti-religious, and full of sermons. The Vatican and the Mafia were in cahoots. Religion was a racket, it was behind much of the crime and wickedness of the world. Priests, nuns, clergy – all were crooks! On the other hand, what a wonderful scam. He envied their professionalism.

As with our hunting forefathers, Siggie's faith went hand in hand with practical considerations: making a kill, bringing home the bacon.

He listened with some impatience to Hercule's fears for the Colonel's Lady. The Colonel combined two marks which Siggie detested more than all others, he was a soldier, and a Catholic – what on earth did Hercule expect from a man like that?

One night, said Hercule, the Colonel would go too far. Hercule's eyes filled with tears.

Siggie said, 'Hercule, if you weep, you can't drive.'

*　*　*

So we drove back in convoy and on the way we stopped for a meal in an eerily deserted valley, near Castres. We found a simple *auberge*, a farm-kitchen, where the farmer's wife cooked. She was not supposed to serve us, since we weren't guests staying overnight. But locals used it and so no one had complained. A couple of farm workers were eating; a table of card-players and a solitary gendarme. The farmer's wife ran between the tables, plonking down carafes of red wine between servings of pigeon-breast salad, rabbit and goat's cheese.

Siggie said, 'Could you dine like this in Paris or London? For sixty Francs? And the wine is given!'

And to cheer Hercule he rummaged around for a joke. He had a big repertoire, but limited categories. Sex and death were favourites, followed by cripples, women, and people with speech impediments.

Hercule, Siggie believed, was *très timide*, and that disturbed Siggie who wanted everyone in the world to enjoy his laughter and his pleasure, to have as much fun as he did, and – while he knew this was impossible, and the loss was ours – he wanted us to *try*.

He told a story about the hunchback who met a ghost in a graveyard and the ghost promised to remove his hump.

Siggie played the ghost, the hunchback, the graveyard, opening his arms wide and hooting like an owl when the ghost reneged on his promise.

Hercule did not mind in the least; his dark, intelligent eyes sparkled all through the telling, and the ecstatic audience reaction – also provided by Siggie. He clapped and stamped and wiped his eyes. Siggie was the best audience his jokes could ever have.

Hercule winked. 'I heard it before.' Hercule wagged his huge head on his broad shoulders. 'But you're in fine form. Not even a gypsy could dent you today.'

The talk turned to the big gypsy encampment, in Lézignan. The gypsy vote, Siggie maintained, kept the Socialist council in power.

There began his litany: gypsies rode from place to place in Mercedes and paid no taxes. Gypsies roamed the roads looking for things to steal.

'Hercule grew up with them. He knows all about gypsies.'

He waved a hand at the hunchback, who blushed violently, he hated being singled out: his embarrassment was terrible.

Siggie did not notice. 'You can live in the pocket of a gypsy and still never understand him. Isn't that right,

Hercule? Don't you say that? Gypsies are stranger than women!'

Hercule wrinkled his big, broad thoughtful forehead.

'I was at school with one or two. And I worked with them in the fairs. People like Pujols. You get on – but a gypsy cannot be your friend. A gypsy sticks to his own.'

Talk of gypsies reminded Siggie of the man who sold him a Venetian mirror, a lovely silvery bevelled fish pond of a mirror. The man who'd sold it to him had told him about an English artist in Lézignan.

'She's a painter and she likes living in France. But her paintings don't sell. She has to do something. So she sells herself.'

Hercule said, 'That's a terrible thing.'

'Why?' Siggie was astonished. 'She doesn't have anything else to sell. It's sensible.'

Hercule specialized in paraffin lamps, old brass farming equipment, wine barrels, petrol pumps from the 30s. It was personal, in the way it can be in Languedoc. He would not sell you a picture frame unless he thought you were kind.

'You can't sell love. Never! What is love? It's myself. My memories, my mother, my sister. Love's not a shop.'

'What is it then?'

Siggie's accent was so strange and his talk so wild and the hunchback so pink in the face that card-players and gendarme and farm-workers crumbled their bread and stared: openly, unashamedly, hooking their legs around their chairs, tilting towards the rush of his talk, leaning into the wind of it.

Hercule had his shoulder blades up around his big ears, so his head looked like a burrowing mole.

'It's a circus.'

Siggie was delighted. 'Hercule, you're crazy! Circuses are for kids – and dreamers. She sells herself – why not? This woman doesn't have any luck – OK, so she makes her own. Wouldn't you?'

The room was suddenly quiet. Looking at the farmer's wife – she was a woman, what did she say? But she wasn't being drawn – she cleared dishes, pretending she hadn't been listening.

The hunchback had no answer, shook his big head and his hump shook too. His shovel face began to break up, ripple after ripple flowed across its broad acreage. The thought of the artist trading herself hurt him. His eyes got their tell-tale shine. And, this was the strange thing, no one turned a hair; Hercule sat there pouring tears, Siggie finished his coffee, I looked out of the window, embarrassed – but alone in this; the waitress cleared our plates, the other diners went back to talking about rugby and it was all perfectly fine; men cry, just as men kiss.

Later we went back to Hercule's place, an old and very ugly house on the main road, near Castres; a big bulky villa in a fenced-off yard, among a mess of roof beams and bricks, and a big steel barn, where Hercule stored the bits and pieces he bought and sold.

In a large bare living room, with a sink in the corner, the hunchback's brother sat watching television. He did not speak or seem to notice us. Hercule carefully removed his white shirt and hung it on the washing line looped above the kitchen sink and put on a denim working shirt;

he took a bottle of Paul Ricard from the shelf beside a statue of the Virgin Mary, and glanced across at his brother. He was watching a programme on the killer capacities of the ladybird. She was eating someone and her jaws crunched – followed by a squeak – like shoes on snow. We drained our milky *pastis* standing up, as is the way, and headed out into the night.

In the car Siggie blew softly through his teeth. The car filled with the liquorice fumes of the *pastis*. He was worried. Hercule had told him that he thought, deep down, he might be Jewish.

'As if he didn't have enough problems,' said Siggie.

CHAPTER 10

———◆———

WEDNESDAY WAS SIGGIE'S sabbath.

Up early as always, he dressed in his Wednesday best, dark blue jersey with clean green corduroy pants; after the usual six glasses of spring water, and morning ablutions, he toddled across the road to his Volkswagen, rubbing his hands.

Oh, that rub — it sent Ria mad.

She would say, 'I can hear it across the road.'

She couldn't, of course, but I knew what she meant. The sound drowned out everything, it semaphored Siggie's belief that all the world hung like some gorgeous bauble from the lower branches of the tree of life — and he was off to pluck it! Wasn't he lucky?

And why, asked Siggie's palms, moving ecstatically upon each other, can't you be more like me? We could, if we wanted to, but we didn't try; that was the problem.

Siggie pushed The Beachboys into the cassette-player — he'd bought an entire archive, as a job lot, on one of his Wednesdays. He didn't like the Beach Boys much, but music was music and a dozen cassettes for fifty francs — it was for nothing! He whistled as he warmed up the Golf. What a day!

He never missed a Wednesday, never altered his battle plan; he performed very well if someone was along to watch him, and he often invited visitors to observe him doing what he did best; but he never changed his style or his timetable. My first exposure to Siggie's Wednesday was repeated many times, but it never changed by so much as a new stopover; like religious observance, like church-going, it ran to formula, and it held Siggie spellbound.

He called it 'turning about' – lightning raids on the junk shops, *brocantes*, cellars, attics, *antiquités*, flea markets of the Black Mountains, finding treasures among the dealers in towns like Mazamet, Castres, Albi. Siggie's faith never faltered. No passionate pilgrim set off for Compostella or Canterbury with more hope in his heart and a greater longing for miracles than Siggie, warming up the VW Golf early on Wednesday morning.

The Beach Boys sang of the surf as I got in beside Siggie that first morning, and we were off. Siggie drove fast and well – the turbo whining up the steep, snaking approaches to the Pic de Nore. And all the time he sang the praises of the country – heavenly salesman of all he surveyed. Everything was better and brighter on his side of the mountain: wine cheaper, apples crisper, onions sweeter, pines taller, dwarf oaks greener, mushrooms fatter, the tigerish, early summer leaves more flamingly beautiful.

The litany never altered, he drummed his fingers on the wheel; the Beach Boys worshipped love and California. Siggie adored luck and Languedoc.

Like all true faith, his swung a load of dogma, the way a cosh swings lead. He brooked no argument; did not know there *was* an argument. It was so satisfyingly circular; so

clinchingly convincing, as it is for those who deal in answers
– a good faith – it consoled the believer, it k-o'd the sceptic.
It was beautiful, it was lucky, it was like California – and
it went like this: all Siggie looked on was good, because he
had chosen it; and he had chosen it because it was good.

End of story.

On that first Wednesday, and ever after, I was shocked
at how suddenly, completely, the country changed. At the
top of the Black Mountains the scratchy chalky textures,
the scrub, rock and vineyards of the coastal plain gave way
to grassy hills, dairy farms and greystone hamlets. The Midi
was left behind and we were in fat, wet country, made
green by rains and mist and snow.

Siggie did not like the other side of the mountain. He
searched for the word to describe it – and it surprised me
then, it still does, when he found it – '*triste*'. He shook his
head, sorry for people who had to live in a land so 'sad'.
Siggie's reactions were often deeply original – perhaps
'forlorn' would be a better translation of what he felt.

On the crest of the peak, he pulled onto the grass verge.
He jumped out of the car, hopped a fence, calling to me
to follow, and set off at his jerky trot, arms held high for
balance. In the middle of a meadow he stopped, stooped
and pointed to his toes.

'Take a look!'

I saw a deep opening in the grass, a chamber lined with
stones.

'Know what it is? A *glacière*. They stored ice down
there. In the old days.'

He was down on his knees before the hole in the
ground, words tumbling out, flying – he talked the way he

ran – redness rising in his cheeks, as he told me the beautiful story. Siggie's Sermon on the Mount.

Long ago, when the world was young and folks were smart, God gave the mountain dwellers lots of rain, followed by a cold winter to freeze it solid. The mountain dwellers farmed the ice, cut it into blocks and stored it underground in a natural freezer. God was pleased and sent the raging summer heat. And when, in stifling August, the townspeople down in Carcassonne and Castres cried out for something to cool their fish, the mountain dwellers opened their deep freeze and sold up a storm.

What a business: water into ice, ice into cash – the brilliance of the deal entranced him, he rocked to and fro before the hole in ecstasy.

'By horse and cart they'd haul slabs of ice down the mountains to the towns. Imagine! That's smart. They cleaned up.'

And it was all – for nothing.

Siggie's highest praise. That was how miracles were made. That was what lay behind his raids on the junk shops in the mountains and the incredible once-in-a-lifetime bargains he brought back every Wednesday. Never missed, never failed, never for a moment considered he was anything but the luckiest man on earth – more, he *made* his luck.

Every Wednesday? Yes. That's why Ria ran into the cherry orchard to shut out the sound, and Gretel became dreamier and dreamier, and even Plusbelle the donkey kept her head stubbornly down when Siggie began rubbing his hands.

* * *

The route was also laid down. His first stop was Loud Lilly's Emporium of Junk, in Mazamet. It was a shed the size of an aircraft hangar, probably an old tanning shed, a reminder of the days when merchants grew rich on the leather trade.

Loud Lilly lay on the very summit of a great heap of bedclothing, mouldy curtains, cotton shifts, camisoles and nightdresses of the last century. The beautiful handstitched, embroidered trousseaus of ghostly brides.

Lilly chose not to reveal herself while she studied the customer. If she approved, she materialized among the roof beams of her barn and hovered like an unkempt genie over a mountain of lamps, commodes, and squads of plaster Madonnas with pink roses in their hair. On top of her mountain, the beams of the great roof were slung with pulleys for moving heavy goods, perhaps even her.

Lilly ceremoniously refused to see the King.

He was not at all put out.

'She stopped seeing me when she heard I lived in a castle – a chateau. Even though it's years since I left and came to live in Kissac, she still thinks I'm some kind of prince.'

But she allowed her husband to deal – a round, jolly man whose only sign of nerves was the glance he threw, now and then, at the roof where unseen Lilly lay on her sky-platform.

You do not easily find treasures in Loud Lilly's; you need 'the eye'.

Siggie bought a clock: 'Very rare movement, it takes four keys. Never have I seen something so rare.'

And a couple of flat-irons: 'Eighteenth century.' He whispers, 'Don't tell them!'

He loved being taken for a rich man in his castle. He enjoyed the status without any of the pain endured in his wars with Him the Horrible.

'She's a *big* communist. A believer. Her communism won't let her see me.'

Then he was off again, ferreting through the junk mountain: paraffin lamps, stone angels, candlesticks, wrought-iron, cameras, duelling pistols, sword sticks. He was hungriest for timepieces: chronometers, grandfather clocks, cuckoo clocks, fobwatches, church and station clocks.

Siggie's eye was as sharp as an aboriginal tracker's; disperse the whiff of profit in thousands of cubic metres of thin air and Siggie sniffed it out, the way a shark smelt blood; just as a bushman can tell, from a glance at a spoor, when the lion passed this way and what he had for dinner. A little bit would do, a wreck, the remains, a corpse. Quick as a butcher-bird, a buzzard, a hyena (that's where I'd heard that cackle before), Siggie snapped up a windfall – something I wouldn't have glanced at – his meal ticket.

Loud Lilly's husband watched nervously.

Siggie's eye was scything past walnut card tables, yellowing pianolas, limbless dolls, bayonets, headless Joans of Arc, German helmets, portraits of Marshal Pétain – and swooped precisely. From a hedge of crucifixes, he pulled out a worm-eaten clock from the Black Forest.

'Not bad.' He opened the door and dug a finger into the empty nest. 'But where's the cuckoo? *En vacance?*'

* * *

Behind it all, in the Platonic sense, was the Great Bargain from which all lesser earthly bargains take their lustre, beside which they are pale shadows – a sleeping beauty . . . lost in the mountains.

'Somewhere, there is a Princess . . .'

He told me about her that first Wednesday, as we were on our way back from a small flea market that sometimes unfolded in Lautrec, and traded in the avenue of plane trees, in a parking lot on the edge of the town. It was a simple affair – each dealer's pitch, numbered in orange paint on the tree trunk, might be a parked van, a trestle-table, sometimes just a tarpaulin stretched on the gravel.

I liked the gambler: a bearded man in a black hat. He arrived late, empty-handed, and raided his neighbours' tables, buying a candlestick, a couple of firedogs, a flat-iron, carried them to his pitch and sold them – at a small mark-up.

If his colleagues saw him moving the stuff, they began to worry they'd let him have it too cheaply and bought it back – at his mark-up. It was a crazy gamble.

But then the best dealers were as driven as their customers by the dream of some perfect bargain, some lovely prize. Like a little gypsy in a broad-collared, white shirt, a big gold earring swinging from his left lobe. He sold old door knockers: swans' necks curving back on themselves like whips; long ladies' fingers clasping in their tips a heavy globe; and serviceable truncheons of battered cast-iron that seemed to come from cell doors.

One day I saw him find heaven: he'd bought a huge lion's head from a dealer in mirrors. The lion had a flaming brassy mane, shining jaws clamped around the ring, as big as a child's waist. The effect was overwhelming; it was the sort of thunderer for a giant's front door he'd been longing for all his life.

The gypsy kept hugging it to his chest, stroking the lion's mane, almost unable to speak, whispering over and over, 'It weighs fifteen kilograms!'

I said it was beautiful.

He looked amazed. 'More than beautiful – magnificent!' His eyes were wet.

* * *

Five, six, seven stops, no time wasted, a brief look, the searching eye; sometimes he didn't even seem to look, he knew there was nothing. The last foray, once we were back on the right side of the mountains, was a sweep through Carcassonne where a couple of junk shops hugged the small streets at the top of the town.

We were passing Leclerc, the *hypermarché* outside Carcassonne, where a long straight stretch of road howling with traffic was adorned with a brand-new traffic island. A big mound of grass, with six small trees stuck in its crest, had grown up from one day to the next.

Siggie said, 'See the tyre tracks?'

Sure enough there were muddy skid marks running straight up the side of the grassy hump.

'You always get this,' he said. 'Someone is racing along at night. He knows the road. But the island's new. He can't stop. Suddenly he's halfway up the hill. See those trees? That's the third set they've planted. People round here—' – he pointed to the sandy little housing estate straggling down to the bypass – 'they come after dark and help themselves.' He did not approve – but he knew why they did it. 'Plants are expensive in France!'

At the edge of the little housing estate of sepia bungalows was a ruined villa; tumbled in a rash of skinny red bricks.

'That was the naked woman's house.'

His voice dropped, a story was coming on. And, again, the pattern was ancient. The songs and stories of our hunting fathers needed a special voice: a fireside voice; the night-time tale was sacred to the holy gods of the hunt, when animals and rocks and rain were also people; talk of them properly and they might help you to make a kill. Or save you from ending up as one.

'One Christmas Eve, a woman was alone and unhappy in that house. Her husband had left her; her children had grown up, and gone: and so she decided to kill herself. She opened the oven and filled the house with gas and struck a match. It was a big bang, the bricks came raining down. She was blown out of the room, clean into the garden. Without a stitch on! And she's not even scratched! But the house is a wreck. Completely destroyed.'

Siggie shook his head. He was sorry for her but he was angry, contemptuous of her mistake. Never try to strike a deal with Death; Death takes all, on his own terms. Death not only kills you, he rips you off. Decent people do it right back. We all tumble towards the grave, OK – but we go down fighting.

'Poor woman! Now she has nothing: no husband, no children, and no house.'

The naked flying woman is what one did not want to be. And an object lesson – love people and you lose. The trick is to go for what holds its value. Lasting stuff. Hidden bargains, the genius of junk; unlikely goods, things thrown away, forgotten, just waiting to be found – like the lost Princess.

She was the best, truest, most beautiful thing he never got his hands on. He talked about her with reverence and longing.

'An Austin Princess! An English classic. A car that no longer exists. Beautiful as the day she was born. Well, almost. She has a small dent on her right bumper.'

She spoke to him, too – and she was the only car that had done that since, well, since he bought the hearse from Azille, a village about twenty kilometres away. He had loved her, too.

'The death-car! Only 50,000 on the clock. And lots of space in the back – for clocks and things. And curtains, so no one can spy inside her. I got so excited I drove her over to Olonzac, and had a glass of wine in the Café du Commerce. On the way back to Kissac, I was passing through Azille and she runs out of gas – right outside the graveyard! Like a dog that finds its way home! I knew then I couldn't keep her.'

The hearse he gave back to the dead; the Princess he had never seen and yet she haunted him; he loved her legend, she was hidden in some barn in the mountains, waiting for Siggie to wake her with a kiss.

He knew everything about her right down to the sound of her horn. How she had once belonged to Florian Fintz. And he bought her back in 1952, when he was courting Lucette Sarda, over in Brennac-Cabardés.

He knew her paint was powder blue; her upholstery

the finest pigskin; her dashboard glossy walnut; he knew her mileage – just twenty miles on the clock – when she 'went inside'. And he knew how she got that dent in her right bumper, one snowy afternoon on the narrow road that runs over the Pic de Nore, when Lucette Sarda hit a wall; and he knows how she screamed and wept.

And he sympathized. His car had slipped when the road iced over, as he was coming down on the Tarn side of the peak.

It wasn't the girl's fault. Up at 1,500 metres, on black ice, in thick mist – it happened again and again.

* * *

But Florian Fintz, on that Sunday, a quarter of a century ago, hadn't been so forgiving. Florian Fintz was an apprentice butcher in Villefranche and he worked all the hours God sent for a year to save money to buy that Austin. And all because Lucette admired the English style. And she wanted to be free.

Lucette was pert; with very dark eyes above cherry cheeks in a round face, and strong shoulders. She told her lover that what she wanted most in the world was an independent man; and in her book independence meant the ability to move; and in her case that meant moving as far as possible from the farm where she lived with five sisters and two brothers.

Florian had the brand-new Princess delivered to the farm and garaged her in Lucette's barn. He filled her with petrol and checked the oil and water even if he was not going to risk anything happening to her: so wonderfully, hugely shining.

During the week, he took driving lessons in Carcassonne, using his instructor's Renault.

He'd spend Sunday at Lucette's place and, after coffee and cake, they would go out to the barn, lock the door, and wash and wax the Princess. Then they would make love on the broad seats of yellow hide, so rich and supple, breathing in the fine English polish of the walnut fascia.

Afterwards, Florian would practise what he'd learnt that week in Carcassonne. Reversing or signalling, sitting behind the wheel, without going anywhere, engine off. Sometimes he'd show Lucette how to work the gears and the clutch, delighting in the oddity of the right-hand drive and planning the trips they would take in the car, when they were married. They were keen to travel, they wanted to see Lourdes and Barcelona and Perpignan.

But there was plenty of time.

'It's hard to believe,' said Siggie, 'but until they got in the car that Sunday and drove over the Pic de Nore in the middle of winter, he'd never had her out of the barn!'

Lucette had talked him into the adventure. 'Just a little ride,' she begged.

And Florian thought – why not? He was driving his teacher's Renault with quiet confidence. And Lucette looked so pretty and the car was his. She swung open the barn door, and climbed in beside him. He turned the key in the ignition, the big engine growled happily, and off they went.

It seemed easy: Lucette loved the smell of the leather, the steady tick of the dashboard clock, the firm and masterly way Florian changed gears as they climbed higher into the mountains. They stopped at the top to admire the view of hills and forests stretching to the Pyrenees. She liked it so much she asked to have a go and before he knew what he was doing, Florian let her take the wheel – thinking, maybe, that going downhill slowly was safe.

They'd just cleared the Col, and the green valleys of the Tarn opened below them, Lucette was doing fine, never faster than twenty miles an hour, never above second gear, when suddenly the car hit ice, and began sliding. Lucette screamed, Florian groaned – the Princess went on sliding, majestically but unstoppably, into a dry stone wall. There was a tearing, a grunt, and silence.

Always, when he got to this point, Siggie had to stop his car. It was too tense otherwise. He got out, just as Florian had done, went down on his knees and stroked the dent, the scratch, the tear in her blue skin.

Florian could not say a word. Lucette climbed out, came round and looked at the bumper and said – and Siggie would mimic her soft voice, 'Well, it could have been worse.'

It cut her lover to the quick. Was she mad? Look at the bumper! Crumpled, scratched. The ride was a nightmare. How could it be worse?

Lucette was appalled. Siggie got this little mew in his voice when he did Lucette getting angry.

Didn't Florian care that she might have been hurt?

But Florian was too upset to think straight. He heard himself shouting. If people got hurt, they healed. Broken legs would mend. But how on earth was he going to heal the Princess?

Still on his knees, Siggie caught his hysteria very well. And his despair. Florian raised his hurt eyes to the peak, sick with the horror of what he'd done. He had no licence, his car was injured; worse still, so was his future – tied to this foreign Princess. With a sick churning stomach, Florian noticed, for the first time, the Princess's bulges: her ungainliness, her Englishness – she was rather large in the beam, and a bit dowdy, like the English nobility he saw in pictures; she had the big toothy grille. She cost a fortune to run. Her steering wheel was on the wrong side. She counted in miles. She was foreign, her ways were not his – he must have been mad to buy her.

He'd been a fool! He suddenly saw stretching before him a lifetime of arguments and strain – over parts and driving conditions. What was his Princess but *folie des grandeurs*! He would be made to pay for trying to be something other than what he was. He would fall behind, stuck – while all around him sensible people swept past in small cars, quick cars, cheap cars – above all – French cars.

And yet, it seemed that Florian got over his horror – he and Lucette married, and went to live in Florian's village of Villefranche – where they took over a butchery. And did very well. But perhaps there was a form of revenge. Because their car never saw the light of day again. Florian never took his licence. Lucette never learnt to drive. And they locked the Princess in the barn behind the butchery.

'Then they started travelling.'

'How?' I asked.

'By car, naturally,' Siggie said. 'Each Sunday afternoon, just as they had done when they were courting, they went out to the barn, and locked the door and sat in the Austin Princess.'

Florian drove; Lucette was the navigator. She was never again allowed into the driving seat.

Florian would lean over and pretend to start the engine. Lucette would pick up the map and they were off – to places like Rocamadour, or even foreign parts where they would never have thought of travelling. In the Princess, anywhere was fine – Morocco and Guadaloupe and Tunis.

Florian opened his mouth and reproduced the steady growl of the big V6 engine. He changed gears, and sounded the sonorous horn. And the Princess took them safely wherever they wanted to go. Lucette would prepare pâté and cheese and olives and pass them to Florian as he drove.

The butchery business prospered. Lucette's father died and left her money. They bought a second shop in a village nearby. And then a third. There were no children but, as Lucette said, it meant they were free to travel.

One Sunday morning, Florian went walking in the mountains looking for mushrooms with a group of men from the village. He had stopped to pick a *pied-de-mouton* from the roots of a dwarf oak when he pitched forward on his face and lay there without moving. Even though M. Julien, the pharmacist, was in the party and gave artificial respiration and heart massage, and the helicopter came quickly and got him to hospital in Carcassonne within thirty minutes, he never recovered consciousness.

At this point always, Siggie got gloomy. Death, the rip-off merchant, was in town. He had a little sympathy for Lucette, none for Florian. But he brightened whenever he thought of the Princess. *There* was an afterlife worth believing in! If only Lucette had been sensible about things.

After losing her husband – perhaps as a tribute to his

memory (this was Siggie's suggestion; he could be surprisingly sentimental when he felt he might be getting something out of death), Lucette transferred the car to a hiding place. A garage or a shed in one of the villages where they had their shops; or perhaps to an old wine cellar, or barn on the land she'd inherited from her family.

Siggie searched for her for years. He never travels through Villefranche or Brennac-Cabardés without trying his luck, asking in the café for news of the vanished Princess; checking likely sites – cellars, barns, sheds – hoping against hope.

After sealing the car in its sacred hiding place, Lucette closed her husband's butcheries and retired. She holed herself up with her geese and ducks, allowing them to walk in and out of the house all day like dogs. She, who had been sturdy and round, became thin, wore black and walked the street, pulling an ancient three-wheeled perambulator, loaded with potatoes or coal.

That's when I arrived in Kissac, and when we went over to Olonzac for a drink, Siggie used to point her out to me, wheeling the ancient baby carriage past the Credit Agricole.

Nothing happened, until the day came when she tried to put an end to her life by leaping into the well at the bottom of her garden. Only to mistake the water level and fall several metres into a shallow pool and break an ankle.

Had it not been for M. Henri Bonnery who stopped by to try and interest her in life assurance and found her front door open and geese everywhere, and decided to investigate, her feeble cries from the well might never have been heard.

Lucette was taken to a home for the mentally ill where she still lived. If asked where she kept her Princess she merely gazed at her questioner as if he and not she were mad. When social workers cleared her house they found a fortune in notes and coins stuffed beneath the floorboards.

Siggie was torn between horror and admiration. Poor woman, living from hand to mouth, her house filthy from the birds, never washing and going about from one week to the next in the same clothes – while all around her were hundreds of thousands of francs!

Siggie kept an old newspaper picture – one of the few pieces of paper he owned, along with his passport and ID card – in an old cocoa tin. The photograph is of Lucette and Florian, soon after they married and set up shop together in Villefranche. He studied it for clues.

The picture is very fuzzy, the newsprint is breaking up. The young couple pose behind the glass cabinet in their shop, the *charcuterie* is displayed on shelves broad as church steps mounting to the countertop piled with cheese; above which smoked hams swing from the ceiling hooks, like dark chandeliers. Florian wears a butcher's jacket with pointed collar and holds aloft two carving knives, tips touching, as soldiers present sabres over the heads of a bridal couple. Lucette wears a white smock and is plump and shining with good health, her face round, smiling; her hair dark and thick.

Siggie shook his head. What a joke! Florian was gone. Lucette threw herself down a well – and lived. What grim tricks are played on helpless humans. Yet, there was hope – somewhere, a Princess waited, almost perfect.

I knew how he felt. I can't pass Leclerc, sprawled like

a beached white whale beside the traffic island, without seeing the flash in the night when the sad woman lit the gas. Bricks, clothes, TV, Christmas tree all shoot into the air – followed by the flying woman. And then she falls back to earth and bounces in the garden, quite naked.

CHAPTER 11

IN MY CALENDAR, summer had three signs – based, like so much I learnt, on things Siggie pointed out to me. I should say that he pointed out things he believed were of no earthly use to anyone. A dealer does not give away things he can trade.

Siggie didn't like the world; he conducted lightning raids, sight-seeing expeditions, and saw more in a short time than anyone I know, and then he retreated to his safe place.

I preferred to be out in the world, and it was Siggie who introduced me to places and people I would never otherwise have known, or noticed. But I once pointed out to him that I was as much a collector as he was, with all the usual anxieties of the self-employed, and that writers hated waste. I wonder if he understood what I meant?

Perhaps he does now.

Siggie was an extraordinarily tolerant man – who hated change. An adventurous man terrified of the unknown. He had a soaring gift for taking things on the wing. No one I've met was better at milking the moment. Yet any change – to his diet, his routine, his Wednesdays, his siesta (1–3, each afternoon), sundowners (anytime after five) — was intolerable.

He liked to get out and about but his essence was repetition. Improvisation in the service of safety. Charms and magic spells were to be used not to change the world, but to keep it the same. Same routes, same jokes, same terrors; same Siggie. His death-defying bravado was just that; deep down he knew it was a losing gamble, we went to the table with borrowed chips and Death was a big spender. Yes, we all went into the dark — but we owed it to ourselves to pull a trick or two on the way down.

What others made of this was clear. They were uncomfortable. The neighbours suspected him of having no heart; fellow dealers suspected him of pulling a fast one; his friends from the north fell out, just as Him the Horrible fell out, and accused him of lying and thieving and being too damn pleased with himself. All the things one might have said about Rumpelstiltskin. His friends invariably drifted away.

He never seemed to mind. Besides, Ria's rented apartments supplied Siggie with a stream of new friends. Siggie was a great linguist, with four or five languages to hand; his English was fluent — but when he entertained guests from England he liked to invite me along 'to interpret'. There was always, with the English, what he called 'a darkening'.

He appeared to be speaking English yet they didn't understand a damn thing he said. And if they made the mistake of draining their glasses, Siggie pounced with his flask of red wine. The eyes of the guests got progressively blurrier, as the weird nature of Siggie's living room began to dawn. The lumpy leather chairs, with their air of sex mixed with business, brothel and bank; on one wall the old maps of medieval Amsterdam, on another the oil paintings of cows in sylvan settings; Fred, the destructive Dalmatian, worrying a cushion like a rat; the naked bronze torso in the corner, young breasts in the glow of a Phillips economy bulb.

Cue his story of Wolfgang, the German sculptor who drove a Lamborghini, and paid his rent in bronze torsos of his young mistresses; which led to the story of the doctor and the bare-breasted bathers, which led to the joke about, say, the bishop and the penguin. All the while the eyes of the English guests swivelled frantically around the room – seeking, and failing, to find any resting place, sweeping past the line of pewter tankards on the big oaken cupboard, and Fred the Dalmatian now ripping up last night's newspapers; and in the corner, a white marble monument of a reclining woman, the personification of grief. In her outstretched hand a red rose which Siggie had picked that very day.

'I bought the lady from a defrocked priest,' Siggie would announce.

It was the way he spoke that got in the way. As it is in a very young child, Siggie's speech was body movement, shivers, touch, gooseflesh; it reached out, curled its toes, arched its back, tasted the words – while the nice accountant from Beckenham, or the smart lady from Scotland, looked on in disbelief.

And I would sum up by saying something simple: 'Siggie is a dealer.'

'Oh, he's a dealer,' said the accountant from Beckenham.

'And a collector.'

'And a collector,' said the smart lady from Scotland.

They were relieved, they needed me; at last, something made sense.

* * *

The first sign of summer was Madame de la Pipe.

Siggie showed her to me that first year in early June 1991, as we were driving to Carcassonne. He grabbed my sleeve and pointed, delighted as always when some longed-for, delectable species of human absurdity turned up. It was the ritual sighting: like spotting the first cuckoo.

'Look, there she is!'

She was walking along the bank of the Canal du Midi, where it broadens in a wide curve under an avenue of trees, before entering Carcassonne. She was wearing a red skirt and white trainers, and kept glancing at passing cars, as if she was lost or looking for a lift.

'She performs services,' said Siggie proudly, 'for men!'

'What sort of services?'

'Do you know what it means to "*faire la pipe*"?'

'No.'

'She takes them . . .' – he paused – 'in.'

'In where?'

He stared at the sky. He looked hunted. Then he told me a joke about two whores. The first whore, who said 'Honolulu', when she 'took men in', and made a fortune – and the second whore, who said 'Krakatoa', and starved. Then he laughed, a lot.

Looking at the muffled figure in the outsized trainers I wondered how she found clients.

'Do you mean she gives blow jobs?'

He looked terrified now, any sort of pinning-down always worried him. Why ask? About sex? Or business? It was a matter of decorum; you never asked a dealer for his trade secrets any more than you asked a magician to show you his tricks.

It was in that first summer that he made good his promise to introduce me to Lizzie – who sold her body; the woman Hercule felt sorry for. As things turned out, he should have saved his tears. Lizzie didn't need them.

Lizzie was my second sign of summer.

Siggie took me along to meet her, goaded by Ria, who never forgot or forgave his promise, on the day we first met, to visit the generous artist. Ria was always asking, 'So? And did you get some joy from she who sells her body?'

I was astonished to find out he'd never met her – perhaps he'd never have done so if he hadn't persuaded me I needed to see her because 'seeing is believing'.

He got directions from a little gap-toothed moustached ferrety sculptor. He scouted for treasure – an old villa, rich with Provençal tiles and cherrywood bannisters and art-deco lamps, about to go under the wrecker's hammer, or a bunch of marble mantelpieces in a builders' yard, or a job lot of Venetian mirrors. Then he got on the phone to Siggie and took a cut of the cost price.

He had just sold Siggie a large Venetian mirror, bevelled and brooched, and flashing like a fishbowl – framed, it seemed, because of the bevelling, in pink and silver shadows. He hung it on the stairs, a gift to Ria, and it fell one night, the silver fragments flapped and fluttered on stone steps. Siggie took the view that it never happened, swept up the disaster and smiled; he hated the thought of the bad luck the broken mirror might bring, of the gypsies that would follow. Ria was almost hysterical because she said something was sure to happen and he must move his clocks from the cellar to some place of safety, but Siggie said there was no place of safety in the world.

His scout came by one day. Siggie said nothing of the broken mirror but because he'd paid a good price – 3,000 francs – he felt he was entitled to something extra in view of the loss. And he said to the guy, 'You're a sculptor, you'll know about her – the one who sells her body.'

Siggie's scout called himself a sculptor because he carved those wooden cut-out cartoons – the jolly *boulanger* or the fat chef – that stand outside bakeries and pizza-parlours. He lived in a little house right on the railway line, in Lézignan. Siggie said you could always tell his work; it had this wavy line to it because the train passed so close it shook his house like a puppy does a slipper.

The conversation about directions to the artist's house went like this:

'Do you know the market?'

'I know the market.'

'Do you know the madhouse?'

'I know the madhouse.'

'Do you know where the fat gypsy lives, the one who used to trade outside Lézignan – whose son is always in trouble with the cops?'

'Of course.'

I also knew the gypsy: I had once called at his shop

and he'd sold me an ebony cane, a folding card table in cherrywood and two 30s lamps of white glass, frosted like crystallized fruit. His son was sitting behind a roll-top desk; he had a lot of hair and two black eyes and in the semi-darkness he reminded me of a racoon.

'Same street as the gypsy's warehouse, three doors down, left hand side. Do I get a commission?'

'Commission?' Siggie was surprised. 'If anybody gives you a cut, she should; for finding her new clients.'

'She won't have you,' said the scout.

* * *

Lézignan is a rumpled, untidy town with a big gypsy crowd at its door and a rough, dark brooding feel. It is in the peculiar plainness of Languedoc that Lézignan excels. A town of high intensity. Anyone not seeing that would see only a rather ugly misshapen place but it is such misviewings, thank God, that keep the tourist population down.

The 'mad house' is in the centre of Lézignan; a home-made palace, a gingerbread house, witch's cottage, patch-work quilt and a junk heap fashioned from odd tiles, wire, chimney pots, glass, thrown up in a quiet suburban street. It is a hobby house built by an amiable lunatic. No one lives there any more; no one seems to know who built it.

We found the artist a few doors down, as the scout promised.

Elizabeth – as she signs her paintings, Eliza to her neighbours, Lizzie to her clients and friends – was little, with dark brown hair and very small ears. She wore her hair caught up in scotty dog clips and favoured black body stockings, over good breasts.

She was from the north of England, from Oldham, and wore her accent like a badge. Even after years in Lézignan her French had a broad Mancunian burr; she did not so much speak it as broadcast it, slowly and calmly, pausing between the words. She spoke comforting Bolton French: no nonsense, nothing to be scared of, nothing fancy – above all nothing foreign.

It was part of her reassurance technique.

She offered us tea: what she said was:

'I'll put on the kettle – you don't mind bags?'

Siggie kept getting up and sitting down again and saying things like: 'Well, I suppose we all have to earn a living, don't we?'

He kept waiting, hoping she would say or do something that explained or backed up what he'd heard about her *real* work. Her magical, fairytale other life. Well, where was it? He was faced by this comfortable, cosy, friendly woman who called him 'love'.

Love was something she was supposed to sell, not something she said. He was trapped into pleasantries, it made him frantic – he hated sitting around, he did not drink tea. Then she showed us her paintings and he had to say things like: 'So this is what you do?' with a big pause to give her time to say it wasn't – that she took men upstairs to bed.

And then he had to say: 'Is there much money in painting?' When what he was dying to ask was: 'OK, they say you sell yourself for cash – is it so?'

He kept swivelling in his seat thinking, praying some client would knock, a guy already unbuttoning in his hurry to get on with it. The lights would go down, music up,

Lizzie would strip, do a bit of bump and grind, and vanish upstairs. And we'd be where he knew we were – in a brothel, a *maison close*.

But nothing happened. We just went on sipping tea and eating biscuits. Bath biscuits.

She had a studio on the ground floor. Her paintings were pleasant in a Cezannish way: landscapes, frequently mountains; the Black Mountains, the Corbières, the Pyrenees, often with small figures, hikers, climbers lost in the hills' fur, like little beetles.

I admired a painting: a solitary walker, tiny, cusped in the hollow of the foothills, climbs into the round dark bulk of the Corbières. He is blond as a wheatsheaf and the mountains are built of green and blue shadows, huge and shapely.

Siggie whispered, 'Two thousand francs! I can buy a box full of pictures at that price! It's not even in a frame, Christopher!'

He said it in the same tone of outrage he might have used if Lizzie had been what he hoped she was – and I was going upstairs with her. 'She charges – *what*?'

I understood his disappointment; there in that house with its Roses Marmalade bottles stuffed with paintbrushes, its Tetley teabags and Bath biscuits and Lizzie's plain, flat way of being was a kind of sober reality that ground him down, drove him crazy. Lizzie with her Bovril jars and Quality Street toffee tins was crushing the life out of him – it robbed him of joy; the cosiness closed around his throat, the weather of the house made him ill, it rained on his dreams, it put out his fire.

The business of Lizzie's house was even more profoundly foreign than he dreamed of. Its very air was calculated to shrivel his soul like last year's almonds . . .

Afterwards, he said we'd been conned; she wasn't a dreamer or a woman who sold her body or even much of an artist. 'Artists have egos – I have an ego, people who get on have egos. You have an ego.'

But Lizzie? She wasn't anything except an Englishwoman!

This was true but in being that – what genius!

The scout was quite right about Lizzie having no interest in us as clients. A Prussian and a South African. Lizzie reserved herself, she specialized.

Lizzie said to me, 'It's all about niches, everyone's in niches now, aren't they? Banks and boutiques have their niches. And I've mine. My unique selling point – and I stick to it.'

She slept only with British men. Her clients who 'stopped'. Anyone else and she might lose the touch – and her clients would know; besides, it wouldn't be fair. With her they could be sure they were getting the real thing – 'one hundred per cent, true-blue Brit'.

It was part of the service.

Usually her clients were English, though she said, 'Far as I'm concerned, love, you can stop – if you're Welsh or Scots or Irish.'

Like all true artists she lifted an idea from someone else and made it her own. The first part she got from a man in a van who sold English home comforts to lonely Brits abroad. His name was Timmo and he worked patches of English settlement, the valley of the Dordogne, the valley of the Tarn. He drove from market to market, selling

Bisto and genuine British bacon and baked beans and Worcester sauce, crisps and pickled onions to marooned expats who said, right out loud, 'Madelaine, you should see the cheese!' They had dogs which they could not take home, and that curious cottagey look of upper middle-class Englishwomen in foreign climes: the fair skin, the flowing look that Being Abroad seemed to call up, the frock and scarf and straw hat; and sons called Tom and Crispian, and a husband with dark hair, and they come and go in a dark green SAAB. They have entirely remade green hillsides into something like Shropshire and to these people Timmo, whom they wouldn't notice, let alone patronize, in England, sold them things they wouldn't usually dream of eating at home: baked beans on toast, bacon butties on slices of real white English bread.

Lizzie studied Timmo.

'I saw what he gave people – comfort, reassurance. Most of them haven't a clue where they are and spend a lot of time over here feeling sore, pained, you know. Like toothache, it is. They don't really know what they're feeling, wouldn't believe it if you told them. No chance of that! But they're homesick. And that's a fact. They love France. It's the French they can't stand. And it makes them sad and slightly silly and disabled; they need help. And that's where Timmo steps in.'

So it was Timmo and his van and his Bird's Eye beefburgers and Findus fish fingers who laid the first seeds of an idea. But the clincher was the estate agent, Lawrence, who dealt on the Internet.

'Lawrence – he lived on English clients. "Thank God for England!" he said. They went to him because he's

English and they're terrified; they want some place in France but – Oh God! – they have to deal with French agents and they don't trust their French – or know the first thing about the country; they've seen magazines – old mills, vineyards, terracotta tiles and lavender. And they point and say: "Lawrence: I want one of those!" '

And that's when it hit her. She would become a service provider, a bridge, a home from home, she would smoothe the passage of homesick Englishmen into France by easing them into the broad and gentle channel of herself. She furnished her room with a bed of English oak, hung up fox-hunting prints, she bought McVities biscuits, she dressed in Laura Ashley gowns, she gave tea and sympathy and sex to people lost or confused, or even happy abroad – but who wanted to make it stop being so damn foreign – just for a bit.

She had a following among the technocrats of the airbus industry around Toulouse; she befriended golfers and canal-boat enthusiasts who cruised the Canal du Midi. Englishmen arrived at Lizzie's door, out of sorts, fearful, aching all over for something friendly and familiar and Lizzie gave it to them, and lashings of it: she cooked them chips, she never allowed any foreign element in her bedroom; even the videos were specially chosen from the best the BBC had to offer: a lot of comedy, 'funny foreign stuff is good. It's therapy.'

She had a plan to pipe in the British news – 'Like they do on aeroplanes.' Why not a home-page on the Internet? Like Lawrence the estate agent. She would call it ' 'Ullo Luv!'

Lizzie's niche was the nice brothel. Homey. She served

Scotch, gin, elderberry wine and bitter from the cask. Wine was a problem. She'd tried English but her clients didn't like it. If they wanted wine she gave them Australian.

'Laugh! Some of them want nothing more than a cup of cocoa when we're tucked up.'

She knew the cricket score and the football results.

'I even use English condoms,' Lizzie said. 'Mates. At least, I think they're British.'

And she once unbuttoned her top to show me her bra. 'Marks and Sparks! Knickers too.'

Lizzie, over in Lézignan, sold her body to Englishmen. Lizzie was a philosopher. A Samaritan. She reckoned that the more 'we go into Europe the more confused people get' and she said someone had to help.

I thought of her painting: and I began to see what she's driving at. The big dark looming hills are not the Corbières, that mass of shadows, that deep rich soft mass – it's Lizzie's bed upstairs: and the blond climber is not a climber after all, he's a client.

CHAPTER 12

EVER AFTERWARDS SIGGIE denied meeting Lizzie. If Ria
needled him, he got flustered.

'The scout couldn't remember where she lived. I never
saw her in my life. Maybe Christopher did. Me – never!'

With Madame de la Pipe it was different – he spoke
of her with warmth, even pride. He was proud of her
precisely because he hadn't met her. She remained his – to
imagine as he liked. Such imaginary items, like complex
financial instruments, he valued and traded. Like futures.
Madame de la Pipe's value was tied to the fun she gave
him, but he didn't want her on his hands. He felt much
the same about clocks: find them, fix them, sell them on.
Always the hunt – never the keeping.

The day he pointed out the walker by the canal Siggie
gave me another sign of summer – pink garlic. It came
from Lautrec, a village over towards Albi. Not to be confused with the imposter variety from China.

'What's the difference?' I asked.

'Sex,' said Siggie.

We had driven to Carcassonne for the ritual buying of
radishes. It was a Tuesday morning in July, and the market
was pared down to mid-week strength. Gone were the

rabbits and roosters, the oysters and the frantic fruit-sellers of Saturday morning. A few vegetables, and much leisure, around the fountain where Neptune poses like a beauty queen.

The new pink garlic was laid out next to big Spanish onions. Strange bedfellows. At first sight the scarlet onions looked more brazen; whores hanging out with convent girls. But look closer and there was something perverse about the demure knobs of pink garlic. They were deliberately, carefully lewd; they were naked beneath the tight see-through sheaths of skin. Nuns in négligés, striptease in church; and what Claire did to that automaton.

Siggie shook his head. 'Oy, yoi, yoi, yoi . . .'

Custom decreed that he'd have one beer at Chez Jim, always outdoors, on the square. Indoors made him uncomfortable. Escape was difficult; in a room he always sat facing the door.

His beer drained, lunch called, there was not a moment to lose, and Siggie literally ran back to his car.

But I kept coming back and in time I became as regular there as that irregular place would allow.

* * *

Chez Jim is that rare thing, a working café of the southern kind; perhaps being so far south has kept it going; it is nothing special, that is its genius – it just is. It is so much itself, I think sometimes it can't last much longer. Its time has passed. But the news hasn't reached the patron or the waiters or the customers. Or they've been too busy to notice.

At first sight it seems a small place. Customers sit close

at the tiny tables. Flower-sellers, readers, sleepers, the madly quiet, the old and lonely, tourists, lovers, tramps, students, the very drunk, the mildly thirsty and the quietly mad. The waiters are some of the last to wear black waistcoats and white shirts, and run between tables. Didiér, Eric and Bruno took over from their fathers or uncles – a job at Chez Jim is never advertised, it passes down the family. Low wages, big tips, long hours – in all weathers.

Chez Jim seems small only because it holds so many. There are tables in the main well, below the giant TV bolted into the corner above our heads. Up two steps, beneath a big fake wristwatch, nailed by its strap to the ceiling, courtesy of Belgian Brewery, is the rear section; six tables beside the back door, and the single WC. The TV may be seen from every point – and it is running the Tour de France. Along the bar, the steady drinkers turn their backs but they hear the boom from the box roosting high in the corner, where the wall hits the roof.

I've made a point every summer of not watching the Tour in Chez Jim.

Behind some fancy trellis work is the tiny alcove, raised into a gallery, where lovers sometimes sit hidden, like the kitchen door, by a few strands of plastic ivy. On the narrow pavement outside the front door is a line of tables; and across the street, on the edge of the square, more tables under chocolate awnings.

Traffic drones past the front door, so close sometimes diesel fumes mix with the *pastis*.

This morning, gangly Didiér is working a four-hour shift. One waiter is often enough before lunch. Eric and Bruno will take over at noon. Later, all three may be needed. Everyone in Chez Jim knows what to do – including the clientele.

There is no Jim – there is only Madame. She is a perfectionist. We may do as we like so long as we do as expected. Her perch is a skinny, steel bar stool, on the round corner of the marble bar, beneath the giant wristwatch that hangs from the ceiling; and stands now at 11.13. Madame is plump, powdered, pale but you can sense the steel in her spine. She reminds me of a genie; it's her colouring: red hair and green eyes. A genie who escaped and they forgot to put back in the bottle.

She looks like any other customer. That is part of her charm and her terror. She is bored and soft and smooth and tough and very, very silent. Madame needs only to raise an eyebrow and everyone understands. She never interferes, so long as she is obeyed. She is ever-present but never offensive, dormant unless there is a little ripple on the surface of her universe, where some insignificant planet burns up or some war among petty worlds begins in some back corner of her creation.

Then she shows herself . . . lifts her head, an eyebrow, and the trouble is over, it has been annihilated. She moves from Divine Indifference to the Last Judgement in an instant. It is not for nothing that the Bible reminds us that when God wishes to terrify his creation it is enough to show his face.

Madame brings order, and she brings relief. The single unisex WC, the hole in the floor, is strictly reserved for customers. They must catch her eye. Even her waiters must call for permission. Madame controls the door lock with a secret buzzer hidden behind the bar. She has had enough of tramps, chancers, market stall-keepers sneaking in to use the loo. No more! Let them use the public *pissoir* across on the square.

And what is her universe founded upon? Love. Her love encompasses all, it reaches from the cash-till beside the eight hard-boiled eggs in their circular stand to big Dolores, the chef, toiling in the tiny kitchen, and now chalking up the *plat du jour* on the tiny blackboard hung outside the front door . . . *BLANQUETTE DE VEAU AVEC RIZ.* It reaches from the lovers behind the plastic ivy, to the tourists drinking in the sunshine on the square.

Madame is the tiger ready to pounce; she is love, yes – and control, and cruelty. But she treats with a certain rough kindness those who have fallen into her claws.

Didiér is stirring the Duchess's beer. The Duchess is about seventy, very white, very wiry, she has the angular poise of a fish-hook, she dresses in a fawn overcoat and smart brown pumps and a silk scarf in biscuit and periwinkle blue. She sips her beer with gravity.

The Duchess has had four in a row. Her eyes are beginning to glitter, she grows more haughty by the minute. Didiér knows the signs – she is a little *allumé.* Madame's standing orders are clear – from this point, she is not to have another.

The Duchess calls for another.

Didiér takes her order, and her glass, with the courtesy he always shows an old customer. At the counter he reaches for a clean glass, opens the silver tap on the keg of draught and pours an inch or so and then, with the spatula used to skim the head off a good beer, he whips up the few drops till froth rises to the brim of the Duchess's glass:

'What's this?' the Duchess demands.

'Madame's order.'

'Doesn't look very full to me.'

'Full! It is a lake in there.'

'Good.' The Duchess tastes a little foam and licks her lips. 'Very good.'

The newspapers are furled like flags around oaken staves. They are passing from hand to hand: *La Dépêche*, *L'Indépendant*, *Midi-Libre* – the last reader scrolls the pages round the stick and drops it back into the plastic box. We wait for nothing to happen.

And nothing happens. Chez Jim is reliable. And for reasons I don't understand, out of that nothing comes peace and contentment and joy.

I know that according to the increasingly threatening explanations of physics, we have no reason for being here – our universe just happened, it occurred for no purpose – it does not need us, or God, to explain how it came about. And we do not, should not, feel curious, grateful or even particularly puzzled. It wasn't and then it was and one day it won't be.

The same cannot be said of Chez Jim. Without Madame it would not be here and nor would we. Madame created it and it obeys the laws of its creator. And I believe in it; and so do a lot of other people, and I suppose we're an underground church. But we're not a support group, as we are at the Circus of Dreams – the Circus is dying: Chez Jim is in rough good health.

Put another way, Chez Jim is not in the real world – where sense and sobriety rules and science is king; where God is officially dead and life is run from California. But then I don't care about these things, I care about signs of the heart.

Chez Jim goes further – it doesn't even *not* care – it simply doesn't notice it is supposed to be something else. If I can't escape the tedious reductionism of science, the frantic need to kill by analysis anything that won't conform to the laws of physics, I can drink coffee at Chez Jim. As some American goldshops make you disarm before entering: before entering Chez Jim you must leave your science outside. You dump the reasonable, the practical, the common-sensical at the door. Walk in with curiosity, gratitude, puzzlement, and sit down with them.

Does the real world have Madame to run it, with her severely tolerant eye? The real world should be so lucky.

Chez Jim is distant, provincial, untidy, you can't do anything with its kitchy clock nailed to the roof, its ugly bar stools, the colour snaps of Neptune's fountain in the market square – when it froze over a few years back. Neptune, framed in plastic, with this huge icicle hanging from his nose, is on the wall. It's *déclassé* – that's Chez Jim all over. It doesn't care to come forward. You'd need to add a lot to Chez Jim to make it halfway decent. It's glamour-poor; it fails the test of the truly modern: it would really bomb as a movie. It would look terrible on TV.

Movies are stuffed with money, stoked up, highly coloured, the way the corpse in the funeral parlour is rouged and flooded with formaldehyde. The movie is another of the mortuary arts, it dresses things up to make them look alive. That's why it thrills its creators and, ultimately, sickens the customers. It deals with handsome corpses. It's a value-added industry.

But what value could you add to Chez Jim? It is so ordinary it hurts. That's its genius and its fate to be genuinely alive. Which means it will genuinely die. And that is where it gets interesting. What's human dies; it leaks.

It's the same with the little antique markets throughout Languedoc. The best are the poor ones; dawn in windy supermarket parking lots. Trestle-tables, old tarpaulin on the tarmac, the back of a van, the boot of the car. And the stuff on offer is poor, broken and sometimes false. Brass lamps ripped from old walls, plaster still sticking to the screws. Broken things, cracked, damaged goods. Grave treasures, still hot from life. Stained linen, picked out in yellow roses; ruined trousseaus; the hundred bits of iron that might make a lamp, jumbled in a plastic bag. Sex and salvation. The naked doll with the cracked skull; and the box of crucifixes. Rags and bones; dealers shivering in the dawn chill, yanking loot out of their cars, like stolen pets.

See these things later, when they've been bought and valued, grouped by speciality, in the square of a bigger, better town, polished, priced, painted and decently laid out, and you know the morticians have been at them.

Chez Jim is a node, a place where the lines lead, where the stories may be glimpsed, in other forms.

A little guy sits at the bar wearing a green shirt. He has this little grey poodle called Chou-Chou on a lead. He is drinking Pernod and he's a friend of Hassan, a North African, who lived over near the goldmine in Salsigne. It's the only goldmine in Western Europe, has been since the Romans were here. The gold is leached out of the earth with arsenic and the poison flows into the rivers and the inhabitants of Salsigne die of cancer at a terrible rate. It is a stupefyingly grim place of slag heaps, craters, conveyor belts and crushed stone.

Hassan was a lift operator. He made some money and bought a lot of gold fillings.

'He kept his fortune in his teeth,' said the man in the green shirt.

Hassan was married to Nioshe, a woman with a face like all the horses on the merry-go-round. But kind enough, and he kept a donkey in a field at the end of the village and he sent his wife to feed it.

'He was fine – until he got diabetes and they had his leg off. Above the knee, it was. After he lost his leg Hassan wanted to make love to Nioshe three or four times a day. He hopped around the house after her! He believed he was only half a man and he was trying to prove something. Anyway, Nioshe couldn't stand it and she ran away. Don't you think that's hard on a cripple? Running away? Hassan was left alone. The donkey was in a field a kilometre away. He couldn't get there to feed her. So he sold her to Maurice. For just 550 francs.'

' "What do you call her?" Maurice wanted to know.'

' "What do you mean – *call* her? Nothing. She's just a donkey."

' "I'll call her Plusbelle," said Maurice.'

That donkey's life has been concerned with love, one way or another.

The man in the green shirt can't find his poodle. As usual he drops to his knees and begins crawling under the tables and through the legs of the customers calling: 'Chou-Chou!'

We go on doing whatever we're doing; the newspapers

pass from table to table. It's coming up to noon and Madame chalks the blackboard. Today's *plat du jour* is escalope of chicken breast, in a mushroom sauce, and a shallow lake of melted cheese which, since it slips through your fork, you scoop up with bread. (You might be better off with the *plat végétarien* or the *carpaccio de saumon*.) Didiér is stretching the Duchess's beer; his teaspoon tinkles in the glass as he whips froth into a fine head. Madame's all-seeing eye roves; we have fallen through a wormhole in the cosmos, and found ourselves in the universe next door, and we all wait for nothing to happen. Mostly nothing happens.

The commentator's voice speeds up, like an auctioneer at a cattle sale. Everyone turns and stares up at the screen. The two leading cyclists are hurtling for the finishing line – suddenly they bounce, part, claw wildly, grab again, and it looks for an instant as if they must crash. Then it's over and they flash across the line with the commentator shrieking about a 'flagrant irregularity'. The clip is rerun and rerun, the film frozen; the riders clutch each other. Jerk free. Like frantic lovers. Who grabbed whom? Who touched first?

The café is gripped, Didiér stops stirring, the man in the green shirt pokes his head out from under a table and, still on his knees, stares up at the box.

The Duchess gets up, very neat in her cream dress, takes up her tan bag and walking stick and weaves out. Her drug's not booze; it's attention. At Chez Jim she has what she craves – what we all want – love. And someone to stir our beer.

On the big screen in the corner a long line of frantic

ants are racing through the empty streets of some French city, in hats like pointed raindrops. They are flagged on by other adoring ants and sweep under a huge red inflatable Coca-Cola bridge.

And we go back to doing nothing.

CHAPTER 13

SUMMER VISITORS HAD strange effects.

They were needed and spurned all at once. Maybe they reminded people too much of themselves. The Midi was full of invaders who stayed on. Even a little place like Kissac was riddled with them. There were Spaniards who had fled Franco; Neapolitans who had worked the marble quarry; North Africans were from Marseilles; Tomàs, the Serbian ex-blacksmith, came via the Foreign Legion; God was from New Zealand; Thierry came from further off still – Paris; and Siggie from vanished Prussia. A band of English hippies, from whose midst had come the automaton who ran off with Claire, roamed the mountains in a red London bus; Dutch settlers in a neat ghetto near the canal kept a herd of caravans, each chubby rump proudly branded – NL.

'*Niente lire*,' said Siggie. 'That's what it stands for. They don't spend a franc if they can help it. Mean as ticks. They bring even their potatoes from Holland.'

It was a strangeness of Languedoc. People from elsewhere – who had a problem with people from elsewhere.

It went back a long way. How the locals must have detested the Romans! Until they became a fixture, and then everyone detested the Visigoths, then the Moors, the Spanish, and the French kings, who annexed Languedoc in the thirteenth century. Some groups, like the gypsies, were useful because everyone detested them equally.

* * *

Summer brought the beggars or tramps crowding into Carcassonne. The new *clochards* (though I don't like using that noble name for the travellers) came for the sun. Like the tourists.

Many of the new *clochards* were fakes. Hobos, bums – with no talent for it; they were poor, of course, but in Languedoc that was no recommendation. Languedoc was always poor.

They were modern, mobile beggars. It was not a calling – it was a mistake, or a bolt-hole: a part-time job. It was nothing special. It could happen to anyone. A hair's breadth divided pleasure from penury – one moment you were scraping along, the next – you were on the skids. Like Roddie.

I met him when Thierry left for the Tarn and I lost a French teacher. I placed an ad in the local freebie: *Aude Info*.

A man with a round English accent replied, and we arranged to meet at Chez Jim. He was a short, shy, yet somehow forward man with a faint moustache and broad vowels. He was about thirty-five and he'd been a French teacher in the north of England.

'Cathedral school,' said Roddie, swallowing his beer quickly and licking his lips absent-mindedly. 'Have another.'

He called to Didiér, who was polishing glasses behind the bar. Didiér went on polishing.

Ten minutes later we were still sitting over empty glasses, so I called for more beer in my bad French and Didiér jumped into action. But he skirted Roddie when he set up the beers. I'd seen this sort of reaction once before; Thierry did something similar. He simply turned people off, they couldn't look at him. It was as if he gave off some sort of ray that stunned all who walked into it. Roddie had some of that – and something else. The waiters stared at him. The waiters had views about Roddie.

Roddie didn't seem to notice.

'I speak good, sound French. And I play the organ, if you're interested. Or know someone who might be.'

He talked in furtive little rushes. Rolled his eyes back in his head as he made these inter-cranial cross-border raids on sections of his mind open to inspection. A lot of Roddie's mind was off-limits. He had had – his eyes grew misty – a bit of trouble, back at his school.

'Look,' he said, 'I came over here from Lincolnshire, oh – about six months ago and well, I don't have any money left. I don't know how I'll eat today. I've always wanted to live in France. I love it here.'

He flickered his long lashes.

I thought of Siggie and his deep suspicions of 'love'. I remembered Sad Bob – he'd loved French food; and Sophie had loved a vanished father; and there was Thierry; he loved genius.

You had only to look at Roddie to see he was miserable. He was frightened. He'd had an ideal perch in England. The rumpled common room, the gentle consoling malice of men penned together, tea and biscuits, trips to London and the theatre; the whipcord carpet, the view of the cricket pitch; chapel and organ, and the boys. It was hard to think of him anywhere else. Why had he left?

Roddie was in free fall. From the green fields of Lincolnshire to the doss-house in Carcassonne; from sherry in the common room to cadging beers in Chez Jim. Soon he would land on the pavement outside Monoprix, a modern *clochard*, leading a mongrel on a piece of string. If he wasn't there already. Got someone to hold the dog while he saw a man about a job.

I was puzzled by the downcast eyes, the hints sand-wiched between the breathy pauses, the lowered head. There were one to two mentions of 'love' which had to do with life 'over there', but he couldn't talk about the cata-strophe that brought him to France. He also used the word 'love' about France, but I didn't believe it – the word was hollow, achingly insincere and I felt he didn't believe it either. He breathed a kind of defeated unhappiness.

Roddie called for another beer. And again Didiér ignored him.

I began to think the waiters knew Roddie, that he was often in Chez Jim, begging drinks off people. True, Didiér did not like or trust the Englishman but that wasn't why he ignored him when he lifted his chin and called in French for more beer.

Once again I ordered and Didiér gave me a look, as if to say, *d'accord, monsieur*, but I hope you know what you're doing.

It hit me hard. Not often am I that lucky. The reason why Roddie couldn't make himself heard was simple – and exhilarating. Whatever had ruined him back in Lincoln-shire, and exiled him to France, was no professional failing. He seemed a fussy, methodical man. I'd have put money on Roddie's teaching, the pass rate in his classes would have been fine. There was just one drawback – Roddie's French. It was correct, it was what French was in Lincolnshire. But neither Roddie nor his boys ever expected to be down and out in Carcassonne. Half the damn time, Didiér hadn't an idea what he was saying.

It was a pretty wonderful achievement.

As gently as I could, because Roddie was very fragile, I said I didn't want lessons.

To my surprise he looked vaguely relieved. There might have been a problem with what he called 'a venue'. No 'digs', said Roddie. He used a flat over in the rue de la Liberté. But there were 'chaps' who also 'stayed over'. Where would we have had lessons?

Then he said, 'Well, at least buy my book.'

I must have looked disbelieving because he said well, not *his* book, exactly. But an essential textbook, the only one he taught from, the only one to have – if he gave me lessons.

'The book costs 200 francs,' said Roddie.

I said, 'But if I'm not taking lessons from you, why do I need your book?'

I really thought he was going to cry then: I kept missing the point. What did I think he was saying? He was dossing in some squat in the rue de la Liberté, where the *clochards* slept in shifts.

Roddie said, 'Tell you what, I'll order the book for you. On trial. If you don't like it, I'll refund your 200.'

I passed him the money.

'I'll phone you.' Roddie swallowed his beer and stood up. 'As soon as the book arrives. You won't be disappointed.'

Then he left and I paid for his beers. He never phoned me and his book never arrived. But he was right – I wasn't disappointed. Roddie gave me something to remember.

* * *

Beggary is not what it was. I think this happened when the religious aspect went out of it.

Consider the prince of beggars, the Beggar from Bram. He gets the mix exactly right. He knows that beggary is a business. He believes that God helps those who help themselves and he never goes downmarket. He knows that beggars go in and out of fashion but their product stays the same: they sell you the means of dumping your guilt, for a while. You don't have to take Siggie's view – that the Vatican is hand in glove with the Mafia – to see the old links between Church and commerce, Christ and cash.

The Beggar from Bram believes the old ways are best, he is a traditionalist. He works at the very top of the tree. His pitch is the Basilica of Saints Nazarius and Celsus, in the old medieval Cité of Carcassonne, the original settlement on a hill overlooking the modern town. La Cité has been here since Roman times; a walled confection, a fairy-tale city; it speaks of knights, Cathars, Crusaders and the death of Simon de Montfort; sieges, burning pitch, prisoners left to rot in *oubliettes*. It has been attacked by Romans, Moors and Crusaders.

The first time I saw Carcassonne it popped up so splendidly, towers and battlements and leaden grey roof, like a dream palace, and it goes on fascinating me; mainly because almost everything about it is fake. Except for the basilica and its beggar. The basilica had its beginnings in a little church built by the Visigoths in the sixth century. Since then it has been rebuilt and messed about many times. The iron ring is still in the column where the Revolutionaries tethered their horses when the basilica became, for a while, a stable. No bad thing for a Church founded by a man born in one.

One in three French people visit La Cité at least once in their lives. And foreign tourists flock – for the restaurants, battlements, the museum of medieval torture, halberds and dungeons. And for the basilica with its fine rose windows, which have survived almost everything.

This is good news for the Beggar from Bram.

Today, he is in his usual place, inside the door; he is wearing a maroon jumper and grey flannels. I arrive just as a bunch of tourists are being given a conducted tour of the basilica. The Beggar who has been lost in the shadows suddenly materializes with his grave face and his neat, woven begging basket. He is quiet and respectful, he might be the sacristan, the verger, the doorkeeper. He has a long grey beard and cloudy white hair and looks a little like John the Baptist.

Of course few think so; visitors don't make such comparisons, they come because the coaches bring them. But he looks holy, fits the setting. The Beggar from Bram is perfectly cast. Like the statues of saints, the candles or the church furniture, he is proper. Eyes down, little brown basket clinking with a few coins, white hair touched with technicolor from the rose windows.

I reckon almost everyone who passes through the door pushes a couple of francs into his basket and he neither thanks them nor acknowledges them. Sometimes people give twice over, because he is still there when they leave. I reckon he must be pulling 200 to 300 francs an hour. And between waves of visitors he transfers the cash to a plastic shopping bag he keeps on a chair, in the deep shadow behind the church door. It is a rare sight, it's almost a miracle – when he thinks no one is watching, the dreamy hermit turns cashier.

I am watching.

And I've seen the saint turn street fighter. He is a magnificent ruin of a man but he guards his patch. Most of the time he is in the shadow by the door but in a dry period he walks around the square outside the church, muttering to himself; he shakes, he has a tic, his cheek twitches and when, once, a competing cripple tried to milk the tourists on the square, even though this was not his turf, he ran at her pecking like a raven and she wheeled herself away.

Is it cruel to spy on this poor muttering man? I don't think so. It's business, and I think he'd understand this.

But I haven't finished with him yet.

There is another story about the Beggar from Bram. It is said that he climbs on the train from Bram each morning, dressed like any other civil servant, or *fonctionnaire*. He gets off at Carcassonne station, and walks up the hill to La Cité carrying his plastic supermarket bag which holds his working clothes. In the public toilets he changes into the crumpled grey flannels and signature maroon or black jumper, and when the church doors open at 9.30, he starts work.

At the end of the day, he packs up, changes again, and dressed like any other office worker, he takes supper in a restaurant in Carcassonne before catching the train back to Bram. It is said he likes to eat well.

Compare his magnificence with beggary *nouveau*, the young drunks outside the Church of St Louis. It lies just within the old walls of lower Carcassonne, near the west gate. Theirs is semi-political, vaguely unionized, beggary with menaces.

I visited the Church of St Louis regularly, dodging the occupying forces in the little garden outside the door. Wearing military anoraks or duffel coats, they slept stretched out on the metal bench in the war memorial garden, or lay in wait like footpads. A young red-headed woman with a baby and a plastic cup was hard to get by.

But once inside, the church was a sanctuary, painted with chevrons of gold and maroon, warm and soaring to golden stars on the ceiling; even the usual bad nineteenth-century statuary and piped plain chant were perfect. St Louis was a great good place.

As there are churches and churches, there are beggars and beggars; a pecking order operates. St Louis is not in the first rank; neglected now – shipwrecked on the old walls that circled Carcassonne – though there is still a link with commerce.

Yet even as I write that I detect an element of wishful thinking: I know that the reality is elsewhere, or moving away. The Church of St Louis has a *fripés* market nearby. Used clothes spill off trestle-tables for thirty metres. Second-hand, second-best. Goods are cheap, the sellers dodgy. The oyster-seller, knife to hand, with his ready lemon, and a glass of white; the olive man; the singing baker who calls you to taste before you buy: 'It's essential.'

On the road around the square, stand the small producers. A fellow at a card table selling leeks and thyme; a woman with a basin of eggs; a box of wild mushrooms; the *fromager* in his huge brown hat and his goat's cheese; six brown hens in a basket; four white rabbits trembling in a cage; the honey-seller; the gypsy who sells baskets.

But real business is done further down the road, where the smiling, sleepy retro-beggars wait outside the supermarket. The impulse is still religious, but now shopping brings salvation.

Beggary began in Church but it ends in Monoprix.

Beggary *nouveau* belongs to Roddie's lot. Curiously ancient young people, kippery-brown, smeared at the edges, who arrived at the ice-cream pink railway station, with the air of emigrants arriving in the New World.

They looked like survivors of the last great love-in, the swinging 60s, hippies who fell asleep after one joint too many around 1965, and woke up in the Midi, last of the big-hairs.

Except they were too young for that. And too poor. 60s hippies were middle class, like their revolution – gear and music needed parental bank accounts. These refugees on the pavement outside Monoprix were broke but mobile; retro-hippies; their distinguishing badges were nose-rings, tartan trousers, shirt tails, neck-chains, jumpers knotted around their hips, scuffed Doc Martens, little dogs on strings.

There was the juggler and the spinning-top player and the bandmaster of plastic sparrows that chirruped when you filled them with water; the solitary young flautist in the hat-shop doorway, who closed her eyes when she played Bellini; and the phony collectors for Aids victims, and the bad violinist. There were four bald boys playing didgeridoos and a silent man sitting in front of a small notice written in crayon on a scrap of brown cardboard: I'M HUNGRY. Eyes downcast – humility was essential – stroking the mongrel in his lap.

They nipped into the supermarket now and then. The manager patrolled the aisles with a muzzled Alsatian, hiding behind the wine bottles, stalking his victims. They were easily caught. They're bad artists, bad beggars. Not bad people. Lousy shoplifters with expensive tastes. The newspapers sometimes printed roguish little paragraphs about the thief whose 'love for foie gras' did her down: she was caught with a couple of cans in her bra.

Every so often the cops moved them off the Monoprix steps, the way they hosed the dog-shit off the pavement once a week, but the *clochards* were sticky, stubborn, hard to remove.

* * *

I returned to Chez Jim, with relief.

Mrs Pram arrived. She was a familiar soul. She wandered through town, short grey socks around her ankles, a dumpy, brown, splay-legged old person pushing an old-fashioned big-wheeled pram.

She worked the pedestrian precinct, the *piéton*. She anchored herself in the middle of the *piéton* like a rock, and the passers-by split as they flowed by on either side of her outstretched hands, as she gave out her unvarying call: '*Une pièce, s'il vous plaît, monsieur.*'

I watched her as she parked her vehicle outside the door and checked the *plat du jour*. Mrs Pram was wearing her light green summer dress and, for some reason, she had stretched a green pinafore or petticoat or tablecloth over the mouth of the pram, maybe to protect an imaginary baby from the sun.

Everyone knew she carried firewood in the pram.

When her morning had gone well she would lunch at Chez Jim, choosing a table on the pavement, eating with her hands, a sliver of rabbit grease running down her chin, blind to the furious stares of those passers-by who had given something earlier and now saw her stuffing herself on their money.

Mrs Pram was wonderful – but perhaps not wise. We don't like seeing our charity so blatantly enjoyed. As far as I knew, the Beggar from Bram had never been seen eating his legendary dinner in a good restaurant. With beggars, as with monarchs, one should not let too much light fall on the magic.

CHAPTER 14

THE THING I loved about Kissac was its compactness; when I walked into the mountains and looked back I saw how it found its level, like water, hugging the hollows of the foothills.

From my apartment at the top of Siggie's house, I had a view of cherry trees; and through the small window of my workroom I looked into the next-door garden, where a soldierly woman with auburn hair marched along the bean rows, inspecting the work of her gardener. He was a grey-haired, round man in an old green jersey and grey flannels who stood to attention beside his rake . . .

It was a tableau: the general and her prisoner of war.

Lovers, said Siggie. They were both widowed, and met at old-time dancing. Now he lived with her and kept the garden.

'A passionate business,' he said with exasperation.

For a man who never went anywhere, except on buying raids, he was amazingly well-informed; he knew where to find the best wine from the barrel (the co-op at Félines); the price of every mouldering chateau or *maison de maître* for miles around, and he could be relied on to supply some essential piece of information about love or futility.

How he knew what he did I can't say; he never read the papers, never walked into the heart of the village or shopped at the baker. He picked up scraps of news in the Hotel des Cathars, when Nicolas was in his Radio Kissac mode. Local TV news gave him some joy: when the Bible Society sent out free videos – and what arrived were pornographic tapes – Siggie was so pleased you'd have thought he did it himself.

And he relied heavily on the loudspeakers.

Then the local elections came along. Kissac turned out the mayor, M. Santiago, and chose M. le May instead. His first act was to silence the loudspeakers. M. Santiago said it was a terrrible thing to strangle the public-address system. M. le May said we had to move with the times, it was demeaning, and out of date, to have information force-fed us from the *Mairie*.

M. Santiago called the new Mayor a neo-Gaullist rightist, and the new Mayor said M. Santiago was an infantile leftist. And there the matter rested.

It was simply that those loudspeakers mattered less and less. Old Kissac – crumbling arches, tiny squares, small dark houses with sagging shutters – sheltered an audience of the elderly, the ill, the poor. Those with money escaped to the new villas on the hillsides – plastic roofs and steel shutters that brutally aped the tightly clustered stone and red tile of village houses. Modern people had cars, newspapers, TV; they had outgrown the town-crier.

Old Madame Cabrol, beside the ancient *horlogerie*, pulled her chair onto the pavement to take the sun and watched me come and go. She had the face of an intelligent fish.

'Why don't you get a bicycle?' she asked.

What would happen, I asked, now that the loudspeakers had shut down?

Madame Cabrol looked surprised. 'People will still talk.'

People talked in Mimi's tiny grocery, opposite the *Mairie* and the Hotel des Cathars. And in the Lapin. People talked in the bakery, run by a woman shaped like a bag of cement. So stuck-up, her customers said, she kept 'her nose in the attic'. She had the bread – the village had nothing – to know her was to understand why Marie Antoinette had to go . . . The street, the café, and Radio Kissac, sent the real news around town.

But Siggie worried: 'Who'll tell me when someone dies?'

Friends offered to plug the gap. Little Humph-Humph, the print dealer who lived with his ancient father, promised to phone – in the event. Pascal said he'd do the same – the moment his dad pulled it off. And Siggie's scout, over in Lézignan, said he'd do deaths, for the same cut he took on house demolitions.

But for a while Siggie was inconsolable. As he said, 'It's not known deaths I care about. It is the surprise. The stranger. That's where you find a windfall.'

Death notices were still posted at the post office, so he took to haunting the place. 'You never know your luck.'

And he got lucky. He met a couple of visitors who planned to buy a house in Kissac – did he know an apartment they might rent while they looked around? He took them home and handed them over to Ria, whose 'part of the world' that was.

* * *

Nathalie and Thor moved into Sophie's old apartment, above Siggie's workshop. Siggie summed them up. They were unmarried, rich and – he lifted his outstretched hand to form a stiff wedge below his nose – a bit stuck-up.

He was retiring; she was coming home. They planned to buy a house in Kissac.

Nathalie was from Montpellier – but years in New York gave her a monied American smoothness which almost, but not quite, ironed out her French particularity. She was very brown, very pert, and she said what she thought. After years away, Nathalie wanted to live once again in France.

Thor was a Dane who had worked for the World Bank in Geneva; he met Nathalie, and fell in love. He was very tall, with a shock of white hair, and he wore Dior by day and Hermés by night. Thor was an Anglophile, he had a great collection of Gilbert and Sullivan videos. He kept a beach house in Capri. But the most magical thing about him was his shoes; he owned fat black loafers and brown pumps, luscious and rich; his feet were shod in starlight, in cream.

Oh, the glory of those shoes! No one in Kissac will forget Thor and his footwear. He was the sort of fellow who honoured Kissac by walking down the road. He breathed big city, you had the feeling he'd gone to sleep in New York or Berlin and woken up in our village, still dressed to go on the town.

'He could have lived anywhere!' said M. Banet.

M. Banet had a foul temper and hardly a good word to say about anyone. He kept the little butcher shop as one would a fortress; he had a couple of parking spaces over the road and he patrolled them. Anyone who parked so as to intrude on these spaces, and take more room than allowed, would be assailed by M. Banet, who ran out shouting, 'You disregardful person. You ruin me! How can one be such a thief, a boor, a pig!'

But of Thor he said, 'He walks about in those shoes, as if he owns them!'

Thor had spent his life advancing large loans to poor countries. And now he walked about in his miraculous shoes, nodding and smiling at passers-by and adjusting the collar of his mustard polo shirt to show just a hint of chest hair over the breastbone. He smoothed his hands through his crisp white Danish hair and smiled ruefully as he walked between the Lapin Fou and the Bar à Go-Go.

That ruefulness had a reason; though we did not know it then. Nathalie was very busy. Every day was given over to lavishing a little something on the prize of herself. And yet despite this constant care she was never well. She talked in long winding sentences with huge affection about herself.

'I think because I'm so small men love to do things for me.'

She was obsessed with her frames of mind, her history, her body. The injustices done to her by friends, time, tax-officials. Her watchwords were 'defend', 'repair', 'pamper', her holy land was – herself; it stretched from her heart to the boundaries of her being. To the fluted tips of her shell-pink nails, to the strawberry tints of her short blonde hair, the tip of her little nose, the points of her important nipples. Every turn and pirouette was calculated to place her in a position where she looked better, or got a better look at herself. She issued daily reports on her health, her aches, nerves, muscle strain, headaches.

Lumbago hit her and she began the search for treatment. All her time and effort and talk went into it. Nothing was more difficult. Or more vital.

She found a chiropractor, a little woman a few villages away, over in Villegly.

'Such soft hands, my dear. So very careful with me.'

But not careful enough for long enough; and the little woman from Villegly was replaced by big butch Madelaine, over in Rieux.

'She rang me like a bell.' Nathalie's pretty elfin face began creasing with the relief, the joy, of having saved herself.

She was clenching her bare brown toes; her cherry-red toenails dug into her neat new patent leather sandals, and her sturdy body flexed with the effort of recalling the odd mixture of pain and pleasure it enjoyed under Madelaine's steel fingers.

On and on Nathalie's story spun, smiling happily to herself, a gentle unstoppable wave of concern, and joy and relief at having fought lumbago and won, of how, at last, she found Maia, in the nearby village of Trausse. A diamond in the dirt. A slovenly room, so dirty – she growled in her throat to show how the dirt set her teeth on edge – 'Grrrr! Grrr!'

Maia was forgiven all for her gift of healing – she moved the heatfields of her hands like ultraviolet lamps over Nathalie's aching back.

Siggie and I watched in astonishment. Unstoppable

Nathalie, nodding at the memory of having done the very best (which was the very *least* she could do) for herself.

* * *

Siggie was nonplussed by tall Thor, in his brilliant shoes; Nathalie purring and repairing, grooming and glittering, arching her back, her eyebrows and gently rubbing herself – against herself. Siggie found her merciless flow of talk unsettling and, somehow, improper. He said, rather help-lessly, that Thor should have a hobby. Thor did not add up. Thor drank only the occasional Scotch and would not touch Siggie's wine or his *grenache* or his colourless cognac. Siggie had never met a man who spent his time watching Gilbert and Sullivan videos and walking about in a grand fashion.

Nathalie and Thor bought the old mill by the river, and work started on the big revamp. From then on, things got really bad.

Fred, the Dalmatian, had started stealing food from their apartment. He ran off with *saucisson* and cheese, when they were in; and when they were out he rooted around in the rubbish bin.

Siggie was amused, even, I felt, rather proud. A good scavenger! Then Fred started sneaking into the apartment at night. One morning Thor woke to find the dog between Nathalie and himself. He told Siggie he didn't like that.

Siggie simply said, 'Dogs are dogs' – he never disci-plined Fred.

Then it rained and water poured through the roof of the back room and fell on Thor's shoes and ruined every pair but one.

Thor hated dirt. He was Danish, he had been a banker, he had a house in Capri, he wrote in a sloping hand with a Mont Blanc, which he closed with precision; he shopped at Hermés and he had lived in Geneva; the last thing he wanted in retirement was mess.

He walked into Siggie's house and attacked without warning, pinned him to the wall and screamed at him in Danish. There were dog hairs in his bed, his shoes were wrecked, gas was leaking from the bottle beneath the sink, Sigismund was a crook and took money from lodgers under false pretences. His place was filthy, badly made, ugly.

Siggie liked displays of strong emotion; but he never did anything about them – as Ria had found to her frustration. He caved in and enjoyed the spectacle, like a boy who crept under the circus tent and watched – free – the passion, the colours, the noise. He would swap any amount of abuse for the show the attacker was forced to put on.

He had never seen Thor so livid, so loud! Hugging himself happily, Siggie used a phrase he reserved for special instances of madness – when the doctor exposed himself on the hillside – Thor, said Siggie, had been 'completely out of order'.

After the storm, Siggie felt a lot better and Thor felt worse.

* * *

Poor Thor. Perhaps we should have known then that he was, in his way, as desperate as any man could be.

Then Nathalie took to her bed with an attack of sciatica and Thor came and sat in my place, in his one pair of beautiful black moccasins, with tassels, that the rain hadn't ruined, a blood-red shirt, white socks and the sort of pants that seem to have been sketched by pencil, the creases drawn with a ruler, and he said he really didn't know what to do about Nathalie.

He was pretty low; his big square face was breaking up and he seemed to have trouble lifting his big Danish jaw from his chest.

The next day he was gone.

After a month he still wasn't back.

And when I asked Nathalie where he was, she said, 'In Capri. In the sun. Trying to make up his mind whether or not to leave me.'

Her need was so strong, so blind. Those who came too near realized too late. They started out strong, neat, tall; she took them in her arms, squeezed, swallowed and reduced them to mush. Nathalie cast herself as bread upon the waters. She gathered lovers like herbs, searching through them for a cure, pressing them to her needy body. By the time she felt better they were finished.

*   *   *

Thor came back from Capri and Nathalie didn't say a word.

They moved into their new house by the river. You might have thought Thor would be pleased to get out of Siggie's place, and into somewhere decent, where his shoes and his shirts and his videos would be safe and his terrible rising temper would be contained. Because he was getting madder and madder at Nathalie and he couldn't stop it.

The old mill looked beautiful in its steely settled way; Nathalie had designed the interior, and it reminded me of a throat, pink and deep and slightly slippery. Nathalie was planning and fixing and grooming her house with the same obsessive attention she gave to her body, and switching builders whenever one fell below her expectation. Thor's job, she kept saying, was the garden.

Thor took the garden in hand and it was terrible to behold.

He ordered in workmen and removed all the trees along the side of the house. It did no good for Siggie to tell him they were essential protection against the summer sun.

Sun is what he wanted, to lie in the sun; he dreamed of just two things: Danish snow and blazing heat.

Next he ordered in a gang of workers and laid a huge concrete apron over half the garden; big as a tennis court, or a helicopter landing pad, and where he planned to sit in a deckchair and soak up the sun.

Thor began staying in bed for longer and longer and got up only to stand at the window; he looked out at the great slab of concrete in the garden, and grieved. Even though his shoes were safe now and there were no dog hairs in his bed, Thor walked through the village in his best cream slacks and his blood-red Hermés shirt, and people were as proud of him as ever; but he was unhappy. She was killing him, he believed.

I would meet him in the village, humming snatches from *The Mikado*, or 'I Am the Very Model of a Modern Major-General', so upright, so Nordic, so despairing.

When Nathalie suggested he go somewhere to brighten his day – like having a Sunday morning drink over in Olonzac at the Café du Sport, with Siggie and his friends – Thor groaned and knew he couldn't manage any longer.

He was a banker and a Dane; he seldom drank more

than a single very good whisky, he did not smoke or keep pets, he respected his elderly parents back in Copenhagen. Indeed he had probably neglected them for this woman. He had decent clothes and his shoes alone were worth thousands. He had been a person of importance in Geneva and now, here he was, in a rumpled French village surrounded by rumpled people who wore the most appalling clothes, tracksuits and shell suits and trainers. They were dark, frizzy, loud, short; he was tall and silver; they were happy and he was going mad.

One morning in winter he got up early and spent the day marking all his books and his furniture and his paintings and his videos and his shoes, and shirts. After telling Nathalie he would send in the movers just as soon as he could, he left her and flew to Denmark.

He phoned me in tears. When he came down the steps of the aircraft in Copenhagen – Thor felt like crying, there was snow on the ground. He had escaped, he was home!

* * *

But back in Kissac they didn't see things that way. For a start, they were already at home and if anyone had told them that the tall Dane with the miraculous shoes and the fine hair had fled in terror, like a man escaping from a prison camp, they would never have believed it.

They missed Thor's shining walk between the Lapin Fou and the Bar à Go-Go. And they decided he must be ill; the bad-tempered butcher told people that Monsieur was 'très fatigué'.

So fatigued that he never ever appeared and the butcher drew people's attention to the shutters, which Nathalie had kept closed since Thor left. She had moved out of their bedroom and made a tiny suite in the top-floor corner of the huge house.

She kept the shutters closed 'Because men, coming out of the Lapin, in the evening, are spying when I get out of the bath!'

Now the café was a hundred metres away from her house and the idea of peeping Toms at that range seemed unlikely but Nathalie knew that a crowd of voyeurs stood each night, around the fountain, and watched every fold of flesh as she towelled her body, after a bath of camomile and jasmine.

Nathalie told everyone, above a certain level, that Thor had left her; but she, and her confidantes, never spoke to the locals in case they gossiped.

Meanwhile the village grew more and more concerned about Thor's health and no one was surprised when the butcher reported that Monsieur was dead. Adding that Nathalie had been so heartbroken she had him secretly buried in another village.

And Nathalie went on being much as she was and never noticed the looks of sympathy as she drove out in her big new car – too big, people said, for a widow. Poor thing! She never knew they thought he was dead.

She told me she was really quite relieved Thor had gone. He'd been getting more and more depressed and she simply hadn't known what to do with him. If only he'd had some little hobby. Like Siggie, who collected things. But she was not too sad.

'Now I can live as I want to. Perhaps sell the house. Enjoy myself, on my own.'

So it was a surprise when, just before Christmas, I met her in the *hypermarché*. She had with her a man and at first glance I thought Thor was back. But it wasn't him. Almost as tall, with a thatch of white hair. She had her arm around his neck, her elbow was crooked. Nathalie tightened her hold and introduced me. She laid him out the way a carpet-seller will exhibit a rug and he smiled and stammered and looked stunned and Nathalie was radiant. There was a big freezer behind her, full of cold ducks, and the icy light was on her teeth.

'This is Allan,' she said.

Allan. His hair was whiter than Thor's and his cheeks ruddier; he opened his lips to say something but perhaps he was just too stupidly happy or perhaps Nathalie's hold on his windpipe made it impossible because all that came out was something like a little growl: 'Grrrr, Grrr.'

It didn't matter though. Nathalie had said it all for him.

* * *

One Wednesday Siggie and I were in Loud Lilly's emporium, over in Mazamet. Loud Lilly, as usual, had not deigned to see us but the moment the King slipped away into another of her barns to hunt for clocks, she stuck her head over the edge of her tall bed. I was inspecting the piles of junk in the general warehouse, where a hundred francs was top price.

I watched her, watching me from her perch, propped on an elbow. She wore a creased and rather smudged green robe. Loud Lilly, with eyes like cooling volcanic ash – and all the sensitivity of a crow who feeds on road kills. Yet she was a princess on her tall bed, she could feel the bump of profit six shelves below, a little windfall no bigger than a pea . . .

Jammed into Lilly's shelves were the most beautiful and terrible things. Beside a porcelain lion with yawning jaws sat a bald doll in a short pink dress, with wide blue eyes and a cracked skull. A fat little egg-timer, with Humpty-Dumpty's face, leered as her dress went riding up her thighs. Our Lady of Lourdes wore a Nazi helmet. The bust of Mussolini rested in a baby carriage, its plinth five volumes of Diderot. Cherished bridal sheets lay mouldering in an elmwood box: embroidered with a blindfolded boy chasing a milkmaid across a flowering meadow, signed in looping stitching: '*Anne-Marie LeCastres*'. I picked off the snails bedded in the damp sheets; and stamped on them. We should burn, or bury the precious possessions of the dead along with the owners. Anything is better than snails in the wedding chest . . .

I found it strange and terrible, this half-life of once-precious objects: cracked, crazed, jumbled, thrown together – the naked and the furry; the sacred and profane. The way these things, bits and pieces, once-loved junk kept faith, while the owners did the human thing – and vanished.

Siggie's point – the deep unreliability of human beings . . . the way of all flesh – desertion, betrayal, disloyalty; people grew up, or old, or away – they gave in, went under, quit the field.

Yet our prints are on the goods; they've got our number: they're us – scratch them and, like the scent advertisement buried in the page of a magazine, the touch of a fingernail releases the perfume of the past. And where are the absent owners? Who was happy in this bridal finery? Brave in those war medals, laid out on a field of red plush, under a glass bell? Who looked pretty in this mirror, or silly in that hat?

The shelves were thick with rumours. The absent owners? The lovers? Vanished, decamped, absent without leave. Missing – presumed dead.

Now I know there are those for whom a roomful of junk is just that: objects, bits and pieces. I'm sure such people are the majority. That's their consolation.

But there are those who are haunted, as I am, by spirits: just brushing past these things raises ghosts, like Aladdin's lamp. The junk in Loud Lilly's is so terrible because it all talks at once, it pulls at your sleeve. It's what we once were. Worse, it is all there is left of us.

* * *

I don't know why they caught my eye. But there they were – standing on end, like books, supported by two heavy crucifixes as bookends, a shelf of shoes – loafers, brogues, slim Italian slip-ons with tassels – so rich, so supple, so splendid despite a tattoo, or two, of raindrops. When Thor went walking in those shoes, people said he looked as if he owned them. And here they were on Lilly's shelves, a costly leather sandwich, pressed between two Christs.

When Siggie came back I raised an eye in their direction, carefully turning my back. I didn't want Lilly to know what I'd seen.

He led me into the backyard; followed discreetly, as always, by Lilly's husband – ready to deal. In the yard, beyond the cracked bidets and washbasins and lavatory bowls, a tangle of chipped and flaking farmhouse lamps swung from a cherry tree; painted roses and lavender and wild irises, on milky glass. Siggie fell to examining them with such fierce attention that his watchdog backed off and did a circuit of the yard, trying to work out if the King was pulling a fast one, terrified that the 'eye' had spied some hidden bargain, and he was going to get it in the neck from She who Rested in the Rafters.

When we were alone Siggie said, 'I found them in the apartment – Thor left them. Because of the water stains.'

'Are you saying you flogged his shoes to Lilly?'

'Christopher – it was practically for nothing.'

'How much?'

'You can't even see the rain damage. If you bought those shoes in Toulouse . . . they'd cost thousands.'

'I can't believe this. How much did you sell them for?'

'What could I do? Thor didn't want them. Me neither. So what to do? Think of the waste – to leave them. I told Lilly – make me a price.'

'Siggie – how *much?*'

'One hundred francs.'

He got this bristling look; his face, usually so open and placid, shifted under waves of cunning and defiance; I saw a curious bruising around the eyes he got when he was about to tell the truth – and doing it only because the truth was too wonderful to keep to himself. The look of a contented hedgehog, who has done what comes naturally. Stung the hand that stroked him. An angry delight that was as close as Siggie ever came to aggression.

'She thought they were mine. D'you see?'

I did see. Once there was a rich man, an aristocrat, who lived in a castle. Then there was Lilly, the poor peasant who lived on a rubbish dump. Good communist that she was, she dreamed of his fall. And *voilà!* It came to pass that the King fell on hard times. Loud Lilly looked down from her hill of swag and graciously bought the shoes off his feet – his ermine slippers went for a song! How could Lilly resist? It was practically for nothing. Siggie's price had been perfectly pitched.

Anything more, and he was doing business, and that bored him. Flogging Thor's slightly used footwear to the lofty communist – and getting away with it – now that was fun!

'We won't tell Ria – will we?' said Siggie.

CHAPTER 15

IF JUNK, AS someone once suggested, is possessions released from the tyranny of ownership, I'd be happy. But I fear it's more complicated than that. We do not escape so easily. We may disown our possessions but they go on giving the impression that they own us.

In the hilltop village of Montolieu, famous for its second-hand books, there is a *bouquiniste* who keeps a tousled barn of books in the disused factory by the village wall. And one day I found on his crowded tables, where the cheaper torn and fluttering trophies lie like downed birds, the fruit of a recent clearance. He'd bought all the books of the old lady who lived a few doors down the road, and whom I knew to be English.

The Englishwoman's name was Nancy and she sat alone all day long; she had no family. Friends had been keen to visit but they stopped – now she sat in the tall, thin shadowy house from morning till night, and only the doctor came from time to time in his little red Peugeot, and the nurse to exercise her, and the grocer's girl, with the weekly provisions, and the meals-on-wheels lady.

Nancy's friends really tried. But they had no encouragement, she didn't know them – worse, she didn't know who she was – and the pain of reintroducing themselves, each time, to a familiar stranger got too much. 'Alzheimer's,' they said firmly. The bright definition snapped around her, like the electronic bracelet used to tag criminals.

Her neighbours, on the other hand, were more easy; she was 'fading', she was 'confused', she was '*très fatigué*'. They brought her lettuce from time to time and hung it on her door knocker. They shook their heads.

Nancy said nothing. Her eyes were a faint watery blue; her hair had turned from red to auburn. The last time I saw hair like it was on the mummy of Ramses II, when the Pharaoh was taken from his recently discovered grave and flown to Paris, and unwrapped by scientists in front of the TV cameras. He still had his hair. It was very moving, that ancient auburn hair.

The *bouquiniste* in Montolieu was selling her library. There was stuff by Philip Gibbs, Dornford Yates, Cronin and Maugham. I wanted none of it – until I found a bunch of typed pages, glued together, missing a cover. There was no author's name, but there was a date: Cowes, 1951. The title, if it had one, might have been something brilliantly dull: *Getting By In Paris*; or perhaps more slyly amusing: *Paris Regained*.

The dealer wouldn't charge me. 'It's some curiosity,' he said, 'an English cookbook, or a diary.'

It wasn't either. At first glance it was a guidebook to Paris; and a course in French grammar. It was 120 pages; the typing neat – perhaps it had been done on an old Remington. The paper – good but plain stuff you got at any stationer – had held up pretty well, though the type was turning fuzzy. It was a rather satisfying object, solid, well-made, elegantly laid out, and durable – for a book nearly a half-century old.

There was just the one copy – and just one reader. The author was, perhaps, a sailing man. There was the reference to Cowes, after all; and there was bluff sailorliness, a nautical briskness to his clipped pedantries. He was egotistical, pompous, and fussy. It was his achievement to find a way of saying what can not, may not, be said, in a form which does not usually allow for anything true or beautiful; that dull thing, the guidebook-cum-language primer.

I called him Denis – that is the only thing I have invented. Everything else is his.

Denis wrote about Paris, but that was merely his way of talking about France, and France was a way of imagining a heartland, a place where one is well.

The clever thing was to base his ideal city on the real one. And Denis knew it well, he had spent time there, he spoke French, he knew the streets of Paris. But his originality lay in his discovery that reality would be the best cloak for his true feelings; he would be sensible and proper and pompous and make these deadly things work for him. In other words, he began from a position of despair, and moved towards love. He took facts and made them sing.

So he invented the author of this anonymous tract, and what a triumph that creation is. So terribly proper, so prejudiced, so unerringly boring, so completely a caricature of the right-thinking Englishman lost among the Frogs that you almost believe he is what he says he is: a prig, a boor, and a decent fellow, and his only aim is to help people like himself not get lost in Paris.

* * *

'I put down anything', Denis explains in his Introduction, 'that struck me as troublesome, confusing or useful . . .'

Denis builds his book on the rock on which so many Anglo-Saxons stub their toes, the infuriating way hat the French will insist on being themselves. Denis echoes the conviction of English visitors down the ages; France they love – it's the natives they can't stand.

Much turns out to be troublesome or confusing. Denis alone is useful. He begins with a catalogue of warnings: where not to go, what not to do and where not to eat. This is a manual for a tourist who knows nothing, written by a tour leader who has seen everything, and can barely contain his exasperation. Things are never what they seem in Paris; one must be on one's guard – the realities are difficult, disappointing.

But Denis has a plan: he will lay out the difficulties, he will lick them into shape in neat, meticulous chapters.

Problems On The Metro:
You open closed doors, but you never close open doors.

Going to the Cinema:
You must tip the *ouvreuse* (about ten per cent of the cost of your ticket). This is a scandalous system but you feel better when you are told that these tips are the girl's sole source of income. Buy a copy of the script at a railway bookstall as French films are extremely difficult

to follow, particularly as most French cinemas are wretched places.

Eating Out:
Les Halles . . . any night from about midnight onwards. Go to the *Au Chien qui fume* or *Au Pied du Cochon* for onion soup and a glass of excellent Beaujolais.

Getting about:
You should make certain whether what you are looking for is a rue, boulevard, avenue, faubourg, place, square, quai, porte or ponte . . .

But things are tricky; the French are out to trap the unwary and they will deliberately mislead the visitor who finds herself adrift in a faubourg, at sea in a boulevard:

' . . . "St Denis" or "St Michel" can be tacked onto any of these and the fact that they have the same proper name does not mean that the actual places are not miles and miles apart.'

Again and again, Denis comes back to the dangers.

'In walking about keep to your main path. It is tempting to cut across by a side street into what you think must be the parallel street that you are making for.'

At first, the passages about finding, losing, keeping to your way I thought were odd, obsessive. Then I saw they were very strange. Even pathetic. Because they're full of longing and sadness and despair; Denis fusses and disapproves, and, increasingly, you feel – here is suffering; the finicky harping on the right direction hides the raw hurt of a desperate man.

These constant warnings are aimed at someone, a

woman, and she is going off on her own, will go off, will get lost, can never really learn the kind of geography which will keep her safe. She is bound to take the wrong turn: and he will never find her again.

'. . . Paris is laid out like the spokes of a wheel and a deviation like this can leave you hopelessly lost and literally miles from where you are wanting to go.'

Slowly, it began to dawn on me that what I was reading was a love letter, sent to the old lady I know as Nancy; a letter of a most secret and original kind.

It was when I got to the grammar sections, possibly even more brilliantly boring still, that I began to see the extent of his achievement: Denis had found a way of pouring out his heart in banalities.

The French like a lot of things, all in the same word. You may 'like' your mistress just as you may 'like' minestrone. But you cannot be bats about her, crazy for her, dying for her, lost without her, keen on her or even 'pretty smitten'. You cannot play with a thousand forms of saying *I love you!*

You soon come to realize the comparative poverty of the French vocabulary (particularly in adjectives) compared with the English. Everything, from a mild fondness for beer to a passion for cheese and a devotion to your wife, is usually expressed with forms of *aimer*.

Denis's curious grammar book is a series of variations on 'forms of *aimer*'. Denis does with French grammar what he does with Anglo-Saxon propriety, he bends, subverts and gives to the forms a reach and a heart. He has hit on a way of speaking his love that is safe, secret and strangely sexy; he buries passion in rules, directions, grammar, geography; he makes love while giving French lessons. He writes in code on ineffable banalities in which there is seeded a confession of terrible yearning.

And, of course, she understood. That's why the cover is missing. It has been neatly torn off. Anyone opening it – a husband? a daughter? – would find nothing but boringly good advice by an anonymous author. Only its intended reader had the key. No one else would want to read much further. The author simply tells you much more than you ever want to know about the streets, soups and semi-naked reviews of Paris.

Entertainment.
If you're interested in semi-naked reviews, try one of the smaller places, like the Mayol or the Danau – they are much better than the dreary Folies Bergère or Casino de Paris.

There is an immediacy about Denis's directions. It is evident that he is writing from the city, while Nancy is somewhere else, and it seems she had never been to Paris before. Who knows what happened between the two of them – but something, perhaps, like this: Many years ago, Nancy was a young woman living in Cowes. She was almost certainly married. She met and fell in love with a man. Maybe he wanted her to leave her husband; maybe he was also married. Certainly they planned to run away. Were they going to live in Paris? Or perhaps just to meet there?

I think a longer stay is indicated. Consider how Denis

approaches the delicate operation of actually saying he needs to touch her, to put his arms around her, to sleep with her. How to tell her this intimate thing in the public pages of his primer – in a way no one else can see?

Denis's solution is to write about Parisian pleasures: about food, sex, semi-naked reviews, whores – but only in order to advise against them all. Nancy, he warns, must be very careful with French words. There are words and 'words', just as there are girls and 'girls'.

'Do not ever', he warns, 'use the naked form of the word "to kiss".'

Above all, she must never, never confuse the words 'embracing' with 'kissing'.

'*Embrasser* is to kiss,' Denis explains.

And then with a nod across the miles that separate them, he adds quickly, ' . . . as in, for example, *embrassez-moi.*'

It is so quick you barely see it; but she has been kissed and Denis is back to the usual drone.

French, he sighs, is 'extraordinarily troublesome'. If words for 'liking' are used for everything, and seldom very apt, and words for kissing are damn awkward then words for 'sleeping' are the most difficult of all.

'The use of *coucher,* by itself, is dangerous.'

Then there is swearing. Denis is as precise as he always is:

'The equivalent of a fairly strong expression like "bloody" is probably *merde!*'

But he thinks better of it and quickly cautions: 'Not to be used.'

Denis grows ever more obsessed with time.

On Place Pigalle:
The best time to see it is from 10.34, onwards.

Not 10.30 . . . or anything so rounded, but a pointed exactitude on which he can impale his uncertainty. He will nail her down. He will have her there and then.

* * *

Nearly half a century has passed since Denis sat at his typewriter banging out his guide. What is left? He is dead by now, almost certainly, and she cannot remember. There is still Paris, a Paris where parking is hell and pollution smothering. It is a city that is quite unrecognizable from Denis's irritable, pedantic, despairing descriptions.

Denis's Paris, the code for all he desires, the illicit, the sexy, that is also still there, more beautiful and more lively, in the pages of his tattered book. We now come to this awful fact: Denis's book and the love it conveys for faraway Nancy are more alive than the two lovers who poured out their hearts to each other. This Paris on paper is more real than the present capital of France.

And long-dead Denis whom I never met is more real to me than faded, fading Nancy whom I've met and talked to, and who must have moved to France many years ago, and now can't tell me why it was.

I've read his despairing guidebook: I know my way round him. I can trace the man in the prose. His grammatical pedantries, his unsplit infinitives, his maddening need to anticipate his beloved's every move and, more than anything, his horror of losing her.

Fuzzy type on yellowing paper – but it speaks. It sounds

like Denis. I can hear his clear, clipped, rather pedantic voice. Nothing but words on the page, yet when I take a page between thumb and forefinger, he begins growing like a genie out of his own lines.

Even his scepticism has a decent, manly quality about it. You get the impression that, in his world, a chap would feel what a chap like Denis feels. And a chap who asked a lady to Paris would be honour-bound to give her proper directions about those loosely named rues and boulevards.

Denis is a fact fetishist; details turn him on, giving directions arouses him, correction excites him; his blustering concern, his jolly good fellowship, is a mask for dark things. Maybe prissiness helps to make it feel more decent. But all the time passion crackles under the dry details.

His favourite words are 'order' and 'strict'. They go together and are often partnered by his other big thing: nudity. These obsessions show up in the most unexpected places. Here is Denis on *French Food:*

The standard French meal is formed something like this, strictly in this order:

1. Something in advance, either soup or hors-d'oeuvre. The soup is a mighty plateful. There are scores of pleasant things for hors-d'oeuvre – oysters, artichokes, andouille and other kinds of sausage, snails, anchovies, radishes, sardines, foie gras. Without any hesitation the French spread butter on sardines and radishes.

2. The main dish, fish, meat or bird. It is often eaten entirely naked, with the addition only of a sauce. 'Gravy', by the way, is sauce. Butter is seldom put on

bread, which is used for diligently cleaning up the plate after you have finished the main job. You never see fish knives and forks.

3. A vegetable. You throw back a large plate consisting only of beans or potatoes, plus lots of butter.

4. A salad. There seem to be a lot of varieties – the standard lettuce, plus batavias, scarolle, chicorée frisée, cress, romaine, la mâche, l'endive. The salad always has vinegar and oil in it but it is good to give it a hearty stir.

5. Cheese. This is always eaten naked, in a large slab without bread or biscuits.

Everything in the meal is naked. Like all the givers of advice, Denis is talking to himself.

Denis has written a love letter from a sad, silly, yearning man. It tells you next to nothing about the French, but almost everything about Denis.

'Never um and ah,' he urges Nancy. 'This apparently pains the good French. The answer is to prefer total silence – the pause in which just nothing happens while you are trying to decide what to say.'

Denis does not prefer total silence, he never stops talking, he is terrified of silence – her silence, I suspect. His book is a shout in the void, a cry from a suffering heart. A refusal of nothingness. He makes love in verbs and undresses the menu.

* * *

I asked Nancy about Denis and I was treated to an open, revealing and helpless smile. She cannot remember anything; the shadows have crept over her mind and, when she retreats frantically into the dark corners searching for what she cannot remember, her face takes on the cunning of a child who knows she's done something wrong – but doesn't know what it is, and thinks no one notices.

But I had noticed. Everything about Denis and love and Paris was dead to Nancy.

Almost everything.

If I asked Nancy about Paris the mists did not clear, even briefly. But when I asked her if she spoke French, the confused old woman with her Pharaoh's hair smiled herself back to a time when she was happy, for reasons she could not remember.

Then again, I'm not interested in reasons, I care about signs of the heart; and when I asked her if she spoke French, the key turned; the key Denis hid so well in the lessons of his insufferable guide . . .

Nancy sat quietly waiting 'the pause in which just nothing happens' – as Denis always advised. Then she said with her beautiful smile '*J'adore la langue Française.*'

CHAPTER 16

———•———

ONE MORNING, LITTLE Anna arrived at Siggie's place.

Leaving her knocking at his workroom door, he ran into the backyard, up the steps of his summer kitchen, through the cherry orchard where Plusbelle spotted him and shouted loudly for a drink, and stood beneath my window, arms wide like a scarecrow.

Would I come, quickly.

'In case I need a witness. Have you ever seen Anna? Even me, I've seen her only once or twice. You never forget her when you see her.'

I didn't ask why he needed a witness – I knew Anna came from the hills and, so, from the high places of the imagination. She had the dangerous charm of passing strangers – that Siggie needed, and feared. Did the stranger bring riches or ruin? Fortune or folly? He was 'one hundred per cent sure' gypsies had staked out his place. He was forever urging Fred the Dalmatian to take a more aggressive line. Bite on sight, he pleaded. But Fred enjoyed strangers, hated fighting – just like Siggie.

Little Anna must have walked along the old pilgrim's way that leads from the Shrine of Our Lady under the Mountain, over the shoulder of the hill and into the village.

Her heavy boots were scabbed with mud. A thin woman in dungarees, skin with a sheen like olive oil and a fringe of grey hair that hung down to her eyes. She was carrying an old battered cuckoo clock under her arm, and the door of the bird's nest swung on a single hinge.

When he had his witness in place, Siggie lifted the heavy wooden beam that locked his workshop door and scurried out into the road, wiping his hands on his heavy, olive-green apron, his spidery glasses bouncing on the bridge of his good Prussian nose (he bought batches of flimsy reading specs at Narbonne market, none worked very well but he could not resist the wholesale price), his hair was wispy, and tinted here and there with streaks of clock oil, his smoky grey eyes were slightly wild, the pupils black as burnt matchheads. The Sorcerer's Apprentice, on speed.

He held the clock up to the sun and rattled the door on its single hinge.

'Where's the cuckoo? *En vacance?*'

Anna didn't get his joke. She was a serious woman. Like everyone around Kissac she thought Siggie was a crazy Dutchman who ran around the place like a tin man, and knew about clocks. She turned the good half of her face towards him and out of the corner of her mouth she told him the serious truth about how the clock had lost its cuckoo.

There had always been hunters in her family. Long ago her brother Marcel, a boy of ten, had taken aim with his first rifle, waited till the cuckoo popped out of his house and blown the little thing off its perch. Twenty years had passed since her brother shot the cuckoo. No bird, true.

But the clock never missed a beat in all the birdless years. Until yesterday – when it had stopped.

'Died,' said Siggie.

Here began his litany; he was, in horological terms, the poet of the post-mortem. He preached the clockmakers' paradise. His bible was the Book of Hours; he taught the immortality of timepieces. The afterlife of clocks. Throw off that mouldy outer casing! Praise the eternal movement!

Anna's clock had 'given up the ghost and gone cold camping in *le jardin des refroids*'. It had also 'stopped smoking, turned up its toes, bought shares in the last caravan park'. Her clock was not simply 'past repair', it was 'past tense'.

Siggie's peroration grew in majesty: 'I cannot fix this clock. No. But I will resurrect it!'

'That would be kind,' said Anna.

And she turned the ruined side of her face to him; the missing nostril and the vanished eye, the seamed and ridgy plain that spread like thin dough or plasticine from her chin to her hairline.

He laid her clock on his workbench and extracted the movement with the precision of a heart surgeon. Bits would need to be replaced.

'Next week,' said Siggie. 'Come back next week and she will live, this clock.'

When Anna had limped away, he told me, 'The clock got shot, so did she.' Had I looked at Anna? She'd had bits replaced. After she was shot.

'Like the cuckoo.'

Siggie pulled at his cheek, screwed up his right eye and dented his nostril with his finger, so I shouldn't miss a thing. Surgeons had rebuilt her nose and fixed her lips and sewn up the place where her left eye had been, but they could do nothing to replace the tissue, bone, muscle carried away by the bullet.

* * *

Before the shooting, Anna had lived quietly in the mountains and you would never have thought she'd spring to prominence. She kept geese, and a range of cockerels, she bred a few rabbits and she grew sweet onions at the back of the house. You only saw her on market days, behind a table on the square in Carcassonne, where the smallest producers sat; she sold live red roosters, their yellow legs trussed in twine, and trembling rabbits from a cage, wild thyme and fresh eggs from a plastic bag.

All of it was fine, until she met the English boy.

Siggie remembered the boy with admiration. He felt much more well-disposed towards the Englishman than he did towards Anna. He had dark hair, Siggie would insist, as if this were some clue to his homicidal make up, and he was very thin. He told me the story with relish, and a fine appreciation for its magical nuances.

It was a great stroke of good fortune that turned the boy into what Siggie called the 'ex-murderer'. And the word 'fortune' meant exactly that. The saving of the ex-murderer was brought about – as it always is when a poor boy gets lucky – by the miraculous disbursement of money from heaven.

What Siggie called 'real' magic.

'The English guy – did I tell you? He killed a man and went to jail. But after some years, his lawyer got him out.

It seemed that maybe he didn't do the murder. So they had to let him go. So he came here, to Kissac. And he sued his government. They paid out. And he lived with his lawyer, who got him off.'

Siggie was vague on many details. The boy was younger than the lawyer. The lawyer was fat. He sweated a lot. Maybe it was the climate? Siggie couldn't be sure. Anyway, the boy criminal was suddenly rich. The English government had had to pay him lots of money. Thousands. That was a marvel. To go from jail to a fortune in the twinkling of an eye!

But there was something more.

Siggie whispered this to me, 'Christopher, do you know what's a "*Pay-day*"?'

It took me a moment or two. I had to translate what he said – and to do that I had to work out which language Siggie was thinking in. Sometimes Siggie thought in German and spoke in Dutch or English; sometimes he thought in French, the swinging end-stopped French of Kissac. This time he wasn't only thinking – he was spelling – in French. He was talking about *paedophiles*: P-D's.

Touching his fingers to his left earlobe he said, 'A homosexual is a *Pay-day*.'

It did no good to point out that paedophiles were sexually attracted to children. Such details bored him. That's what these men were called, in Kissac, everywhere. That was what everyone called them. It was the slang of the region. A world where men played rugby and women had babies and those who did not were – *Pay-days*.

They had moved around quite a bit, the dark-haired young ex-murderer and his round, perspiring older English friend. They lived for a while in the hotel; then in a room over the Lapin Fou; then in a field on the farm of M. Lamor, who was touched in the head and let his field to hippies and automatons and *Pay-days*.

And they had public fights. Lawyer and ex-murderer fought in public places, like the camping site outside town, or the picnic spot near the river where the Colonel beat his wife. The English boy used to charm a lot of people by explaining 'but we're in love' when the gendarmes hauled him in for breaking up the café. They also fought up in the marble quarry, a magnificent setting, a square amphi-theatre of pink marble, like some Roman coliseum, and remote so that their cries only faintly penetrated the village below.

No one noticed much. Or cared.

Then boy and lawyer-lover fought naked in the foun-tain in the middle of the village and the young one raked his nails down his fat friend's back in bloody scratches, and that was not allowed since the fountain gave drinking water.

The police locked him up for the night and the boy destroyed his cell; first he jumped on the bed and broke it; with a bedleg he shattered the light in the roof and bust up his table and chair; then he set fire to the lot and would have burnt down the entire place had the *pompiers* not been there quickly.

When they let him out he went back to his lawyer and said, as the English will, that he was very sorry and wished to be friends. When his friend said OK, they could live the life of lovers once again and took him to his heart, the boy dumped in the street all his friend's papers, clothes and books, and set them alight in a fire so large it could be seen from the Priory.

The fat lawyer ran off and never came back to Kissac.

That's when the young Englishman fell in with Anna and her brother, Marcel. Marcel was useless at anything but hunting; people agreed he was simply 'not serious'. Though a good lock-forward, by all accounts, in the Kissac rugby fifteen.

The young Englishman still had some of the compensation paid to him by the English government; whatever he hadn't poured down his throat. Marcel, Anna and the boy went into the poultry business. Which suited everyone. For the first time Anna and her brother had some money, the Englishman had a home and the three of them got on fine.

Before the partnership, Marcel worked modestly, raised his birds in the backyard, went out to the markets with his chickens. Now he was able to expand, soon he was selling eggs to the supermarkets in Carcassonne and Narbonne. Next the butchers in three towns were sending their vans to collect Marcel's grain-fed chickens, and his eggs went by truck to the *hypermarchés* of Toulouse.

So successful did he become that when the *routiers*, or long-distance lorry drivers, held their annual strike, as they generally did towards Christmas, and blocked the autoroutes between Kissac and Toulouse, Marcel appeared on television and said the strike was bad for small producers.

People were amazed. Was this the same Marcel who kept a few chickens? Was this Anna's silent brother – suddenly on the *télé*! A small producer! Hadn't he done well on the Englishman's money! Everyone could see that Marcel had his nose deep in the *fromage*.

Marcel was a limp man with a kink to his dark hair. The English boy with his blue eyes was pretty enough, but he was often so drunk you couldn't understand him and he was noisy, dangerous, when well-alight. The trio came to the Lapin on Friday nights and sank a few and the boy danced on the table.

When he looked for fights, Anna used to stroke his cheek and say to him, 'Come along, my little tiger – it's time you were in the arms of Morpheus.'

And they'd be off.

People said they slept together. But who would have slept with Anna, in those boots and with those long grey locks? Marcel was different. He was rich now. He would have slept with the chickens if it increased their egg count. Maybe he had decided the boy was worth a warm friendship.

Maybe. But, as it turned out, Marcel had more of a taste for *fromage*.

He started selling eggs and chickens to a big super-market over in Carcassonne, banking the cash and saying not a word to his partners.

Heaven knows how the boy found out but he turned up one night at the Lapin, just as Marcel was climbing out of his new Renault, a beautiful magenta, and rally stripes and spoilers and tinted glass and central locking. Marcel parked beside the fountain; the English boy came out of the café, where he must have been drinking, and began screaming at Marcel.

Siggie had a range of English insults which he introduced at this point. I have to say that none sounded very real to me: 'You bloody bugger! Filthy swine! Bloody cheater!'

The English boy called him many bad things, said Siggie, and Marcel went for him. He hit him, he pushed him into the fountain, and would have killed him, had it not been for the revolver the ex-murderer produced and was suddenly pointing at his head.

Enter Anna, carrying a basket of eggs, no doubt anxious about the boy; she ran to them and threw herself between the fighting men; the gun went off. The eggs lay everywhere.

Anna fell to the flagstones beside the fountain and bled steadily.

The English boy ran away. He decided to '*faire le valise*', they said in the village.

The doctors had made a good job of Anna though she'd never be beautiful. The bullet carried away half her face. But then again, she'd not been beautiful before the accident with the Englishman. She'd had more face, that was all.

From that point on there was a custom when one met Anna. One turned only half one's face towards her. So as not to embarrass her.

The King refused to observe the custom and offered her both his round and rosy cheeks for the kiss.

And when Anna, in her turn, offered her cheek to be kissed, everyone knew, by instinct, to kiss her on *both* sides of her fringed forehead – so as not to draw attention to the name the children had once called her – 'Little Anna Half-a-face'.

And no one said, as the King did: 'What's the good of pretending to kiss her on both sides? She's only got half a face.'

* * *

Anna and Marcel continued to live together and began breeding cockerels. It might have been as it always was, but one thing was new. Brother and sister began following the French team to international rugby matches in England. Anna would choose one of her roosters, and dye him from tail to comb in red, white and blue. And she'd take her painted rooster to matches.

Midway through the match at Twickenham she'd free her wild and shining tricoloured cockerel from her blouse, send him racing across the pitch, and the French fans went mad.

Anna took those occasions solemnly. This was not something she saw as sporting conviviality, or fun; not at all, said Siggie. It had to do with deeper things. It was, one understood, a matter of honour.

'People around her knew how serious it was for her. After all, there are many people who try to bring the cockerel to French matches,' said Siggie.

But Anna was different. 'Like a nun, or like Jeanne d'Arc.'

She was a regular fixture on the coach that goes from Toulouse to Calais, and on to London; so much so that the English police looked out for her and her mascot. They would board the coach and search everywhere, even in the engine.

Siggie liked this bit of the tale:

'The English hate foreign animals and will allow not a dog, a bird, a hare to cross the water without imprisoning it.'

Anna's hiding places became legendary. They acquired names. Hide the bird in her bosom, and she was 'the nursing mother'; snuggled beneath her long blue skirt and she was 'in the family way'; if she concealed him within the engine housing she was 'roasting the chicken'.

And if the searchers got too close, she had a plan – Anna had no compunction about turning her missing face to them, the dead crater of blind moon.

And, of course, the searchers backed away, mumbling apologies; for the English hate to seem cruel, and Anna knew this having had, as she said, the advantage of living with an Englishman, until he shot her.

CHAPTER 17

———— ✦ ————

I HAD BEEN renting the cockpit apartment, high in Siggie's house, for some years. Now and then, I'd go travelling. Pack up and clear off and Ria would relet the apartment, until next time.

Siggie decided it should stop. All this coming and going. Never settling. These were Romany signs! And besides, why would anyone wish to spend time away from the most beautiful and profitable corner of the world, this rocky patch of Languedoc? If I went to Yugoslavia, he disapproved in principle; Communists ruled the place. And New York – well, when I was there – could I buy *vin ordinaire*, straight from the pump? The Soviet Union fell apart, to his relief: 'Now you won't need to go back.'

His solution to this promiscuous jaunting was simple – I should buy a house.

Curious that – for Siggie, who placed absolutely no importance on owning anything, also believed that only a roof over my head and my name on the door distinguished me from footpads, vagrants, woodcutters, charcoal-burners and other nomads of the forest.

Siggie's routine remained a mixture of lead and quicksilver. He would be in his workshop every day but his sacred Wednesdays – when he sped over the mountains in search of treasure. He might step out of routine upon news of a death. Or when lured by a deal – but he was home by lunch, just as he always bought his wine from M. Villeneuve. The nightly games of solo billiards, applauded by the clocks on the walls, silent spectators wearing national headgear: trilbies replacing stetsons, replacing fezzes, replacing baseball caps. The half-nude jazz trio frozen on the podium in the corner; the scarlet chaise longue on which he took his afternoon siesta waited, the Duke of Wellington's black safe secure in the corner; Ronald Reagan and Simone Signoret arching their eyebrows from their fading posters. The King was in his court. Or God in his heaven – there was little difference.

When I left on my travels, I'd stack my things down in the barn, stored on the row of wooden seats from some lost cinema, or packed beside the giant woodburning stove, with its luscious silver and umber trim, ceramic knobs and aquamarine panels, lovely as a cream cake. Siggie always insisted I use his barn – but maybe my things fell below expectation. I remembered how much he hated Thierry's poor stuff. Only very special objects merited storage in that dark palace, crammed with old blue Portuguese tiles, painted with swains and flagons, and maidens and goats; yellowing skeletons (there was, it seemed, good money in old bones), olive-green municipal drinking-fountains, penny-farthings, ancient perambulators with hoods like the dark blue eyelids of ancient lizards; pinball machines, vintage motorbikes; and the usual mournful statuary of the graveyard. His scavengings from the junk heaps of the Black Mountains were laid down as tenderly as fine champagne, to mature and grow in value, until one day some rich fancier stepped by and . . .

Anyway, I'd no sooner set off than Siggie began giving my things away. Just as he had once given away my books to Sophie – for maddeningly logical reasons; because she spoke English and so did I; and a book was a book was a book.

Why did he give my things away? In part, I think it was cautionary – 'See what happens when you stray?' In part, his own demon, a hatred of waste pushed him to do it; his feeling was – here was all this stuff standing around, doing nothing! And here was a perfectly nice person who needed a chair, a tennis racquet, a typewriter, and – what luck! – Siggie happened to have just the thing in his barn.

Besides, who was to say I'd ever come back? I was a strange man who spent his days in a rented apartment, writing books. Bad enough. And roaming about in foreign lands. Worse still.

Whenever I got back I'd have to sort out what was missing and replace it.

'Very expensive,' the King chided.

He always told me what he'd done, helping some stranger, happy to make use of electric plugs, shoes or CDs, lying there and wasting away. What luck! In his wish to shake me loose from my fond but foolish attachments to distant places and unprofitable activities, he changed the very world I came back to. Leaning this way or that, like Pujols in his wooden booth, I'd walk up the narrow stairs to find another apartment; the same space but a new place. On the walls, where there had hung spidery Spanish etchings of bright-eyed bulls, were lewd monks, members lifting their cassocks, or mournful elms in sodden Dutch fields. The furniture changed too. Chairs and settees alternated between plummy velour thrones to minimalist chrome and leather – from brothel to office, from ecstasy to the executive suite, and back again.

I sometimes wondered if he was saying that business was best done in the bordello, and those who generally screwed their clients worked from the boardroom.

But Siggie did not make moral points; changes in decor were the fruits of a lucky find in the mountains, some irresistible bargain and I was just keeping it warm. And it was a reflection of his curious mind, which was, at base, almost frighteningly practical – if he had morals they were the morals of the tooth fairy. To him, Ria's apartments were just another way of storing stuff – until Siggie found a better buyer. And the lodgers were not people, they were ways of making the storage space pay.

I'd leave in May, when I'd have been sleeping under goosedown duvets; and when I came back in September, it was to worn, very short, skinny sheets, ribbed in blue like a child let loose with a ballpoint; marked SNCF in the left-hand corner – and I'd know that French Railways had flogged off bedding from their Wagonlits.

* * *

I enjoyed Siggie's mind. Its connections were mad. He decided that the very man to find me a house was Hercule. And the reason why Hercule was my man was not, as one might have supposed, because he had any record as an estate agent, but because he had tried so often and failed so miserably. Siggie wished to do Hercule a favour; he needed practice, I needed a house – very well, let him practise on me. Hercule was a no-hoper, a non-doer. A vacant centre. And nullity Siggie could not abide.

'Hercule's always late. If there is money to be made on Monday, he shows up on Tuesday. If St Peter offers to collect all humps handed in by noon, he's there a minute after midday.'

Siggie deplored Hercule's lack of ambition, his unwillingness to take risks. Siggie was a venture capitalist – with this difference: he believed the capital you risked was yourself. There was something sacred about chance-taking. It made for magic. It taught you to be bold – and daring did the trick. As Jack showed when he swapped his poor mother's only pig for the magic beans.

Kill the giant – and make a fortune! That was Siggie's motto.

Close your eyes, and kiss a frog . . .

'OK so in this case, Hercule's the frog. Who wants to kiss him? And that's a problem. So let the frog improvise – and kiss the princess!'

I drove to Hercule's big ugly villa, beside the main road to Castres. Outside was a concrete yard and a concrete barn with an asbestos roof where Hercule stored his stuff. Another scavenger – ancient kitchen lamps, great multi-leaved green things, like electric lettuces; dozens of doors, wine barrels, old petrol pumps, early compressors, early cameras in polished wood.

Often he bought job lots. Statues of the Saviour, a dozen girlish men with painted faces, like a frozen platoon, pointing with manicured fingers to their Sacred Hearts, pierced by spiny thorns. In the semi-darkness of his barn

Hercule's Christs waited like those terracotta armies that were buried with Chinese emperors; except these plaster Messiahs all had pretty faces, rouged lips, pink cheeks. What Siggie referred to as 'Church of Christ – Hairdresser'.

No wonder Hercule never measured up. Hercule was too shy to brag and his slow, sweet pleading way was very likeable.

But now he had a chance to improve his lot; and save me from a gypsy fate.

'Find a house for him,' Siggie said to Hercule. 'You did it before, you can do it again.'

What he did not tell me was how sad finding that house had made Hercule. Nor did he say what kind of house he had in mind. Though I suppose I should have guessed.

A few months before Hercule, working on commission, had found a bargain for a rich German buyer, a nineteenth-century chateau in its own park, on the very summit of the Pic de Nore, a lovely ruin of grand proportions with a wood and meadows.

The buyer was delighted. Only the paperwork remained to be done. When the deal went through, Hercule was to have his commission, many tens of thousands of francs. He had dug a hole in the yard and hidden an old cash box, ready and waiting.

But selling property in France is slow. So the German went to Barcelona, and while he waited, he danced: he loved flamenco and he could not dance flamenco in Germany without people laughing, and dancing took his mind off waiting. In Barcelona he met a posh private banker; the man worked in offices with fine views of the

Gaudi Cathedral, his name was looped in gold on the front door; through that door were hushed spaces, computers and efficient secretaries, good coffee and thick carpets. The banker took the money from the dancing German and invested it at twice the going rate.

The German came home to Languedoc so encouraged by his Spanish visit that he promised to increase Hercule's commission, when the deal went through.

The deal went through and the dancing German rushed to Barcelona. Two months passed without word from him, and then, one day, he pitched up at Hercule's place with a sorry tale to tell.

Not even Pujols of the fairground, of the wooden ball and the wooden world, pulled one as neat.

The dancing German found his way back to the banker's premises easily enough; but he had trouble recognizing the offices. The golden lettering of his name had vanished. Gone were the secretaries, computers, the groomed executives, the good coffee. Nothing remained but empty rooms in an office block, with fine views of Gaudi's Cathedral.

'My brother said it was the punishment of God! My brother – who is an atheist!'

Hercule's brother, Emile, was a little taller, straighter, and buzzed like a bee when he spoke. Two bachelor brothers, together in a big plain house on the edge of the industrial quarter, over the mountain towards Castres.

Emile never married. But he was 'always engaged'.

When a young man, he had fallen in love – with Marxism, and with Soviet communism. A man of the left, who threw off the priests and embraced the commissars.

After the collapse of the Soviet Union – or 'when Emile's mistress ran off', as Hercule said – Emile spent his days watching TV: long documentaries on the sex life of the aphid, and picking fights with Hercule in the commercial breaks.

He stayed faithful to the creed – even after he had been deserted – a lonely lover in a lost world, a believing Stalinist, dreaming of a revolutionary redeemer, a red King Arthur rising from his mausoleum to bump off the bourgeoisie.

Hercule washed his face in the basin, changed into the cleaner of his two white shirts which hung in the rafters, and poured me a *pastis*. Hercule's settled belief, he told me again and again, was that he would never talk politics with his brother.

Emile was watching two praying mantis dangerously courting.

Hercule pointed to me. 'This man has lived in Moscow, and he can tell you the system stank!'

Emile did not rise to the bait, did not even look up from the screen where tiny creatures were now busily mating.

Hercule lifted his broad suffering face; his long soft ears drooped like an elephant's.

'Emile is a fool for love.'

The tiny jaws of an exquisite little monster moved up and down like the leather walls of an accordion accompanied in stereo by a steady crunching bass beat as the body of the victim cracked and popped.

'Siggie says you might want to buy a house. I have a place.'

On the television, the little female went on eating her

lover; she'd been fertilized and now she was being fed: males have their uses – the economy of design was chilling.

Emile's nose almost touched the screen.

We drained our *pastis*.

'Let's go and visit the Hermit. He's expecting us and I think we're late.'

*   *   *

It was a grey chateau behind tumbling walls, looking out towards wet green hills.

A man stuck his head out of an upper-floor window. 'You're early. I'm still having my dinner.'

We waited in his yard while two perfectly motionless cats took the Hermit's place in the window, sitting tail to tail like bookends, and watched us. In the stony yard muddy ducks went scooting across the chocolate water of the pond, gouged out by rain and seepage, between the crumbling *pigeonnier* and the slate-roofed barn with its byres and mouldering straw, still smelling of vanished cows.

'His mother was a doctor and his father a lawyer,' said Hercule. 'An educated man but he lives like a peasant. Don't, whatever you do, tell him you want to buy his house.'

I didn't want to buy the house; it was too big, too old, too dank – it reminded me of the ruined manse in *Kidnapped*, with the same crusty old man pushing his head out of a window and demanding to know our business.

Around 2.30, the Hermit opened the door. His grey hair was long and he was wrapped in a tartan blanket and wore old gumboots. The house smelt of wood-smoke and damp; nothing had changed in fifty years; no electricity, no cleaning, no stove. In the fireplace a black pot hung from a hook over smouldering logs. The Hermit lifted the lid and stirred away every now and then, with a wooden ladle.

'Fricassee of rabbit.'

I wondered why it was *always* fricassee of rabbit? Did he simply add supplies of the same each day? Probably. There were years of ash under the cauldron.

We had barely sat down around the bubbling pot when Hercule told the Hermit I wanted to buy his house.

The Hermit grinned. 'Good decision. For someone with flair, the possibilities are endless. You're a lucky man!'

The Hermit grabbed a broom and began driving it into the rafters to show me how sound they were. The pigeons nesting there began fluttering inside the roof with distressed little cries, shedding feathers. I heard the roof-tiles cracking. He asked me to admire the mullioned windows; these sad little crumbling holes in the walls wore cement bandages under their stubbled chins, pointed like shirt collars.

The Hermit took me into the cellar to view the subterranean water supply. A well in the cellar was a boon. I could hold out for years, if the place were ever besieged. The neighbours were a jealous lot – best have nothing to do with them. The sort of people who poisoned public wells.

'Take the Mayor, now,' said the Hermit, as we wandered out into his sodden yard. 'Lives next door. Got his neighbour's daughter in the family way. Just thirteen. How he's got ahead! Rape a child and run for office. Wonderful, isn't it! Of course, he thinks we don't know because we don't talk about it.'

The tall Hermit stomped through the puddles calling lovingly to his ducks:

'And so what do you say, Princess of the Tarn? Hullo, my little heart, my galloping gorgeous!'

He promised to think about my offer but he hoped I would not be too sad if he decided not to sell. Then he went indoors and waved goodbye from the window with the cats.

I ask Hercule why he told the Hermit I wanted his house.

'To cheer him up. He's got a fine mathematical brain and no chance of using it. Did you see how he brightened when he turned down your offer?'

'I never made an offer.'

'It's a scandal a man so bright should hide in this old wreck of a place. It's love that does it – he wants life to go on just as his parents left it. But he's also a fool for grandeur! The little prince who worshipped his parents. How we fool ourselves!'

* * *

When we got back to Siggie's place, I began to realize I'd been set up. Ria was sitting very quietly, too quietly. Her antennae told her something was brewing. Siggie poured red wine from his glass jug – then began rubbing his hands, always a sign of trouble, of excessive enthusiasm, of plans.

'Well – how was the house?' he asked.

I said, 'It's not for me.'

'Why not?'

'Too big.'

'Too big! That's just it! We share, you and me and

Hercule. We fix it, furnish it — I'll find everything we need. We make five, six apartments. We rent them out. How much does the Hermit want?'

Hercule said, 'A million.'

'What do you say, Christopher?'

'No.'

'But why?'

'I don't have a million.'

'Offer him 600,000, and you will have it. For sure. Hercule and I will come in — for a third apiece. 200,000 each — for a *palais*. That is no money at all. It is practically given! Let's do it.'

Ria had been listening silently. Now there was a dangerous colour in her cheeks, and a pale ring around her lips, then she lifted her eyes to the roof.

'You're mad! Another castle? You think the wars with Him the Horrible weren't enough? I could have taken a gun, I could have shot him. I was going crazy and I was never so unhappy, every day crying and crying and now it's one lifetime later. I am happy, yes; I have my house, my cherries, my apartments . . .'

Outside the windows the tall shadow of the rider in the long cape and cowboy hat went clipping past, nice and leisurely, as Ria's question rang around the room.

'And you want another war?'

I don't think he wanted another war; he hated the idea, even more than Ria. But Siggie certainly dreamed of, hankered after, a great place. To that degree, Loud Lilly was right — he had a regal streak, and a King needs a castle.

We sipped our wine and Hercule, always so easily moved, so shy, kept his eyes down, scarcely daring to look at Siggie. Outside the rider was passing at a steady clip. The lamplight fell on the grieving lady – carrying a sprig of yellow broom to hide her broken finger – and on the coppery breasts of the young torso – the Wolfgang donation – in the corner. Fred was worrying a cushion, round and round on the smooth tiles his long, thin legs skidded; the pewter flagons gleamed on the oaken cupboard.

The castanets of the horse's hooves faded.

'There goes the *koeiboy*,' said Ria.

'*Cow*-boy,' Siggie corrected her.

'Never mind. I know what's true and what isn't. And if Christopher wants a house, I will help him.'

And a few weeks later, she did. When I found a derelict, medieval cottage near the Priory, Ria negotiated the sale with the family who had owned it for centuries. And knocked 15 per cent off the small asking price.

She was joyful, but she was something more – powerful. 'I didn't know I could do it.'

Siggie was appalled. And, suddenly, scared. By her success. But especially by her ruthless bargaining ability. I think he had visions of her moving into his world. She laughed, thrilled. Knowing she was right, the practical one, the engine, the accountant, the one who showed how powerful was the ability to deal in the world, where Siggie's only gift was for dreams, and fairy tales.

Neither of which did his wife have the slightest sympathy for.

Now his fear made him careless and he reached for an extraordinary line of attack. Ria should not have driven the price down.

'They're poor people. Aren't you ashamed of yourself?'

Ria gave a shriek of delighted triumph.

'That's good – coming from you. Poor? They own four houses. They're fat with money.'

Siggie was bested, and he knew it.

A few days before I moved, we stood at the bridge, watching Pascal's dad who was sitting where Lionel had sat, on that night before Christmas – the night he fell backwards and died.

Siggie said nothing but he didn't need to. One saw the problem. There was Pascal's father, a man who had spent his life trying to kill himself – a professional who got nowhere. And along came a rank amateur who did it, first time round – without even trying!

Just as Ria did with my house.

Siggie remembered some old lines of German which his father had been fond of: 'O, what a perilous life he led – following his heart and not his head.'

CHAPTER 18

I HAD SPENT about six years, on and off, in Siggie's apartment by the time I moved out of the big *maison de maître*, and into my cottage in the heart of the village. But there were other moves, deep shifts underfoot, and they made for real changes – for me, for Kissac, perhaps most of all for the King of the Clocks.

For the moment, nothing showed. The village sat under the mountains, below the Priory spire which was wrapped in scaffolding, after years of slow restoration; muffled like some invalid. The village seemed unchanging beneath the huge sky of the South; unmoving, like the old men on the wall, outside the Lapin, all in a row.

But you could hear things stirring. After years of silence, the loudspeakers under the eaves were broadcasting again.

We owed it to Kissac's new Mayor – young M. Angelo, the dentist. In the local elections – an angry contest – he had beaten by a whisker the old incumbent, M. Rivière.

Within days of taking power, the *Mairie* was again pumping out news bulletins. Times of boules matches, the arrival of the pizza van, fishmonger, oyster-seller; meetings of the Club of the Third Age.

M. Angelo honoured his election pledge to restore

power to the speakers. He promised to bring back the old tradition – but the village woke up to find the past was not as remembered, and the future came with a price. Before the sad voice sang the daily announcements over the rooftops, the *Mairie* added a little four-note warning chime; the sort you get in airport announcements followed by the threat to blow up unattended luggage.

What upset Siggie was that the death notices had been dropped.

The Mayor was modern. And sick of old rumours, local legend, parochial scandal. Each village had its own; it was said of Villefranche, for instance, that it was full of thieves – why, only the month before, crooks had backed a truck up to the *Cave Co-operative*, just after the *vendange*, and siphoned off every drop of the new wine and got clean away! Villefranche proved the old story – it had always been, as they said, 'rather careless'.

It was said of Kissac that the old and ill lived there, and the mad and the fickle – and it was said that people died more often in Kissac than anywhere else.

This was something that the new Mayor simply could not accept. Not as a scientist, nor as a socialist. It was statistical nonsense. It did the town no good at all – and it led to the absurd custom of elderly persons preferring the market in Rieu, on a Saturday morning, because local gossip had it you were more likely to die early if you shopped for your *saucisson* in Kissac.

The new Mayor, lean, hurried M. Angelo, flew around town like a whirling dervish. He was fluid and impatient, wore a red sports coat, and had a Catalan flash in his eyes;

he had plans – reopening the Priory, building fountains, bringing in more tourists.

And he had something no mayor ever had – a bodyguard.

'He's been in office five minutes, and he has a cop at his elbow,' people said, in the baker's.

The official explanation was 'security'. Because of recent terrorist bomb attacks in Paris and Marseilles, gendarmes and special forces patrolled rail stations and airports. But a bodyguard in Kissac? Even if he was not a gendarme, but only the municipal policeman in peaked cap, the kindergarten cop, who read the meters and stood guard outside the *maternelle*, when mothers picked up their kids after school.

Certain individuals, in the camp of the defeated Mayor, M. Rivière, called M. Angelo an ambitious upstart, a neurotic modernist – and an *arriviste*.

That last insult stung. Some sixty years before, during the Spanish Civil War, the Mayor's grandfather had fled Franco's murder squads and settled in Kissac. It led him to tell people in his election campaign that he belonged to the village – what he meant – said M. Rivière's people – was that the village belonged to him.

Siggie met the Mayor one morning and asked him to bring back the death notices.

The kindergarten cop, leaning his palm on his pistol butt, stood very close, looking from one face to the other, nodding when the Mayor spoke.

M. Angelo replied that Kissac was looking ahead. 'But we keep the best of the past.'

'But the dead – they *are* the best of the past. How do we keep track?'

'Families, friends, they spread the news. And today we have the phone, newspapers.'

'But M. le Maire, what about deaths we might not hear about? Friends we've forgotten, relatives we've lost touch with? People like to know.'

'Visitors, perhaps.'

'*Visitors?*'

'Tourists.'

'Tourists! Monsieur, I've lived in this village for twenty years!'

So began the misunderstandings between the King of the Clocks and the Mayor of Kissac.

* * *

Siggie was in two minds about my house.

It rankled that Ria had beaten the seller down. But he approved of a settled place because that was what distinguished decent people from Romanies. He looked about for drawbacks and found one – it was a shame the house was so dark as you descended.

I said, 'Yes, it is dark in the cellar. It often is – in cellars.'

'You should let in light,' said Siggie.

He could do nothing about his wife's gift for driving a bargain – but he could do something about the dark. He gave me several oil lamps, brass candlesticks and a pink marble mantel – in several pieces – which, once cemented above my fireplace would be, he promised, 'as good as new'. He advised lighting the lamps early, and the fire; and hanging mirrors to 'spread' the light.

As the year moved towards October, and autumn, I had another piece of luck. The old farmhouse by the stream where I had stayed when I first arrived in Kissac, the floating world of the mysterious Inspector of Weights and Measures, was sold. The owner offered me knives and plates, pots, pans, and a painted parrot or two. I will always be grateful to her for her kindness.

I drove once again down the steep rutted lane to the house by the stream. Cyrille, the *gardien*, was sitting on the wall, sadly eating cherries from a bottle, spitting the pips into the air and catching them like a juggler. He stopped when he saw me, in case I should think he was having a good time.

I told him about my windfall. Cyrille sighed and shook his head – and then brightened; he'd thought of a difficulty. How was I going to transport the stuff?

I said I'd use my Golf.

Cyrille's sad smile disagreed. 'You will need a van.'

When he saw the cobbled lane where my house stood, he was even more pleased.

'You'll never get a van down there. You could be wedged – for ever!'

He advised doing the move in 'sections' – and he hired his friend Aimé, whose Citroën might squeeze down the narrow *ruelles*. Then he wheeled his old *remorque* out of the garage. The skinny, rickety old cart wouldn't have taken any weight – but then it wasn't meant to, any more than Cyrille meant to carry anything, because it – and he – had 'a bad back'. Cyrille and the *remorque* were a double act.

A mutual support system. They went everywhere together during my move.

Cyrille set a fairly stiff price on Aimé's transport service, and asked for cash up front.

Aimé was short, round and breathless – like his car. He winked at me. 'Life's an adventure, not so?'

Cyrille leaned on the *remorque* and regarded us gloomily.

We loaded up, lashed the kitchen chairs to the roofs and bounced up the long, difficult drive. Cyrille led the way in his little Renault, so flimsy it always looked to me as if it had been built from tin playing cards. In the village Cyrille began hooting as we went around corners, and flashing his lights. Just as the gendarmes did when some *convoi exceptionnel* – a giant yacht, or vast wine vat – crawled along the country roads.

We got the Citroën to my front entrance, but so narrow was the lane we could not open its doors. So we backed down to the Priory, and carried the stuff the last few metres.

Then it began to rain. Sheets of water fell.

Cyrille looked at the sky. 'Every few years the deluge arrives. The river and the vineyards flood – the village is up to its neck.'

We stood in my doorway watching the rain drumming on the cobbles; it ran away down the gutters, and slowly stopped.

'Next time.' Cyrille gave his sad, certain nod.

On the second grinding run up the farm track, the Citroën's radiator blew; Aimé opened the bonnet and looked at the geyser of steam.

'Life's an adventure,' I reminded him.

'With many endings,' said Aimé, who was really very charming. 'I'm sorry about this. Of course, I won't take a franc for the work.'

Then he bound the leak in plastic tape and set off to the garage.

Cyrille said, 'A man could be scalded alive, if caught in such an eruption.'

I began humping my stuff alone. Cyrille walked ahead of me pushing the *remorque*, waving people out of the way.

Then a huge man with black hair came from a nearby house, a place set about with scrap-iron and old tiles, and without a word lifted my heavy stuff onto his shoulders.

He said, 'I can do this – as long as I wear my hernia belt.'

It was my first meeting with Tomàs, the ex-blacksmith.

Cyrille said, 'I'll have to charge you for that radiator. Aimé can't afford this sort of wear and tear.'

Then as Tomàs moved down the street, carrying old grape-picker's hods loaded with earth and vines, Cyrille stepped close to my ear and whispered, 'Be very, very careful of that man!'

* * *

My house had an earth-floor cellar, a crumbling terrace covered by a spreading vine, a squat toilet in the corner of the garden, and a pomegranate tree. It sat astride the old village ramparts and looked out across the vineyards towards Corbières and, beyond them, the Pyrenees. Below the ancient fortifying wall, falling sheer to the road some ten metres below, was the open-air public wash-house, a red-tiled roof covering a bath of water, fed by the local spring. People still beat their clothes on the concrete wall, and polite notices deplored the habit of washing car-carpets in the crystal water. Across the road were the vegetable gardens and the river. In the evenings, the Neapolitan voices of quarry workers among the lettuce patches, and the soft buzz of Kisaqienne patois, rose like midges in the warm air.

Little Humph-Humph, the print dealer, came by, with his quill-like hair and his porcupine nose. He held his father's arm. He took his old dad wherever he went – a man well into his eighties, a purple nose and a sleepy smile.

'He missed his siesta,' Humph explained, 'but I can't let him alone. Who knows what he'll get up to, once my back is turned.'

He gave me a Daumier courtroom cartoon; the thin judge on his bench confronts the pale prisoner in the dock; the *maître*, in white bib and important belly, presses close to his client, whispers in his ear; the prisoner in the dock is a wraith, trapped between the brute figures of authority and complacency.

'*Le pauvre bête,*' said Tomàs, of the shivering wretch.

Tomàs, ex-blacksmith, ex-habitué of the Lapin, ex-husband, ex-con, ex-Serb. Tomàs, of the big springy Serb hair, dyed jet black, lifted his long arms and let them drop to his sides, in a flap of apocalyptic wind, as he studied the terrified prisoner.

Tomàs was ex-just-about-everything; boasting, lying, self-pitying, brawling Tomàs. Soldier, artist and – pickle-maker, counting off the presidents he'd served.

He began in Yugoslavia, a soldier for Tito.

When the Czechs, under Alexander Dubček, tried to

break free of Mother Russia's stranglehold, Tomàs marched into Prague with the Warsaw Pact troops.

'We put down the Spring. That was when I served Brezhnev. But I am not a communist. I am a Leninist.'

He defected, fled to France and joined the Foreign Legion, down the road in Castelnaudary. He served in Africa, under Giscard; in the South Pacific, under Mitterrand. He'd rejoin the Legion tomorrow – had tried – *hélas!*: he was too old.

And also too fat, too drunk, too sad, too far gone.

He pulled out his photograph album with shining eyes, convinced that in its images was a wealth of life such as most men can only dream of.

It is a cheap and sticky red book and opened in some South Sea base. A very young Tomàs, in legionnaire's khakis, white kepi and red-fringed epaulettes; he looped his thumbs into his belt and posed. A cocky, somehow sad young man with yearning eyes; that a snap could capture such vanity! Tomàs, again and again: in a brothel with dead-eyed girls; on a beach in ridiculous yellow trunks; acquiring his tattoos; drinking with fellow legionnaires in jungle clearings; lying back in some barrack-room bed, in a dorm wallpapered with pin-ups. In Rwanda, with more ash-eyed camp-followers, babies strapped to their backs.

'Africans', said Tomàs, 'are even more racist than the French. They hate their own kind.'

His tattoos – a blonde in pink panties stood behind his thigh, and a redhead lay naked on his forearm – were exceptionally well-drawn, and mobile. He liked to 'animate' these drawings. He got the blonde's bosom to heave when he clenched his thigh. He could inflate the redhead into momentary pregnancy by tightening his bicep.

He took a proprietorial view of my house – it had belonged to his ex-in-laws and he'd lived there when he first married his ex-wife, became an ex-legionnaire and headed into his career as the ex-blacksmith.

Another album.

Tomàs treasured his crumbling past. Between splitting plastic covers lay his sketches, models, designs for wrought-iron gates, stairs and spidery grilles.

Another folder.

Stuffed with paintings, done when he was in hospital recovering from a bad fall – how and when he had forgotten – he said, simply, 'from a great height'. Paintings of green and chilly meadows, probably distant echoes of the Slovenian Alps; as well as very bad drawings of lions.

His true artistry lay in his survival rate; lasting through his accidents. He nearly sliced off his arm with a saw, he damaged his back, and then there was the hernia belt . . .

He was full of noisy certainties but none convinced even him. Pleasure lay in forceful opinions. Big ideas, big talk. Yes, my house had just one tap. It was probably twelfth or thirteenth century. He pointed to the pomegranate tree at the corner of the ruined terrace, with its fruit among dark green leaves, wonderful globes of pink.

'I planted her. Ten years ago. You'll need shade when the summer sun burns.'

Thus his decline, measured in pomegranates.

He was in the Midi, the South, a world of light, but Tomàs brought his Slavic gloom. Perhaps that's what the

Midi does, welcomes in the visitors, invaders, strangers, refugees, and makes them ever more of what they were.

Tomàs remembered hardly anything of his old languages – Serbo-Croat, Russian – he spoke French, in the patois of Kissac. Furious, thick, slightly Italian or Spanish in inflection, words bitten off in the back palate, rising into the nose, explosive brassy 'n's and 'g's, deadstopped in the nostrils like stifled bells.

And his talk was noisy – with gunshots going off, corks being pulled.

I was warned again and again to be careful of Tomàs; to keep a distance.

For his neighbours, that was out of the question. The flotsam of his lives and failures washed up against our walls. We were in his vicinity – he exploded, we lived with the fallout. How can you keep out smoke, tears, blood, thunder in the night, things that leak?

Gigantic self-pity swilled down the gutters. Chaos spread from his smithy where his bellows groaned in the barn, like some old cow calling to be milked. His house, ten years in the building, was unfinished, and – this said proudly – 'as filthy as a brothel'.

On mornings after, he would wander out of doors in his vest, yawning and describing in a proud disbelieving voice how the night before had gone – he'd had *un peu trop* . . . Dreamily reeling off, in much the same admiring tone he reserved for counting off the presidents he'd served as a soldier, what the 'bit too much' meant: '*du whiskey* . . . *du vin* . . . *du Muscadelle* . . . *du grenache* . . .'

Since being banned from the Lapin, he headed across the fields and hit the Bar Gypsy or the Café du Sport, in some neighbouring village. Staggering home, roaring legionnaires' marching songs, stopping to piss noisily as he passed the public wash-house at the base of the rampart wall below my house; the sight of so much water no doubt bringing on the urge.

In the morning he might have blood on his trousers, a purple eye, cut and crusted. He treated himself, winding long bandages around his head. The neighbours looked at his swaddled head and looked away.

Tomàs set to fixing my ruined terrace, which wind and rain had washed away. He arrived with wheelbarrows of old blue tiles, 'genuine *céramique*' he told me 'from an old chapel in the Black Mountains'.

When he had laid them they glowed, watery blue, the floating floor of a swimming pool.

Tomàs arrived one morning with a cardboard box containing a small, rather modest silver dinner service.

'My mother walked across Germany, when she was released from Dachau, and came to the house of Eichmann, where she found this.'

The name on the box was indeed Eichmann, but Eichmann the cutler, not the killer of the Jews.

It was Tomàs who told me that the Kissac Co-op manager had run off with thousands, money which Kissac wine-farmers owed the government in taxes; the Co-op was broke, the *négociants* for the high jump.

And he was delighted. Tomàs was an outlaw, all forms of lawlessness were reassuring in these tough times when no one gave a desperado an even break. Tomàs saw himself as a golden-hearted rogue, tall and strong and immensely attractive, and I saw no reason to discourage his dream. I was sorry when he let himself go, when he went on a blinder and forgot to dye his hair, and the morning sun cruelly exposed his ashy streaks.

I warmed to his aspirations, his sensitivity, I felt his approaching extinction – rather as I did when I watched the Circus of Dreams, or Madame de la Pipe. Like them, Tomàs was barely holding the line.

When the floating watery floor was in place on my terrace, he replaced the ancient iron railings that strapped the terrace waist-high to the house. He arrived one morning in a welder's mask, looking like Vulcan. That was the thing with Tomàs – the show, the tragic grandeur, but, above all, the uniform. He wore a single black knee-pad, and carried an oxyacetylene torch. Tomàs was an opera, exhausting; he wanted all the parts.

Kneeling, a masked knight, a suitor, ready to cut and weld the railings; he fixed a thick cable to my electricity supply. 'I need more power than you can manage,' said Tomàs. 'Stand back!'

He fired a fusillade of golden sparks and then, amazingly, stopped and lifted a frond of vine away from the terrible torch. Sparks flew again.

The tenderness of his arrangement; the perfection of his placing the frond just there, so it bisected the oval frame, his artist's eye – all so strange in that husk of a man.

It turned out that love had done for Tomàs. The pain – no the *shame*; his wife had run off – with a cop! And he, a man of 'the other side', who'd seen the inside of many cells. His wife did a runner with a *flic*! And robbed him blind. Took off with television, video-player; rifled the money in their joint account. Took their son, too.

No – he would never work again, never take a job. Let his wife get her claws into his wages? Never! Nothing would persuade him to give her a centime.

One night his son returned home, put a ladder up to the bedroom window on the first floor, planning to remove the furniture. Tomàs surprised him. His son pulled a knife, Tomàs reached for his rifle. Nose to nose in the moonlight, father and son slowly retreated from each other, from murder.

If ever she showed up . . . Lifting two fingers, sighting down the barrel of his imaginary pistol, he shoots her and blows smoke from his finger; sad, not because he's killed her, but because he hasn't.

Tomàs, when you got past his violent side, the huge hurt in him that would drive him to murder, was a romantic, even a sentimentalist. His love was dangerous, choking, useless, its end was the destruction of himself.

His true art was escaping with his life – from his brawls, accidents, knife wounds, car-smashes, shootings, the big falls.

Peaceful moments came when he passed out – or when he was pickling. Strange domesticity. Tomàs the pickle-maker. Autumn saw him in the kitchen of his 'bordello', like a good Serb, peeling, stoning, boiling, bottling, putting by for the winter. His ratatouille was particularly good.

* * *

Siggie noted how fine the blue tiles looked. 'I gave those tiles to Tomàs. Stripped them off my cellar floor.'

In the art of disaster, Siggie had no doubt about Tomàs's masterpiece. Becoming Cyclops.

He told me of the time a steel skewer lifted an eye from its socket; it hung there 'by the optic nerve, swinging like a fob-watch'.

And he had 'stereoscopic vision!' With his dislodged eye – Tomàs stared back at his own amazed and frightened one-eyed face.

Siggie was entranced by the idea. Two for the price of one. An independent eye, going its own way. I could see the beauty of the idea – even if I wasn't sure of the division in the brain that would have to occur to split the mind-screen in this way.

But what a good thing for a hunter in Loud Lilly's place, or a clockmaker, who could screw in one glass eye, and send the other on errands.

'What would you look like – if you could look at yourself?'

We were drinking beer in the Lapin, after tennis. One of our regular games, filled with his curious gambits designed to unsettle his opponent. The looping, backwards-over-the-head shot; the kangaroo-hop net charge, his racquet held two-handed, raised like a club; the maroon tracksuit and fancy shoes with horseshoes of winking brake lights around the heels – another buy from the gypsy's place in Lézignan – a little on the big side 'but with two pairs of socks, I fill them nicely. Where else could I find thousand-franc shoes for fifty?'

It was a convention of tennis to mask your pleasure in your opponent's errors. Not for Siggie. Put a service into the net; drop a return a fraction beyond the baseline; fall over your feet – and you got non-stop appreciation: 'Thank you . . . Oh, *thanks* again . . . Many, *many* thanks . . . !'

But his greatest ploy – when the ball bounced into the firs around the court, and vanished among thick needles and brambles – was brutal concern. A warning cry as I reached a hand into the undergrowth:

'You wouldn't do that in the spring. When the vipers wake!'

CHAPTER 19

IF SIGGIE HAD known what lay ahead, he might not have been so keen to call up the vipers.

Without being called, they come, they come . . .

You began seeing them in the spring, slipping from their winter sleeping places. Pencil-slim, quick as whips. Hungry and irritable, greedy to feed and fatten. As summer wore on they got fatter, lazier, happy and stupid, they stretched on the roads, basking on the warm tar, thinking this must be viper heaven. In Languedoc, the roads of summer were streaked with vipers who made the mistake of thinking this. For even vipers have their vipers. One small mistake – of timing, position – and everything ended. The hunters were suddenly history.

* * *

After our tennis match, on the day he talked of snakes in the grass, we went for a beer, as we always did. Siggie paused among the parked cars before entering the café, combed his hair in the wing mirror of Dédé's lime-green Opel Mantra, and adjusted his shirt collar, displaying that curious vanity that overcame him in public. A gleam of arrogance in someone otherwise so utterly plain and unpreening, something Loud Lilly spotted, and made her refuse to deal with an aristocrat.

Siggie and I sat in the Lapin – slightly lost since the café had changed hands. When roly-poly, lazy Bertin had the place it was the village club: packed on Sunday afternoons with card-players, coffee-drinkers, winners and losers from the *boulodrome*. And fat unshaven Bertin, chewing on a matchstick, scratching his chest, moved between tables for a couple of hands of twenty-one, while his wife did the work.

Bertin had sold the place to Dédé – who did it up. In came the new polystyrene ceiling that hid the old custard mouldings and red and silver chevron wallpaper from the 20s; and eyeball halogen spots glared down. Out went the heavy round tables, the spidery chairs; in came imitation leather banquettes in pistacchio, plastic tables, and a fake marble bar.

When Dédé did it up, the old clientele deserted the Lapin for the *Bar à Go-Go*. In the back room were the kids who played video games, table-football and pinball, and who drank nothing. And in the front room was the school of serious gamblers settled into an everlasting poker game. They drank next to nothing. Sometimes as much as a thousand francs rode on a hand, and they preferred to concentrate.

Dédé, like Mayor Angelo, was modern; but Dédé's was the modernity of fear. He was frightened of the future, of his customers, of his luck. In this he had more imagination than the Mayor. M. Angelo believed in the future as a form of force. He was scientific, he believed in knowledge for manipulation. He did not believe in luck, he believed in getting on.

To shake hands with Dédé was to touch a sea-tendril, a watery frond, white as a wishbone. There was something airless about Dédé; as if he never saw the light of day. When he was not playing in the eternal poker school that sat for days, over in the corner, he was at the table just to the left of the picture of the Kissac Rugby XV, playing solo poker on his laptop. Readying himself for the next encounter.

Siggie had nothing but scorn for the poker school. And they were a dreary lot. As boring as drunks, and less amusing; as tiresome as clerics, and less interesting; as silent as the grave, and much less important. There was the thin, beaky-nosed 'journalist' – in fact, he was Kissac's occasional correspondent for *Midi-Libre*. Each village had one, a sad or angry man who'd now and then file a story, usually seasonally driven and steeped in the reader-hating clichés of the roosting hack. There was a form to these pieces, a calculated insult in the well-worn phrases, beginning 'And so the *hirondelles* are on the wing and autumn approaches in her sombre beauty . . .'

Beside the hack sat his unsmiling mistress, in a black leather jacket; she played the game more ferociously than he did. Opposite her sat Dédé. Over his head hung a poster promising free orange juice with breakfast – an offer long defunct. There never was breakfast at the Lapin.

What offended Siggie was that this game was dull, earnest, joyless work; and he always held that work was the richest game imaginable. But there was another reason for his hatred of the poker players.

Pascal, now dark and glowing and successful, made a fourth. Pascal, of the failed father, Pascal who had so little hope for the future he once set up in business with Sad Bob, and humped stones in people's gardens.

And what made for this change in Pascal? Death!

Pascal's father had tried, once again, to put an end to it all. He went out to the barn, flung a rope around a roof beam and jumped off a chair. The result was not quite as he'd intended. The beam had broken, struck him on the head and killed him.

Pascal had found his father stretched out beneath the treacherous wormy wooden beam . . .

People felt for the boy. But it had to be said that his father's accident also provided a curious little *frisson*, close to pleasure. They were sorry for Pascal, but they felt oddly cheered. Strangely alive. The passing of Pascal's dad did everyone a power of good.

There was relief. There was admiration mixed with pity; there was also, in some of us, a dash of something else – rueful solidarity with the dead man. The feeling that, *yes*, we know it happens, and some day it will be our turn to pay the Ferryman. But here was a fellow heading for home before his number was called. He made an honest effort to end it all and what happened? Death pulled a fast one.

Siggie wasn't rueful – not a bit – he was furious. Not since the woman filled her house with gas and set it alight, and was blown into the night sky, stark naked, had he seen such a typical case.

When you thought about what happened to Pascal's dad, said Siggie, you realized Death was a lot of talk, and – contrary to the big talk – often pretty duff at what it did. A botcher, a bragger. Good at the bravura stuff, of course: famine, pestilence, war. But any fool could do those. Yet when it came to something subtle, something special, when you had a man who literally leaped into the very jaws – what did Death do?

'He goes and pulls a lousy trick like that.'

But Pascal had thrived since his dad had pulled it off. He smiled, he won at the poker table – he bluffed well on small pairs and low straights – and he was soon to do his military service. He was about to be posted abroad, further than anyone in Kissac could have dreamed possible, to far-away Martinique. He was longing to leave!

And just behind Pascal sat a smiling shadow who studied his every move.

Siggie ordered a couple more beers.

I followed his eyes across the room, noting the bruising in the grey of what were often very bright eyes – for there sat his daughter, Gretel. She was the shadowy fifth at the poker table. She didn't play, for that matter she didn't speak – she adored. She was in the café every day: and it was a source of pain to Siggie.

'She does nothing! Not school work or housework – nothing!'

Gretel had fallen disastrously for the charms of young Pascal. And Pascal grew in the shadow of his father's passing and became deeply desirable; he flourished, relieved, and his relief was apparent, at last something had been *done*. In death his father redeemed himself. In fact the whole family seemed to pick up after the affair of the falling beam. Pascal's sister kicked out Sad Bob – for good – and Pascal became irresistible to Gretel.

It was her utter exposure that so discomforted Siggie. Pascal had only to breathe, to clear his throat and Gretel giggled and gasped in astonished disbelief that everyone did not see and adore her lover – so beautiful, clever, funny, bold, and sexy. All at once!

And when Pascal raised the ante, or saw someone, or threw in his hand, her amazement at his brilliance turned her lips pale, she clapped her hands to her ears, and groaned in delight. She never spoke but now and then she chimed, bright and silver, she rang with passion. Her lips opened, her breasts strained, her eyes rolled, the table leg was between her knees. 'Oh!' breathed Gretel. 'Ah!' sighed Gretel, like one of those small figures who interprets for the deaf and dumb on television; she was wildly dramatic in the frame but out of the picture. Mewing and pleading and palpitating – and absolutely ignored by the principal players.

She was stupid with desire; she was in heat.

And Pascal never even looked at her.

'Pascal's father didn't kill himself,' said Siggie, 'he was bumped off.'

Siggie swallowed his beer, his hurt eyes still fixed on his daughter, who was laughing, teeth shining, breasts heaving, and he repeated a favourite line: 'Death shouldn't be respected, he should be arrested.'

* * *

The ghost of Pascal's father reminded me of my own.

My father, a bomber-pilot, died in North Africa in 1944; just one of thousands of young men who perished in the Western Desert. I've never found out how he died.

Was he shot down or did he fly into the ground? Mechanical failure or enemy fire? Accident or homicide? Someone I hated once told me he'd 'bought it' because he could never tell up from down.

It was meant to wound but it made me smile: what serious person could tell the difference?

I possessed a fading, black and white studio portrait. Reading anything into the smooth boyish face, much of it hidden under a large air force cap, was quite impossible. I was three months old when he died, far too young to remember anything about him. It was a long time ago. He should have faded like the snows of yesteryear. Yet his passing, I sometimes think, was the most significant event in my life.

Without a father, I was set free. Not entirely free because I took his memory with me wherever I went. Ghosts are portable, they travel very light. He has always been with me. An amiable stranger who has spent much of his death at my elbow; my father who is younger than my sons.

He was a liberating spirit, much as Pascal's father was for him. Not at all like Sophie's dead flier-father, who came back to sit on her bed at night in unhappy Harmony Lodge, in suburban Christchurch, and tell her stories of paradise, and teach her that heaven was made, and unmade, in America.

Pascal was lucky; I was lucky; the ghosts of our fathers did not arrive with marching orders, or instructions about heaven, and how to get there; they set us free.

* * *

In Kissac, the man who failed to hang himself stirred up a heap of trouble for the modern-minded. The ghost of Pascal's father set free other phantoms. It was as if, once the new mayor had decreed that the dead should get no airtime on the loudspeakers, they started turning up quite literally everywhere we looked.

It began innocently enough when the *Mairie* decided to address the parking problem: the Mayor ordered workmen to carve out a chunk or two of a forgotten field to make additional parking bays. A couple of mechanical diggers arrived and munched into the edge of the field on the crest of a small hill above the village, at the top of a tiny lane called the rue des Corps Saints.

It was a squarish patch of empty land. Unremarkable but for its faintly suspicious rectangular neatness. A few gnarled, untended vines grew wild and four feathery cypresses were planted like black quills in the stony soil. No one gave the place much thought; a curious peaceful mound among the backstreets.

The diggers bit deep into the packed yellow-brown sand.

Then it rained. And soon no one could mistake any longer the secret of the new parking lot; all sorts of human bones – knees and forearms, elbow joints and fingers – sometimes cleanly shorn by the diggers' claws, stuck out of the clay. Even skulls were embedded in the bank, snug as peach pips.

It turned out that the patch of land was a fragment of the original medieval graveyard which had escaped the nineteenth-century developers. The tombs and mausoleums, angels and crosses of the crowded burial ground had vanished but many of the dead remained.

The discovery gave Siggie a lot of trouble; he agonized over it, he walked past the diggers, he sighed when he thought of the treasure. Loot was already walking. He pointed out the round indentation where, he said, someone had lifted a skull. Skulls were good business: medical students wanted them, the discotheques used them; he could get a good price in Toulouse for human skeletons.

The loudspeakers ignored the discovery of the bones in the parking lot; and reactions in Kissac were just as interesting. No one suggested suspending operations; or being nicely Anglo-Saxon and apologizing all round, or draping plastic sheeting to hide the offending items; instead they steamed right ahead.

No one fussed about the effect on dogs. Or children.

Nothing was done about the bones because there was nothing to be done about them. They were alarming perhaps, in their nakedness, but they were also normal, natural, unavoidable.

And people did lift them. Stole them away. For souvenirs, or because the custom of gleaning was so strong – the last of the grapes, the wild leeks, snails after rain, cherries, chestnuts, mushrooms, skulls . . .

I walked past the shuttered windows of Kissac in the evening, wondering if someone decorated the mantelpiece of some cosy front room. A cousin's head, because Kissac was crowded with Yoricks. Families have lived in the village for centuries and doubtless their relatives lay in the new parking lot. Those who lifted a tibia or a knee-bone were rifling family tombs. The chances were that the grave-robbers and the missing bones were probably related.

But no one seemed much put out by the implication

that we are all scavengers or ragpickers at heart. Most people would not seriously question that.

'Sad but true,' they would say, 'at least we don't attempt to disguise it. What are archaeologists, for example, but tomb-robbers with degrees?'

If embarrassment was felt it was not for the dead, so cruelly exposed; but for the affront to modernity. There was sympathy for the Mayor. Kissac was ancient and France notionally Catholic but these were modern times and the proper place for such things was out of sight. The future belonged to motor cars and parking bays and crematoria.

Mayor Angelo toured the parking lot and looked displeased. One saw his point but to whom was one to complain?

The passing of Pascal's dad and the parking lot hauntings were strangely encouraging. Perhaps because they disturbed, if only to an exquisitely small degree, the sense that death, while as implacable and inevitable as the police or taxes, was not always an event of woeful normality. Usually it fell on all – like the rain; it was inescapable, and insupportable. But sometimes, in some curious way, though we lost, we humans hit back.

And when we did, then death, even if it did not attain some majesty, at least showed some wit.

'Without us, where the hell would it be?' Siggie demanded.

The loudspeakers under the eaves kept their silence – and into that silence the ghosts poured. Up in the mountains the same heavy rains that had exposed the bones in our churchyard flooded a nearby hamlet. They loosened the earth in the graveyard by the river, and the river became a torrent. Soon coffins were sighted, bobbing their way downstream, a bizarre flotilla, heading for the sea. The dead were taking one final unscheduled cruise, defying every known canon of decency, certainty and even science.

It was a voyage in defiance of our own best hopes and worst fears. Even devout believers do not insist that the dead will literally rise from their graves. And certainly no one expects – or wants – to find them sailing past the front door. But there they were, the brave armada, the little ships.

* * *

And death came like a friend to the Colonel's wife.

The Colonel, her stiff, dry husband, had served in Algiers, and Senegal, and once in Guadeloupe; he had a moustache straighter than a pair of dividers and bright green eyes, expensive tastes in ties and false teeth, and money from his family, who had been minor aristrocrats, somewhere in the Ariège.

The Colonel and his wife retired to Kissac, and bought the big house at the end of the village and there they lived quietly; he seldom went out, she never missed the dromedary in the Circus of Dreams; she would rise in her seat and cheer when he trotted around the ring, the shaggy, evil-smelling, bouncing beast.

I had thought it was admiration. Now I know it was hatred. She could abuse the chocolate dromedary because he looked like her husband who took her down to the lonely stretch of river by the Roman bridge, and assaulted her from time to time.

It was well known that the Colonel beat his wife. Quite

why the Colonel did so, we did not know though some said that he had a bad war record and the urge to violence never left him. Soldiers were everywhere around, the Foreign Legion in Castelnaudary, the Marines in Carcassonne. And everyone an expert on what the military did.

Anyway, the Colonel did not beat her up at home, as might have been expected, since they never went out much. Their house was close to that of better-class neighbours, like M. Belasco the retired *notaire* and a rich Dutchman who has the old farmhouse nearby and has been dying for years.

The Colonel walked his wife down the road to the leisure garden by the river, on the edge of town, before assaulting her. Her cries floated across the village and a lot of people knew what was going on but he never so much as gave the time of day to anyone in the village. So it was that the Colonel kept the sound of it out of the ears of those who mattered.

She never complained. And we never said anything.

Then, one morning, in that October, suddenly and unseasonably cold, the postman coming by, at around eleven o'clock, found the Colonel sitting on the swing that hangs from the cherry tree in his garden.

The postman greeted him and when he got no reply he thought nothing more about it because the Colonel was like that, very taciturn.

And so it was only the next day when he found the Colonel still sitting in the garden that the postman, who is a good fellow and plays flank in the Kissac XV, went over and tapped him on the shoulder. He noticed that his fists were fixed firmly and coldly around the ropes of the swing.

He rang the bell and when the Colonel's Lady came to the door the following conversation, which was soon famous in the village, took place:

'Good morning, madame. I think your husband may be dead.'

'Maybe? Are you sure? Or not sure?'

'Well, madame, he is sitting here on the swing, very cold.'

'Cold he has always been, Monsieur le facteur. But that is not to say he is dead.'

And she closed the door.

The postman went to the Mayor, and the Mayor called the village policeman, and he asked the doctor to accompany him to the Colonel's house. There the doctor confirmed that the Colonel was indeed dead and so they rang the bell and told the Colonel's Lady.

She showed no surprise: 'Yes, I have already heard something of the sort from the postman. But he couldn't be sure.'

And she went inside again.

What seemed to have happened was this. One morning the Colonel died, very suddenly, of a stroke, and the Colonel's Lady did not report his death. What she did was dress him in his best grey suit with a green tie to match his frozen eye and she carried him over to the swing which hung from a branch of the big cherry tree, and there she left him.

It took some time to free the Colonel. She must have clamped his hands around the ropes of the swing and held them there until rigor mortis set in. They had to cut the ropes. M. Belladon, our carpenter, whose father made all the doors in Kissac, built the coffin extra deep.

The Colonel was buried still clutching two lengths of rope – 'holding on to them for dear life,' said the carpenter.

At the funeral, in the Priory, we thought of him in the box with rope in his fists. And we watched the Colonel's Lady for some sign that she knew what she had done but she did not give the slightest hint; rather she looked thoughtful, as if her mind wasn't really on the proceedings or as if she hadn't known the deceased particularly well.

But she had a plan. Oh yes. And from the window of the Lapin, any morning of the week, you could watch her plan unfold. The Colonel's Lady was not finished with the Colonel.

Her year begins in the spring. That is when she walks. She comes out with the cherries, they say around here. When the trees are so fat with fruit they bow and groan – and do not move even when the *tramontane* blows over the Black Mountains, and shivers the shutters. Ladders are propped in the orchards and the pickers balance with buckets, faces show in the trees and the leaves are full of gossip.

The Colonel's Lady goes walking. In a blue coat and cloche hat; sometimes a fox-fur over her shoulders, the paws lifting and falling, playing the drum on her breast as she swings down the Avenue de la Montagne Noire, and turns right for the Bar à Go-Go, without saying a word, a dim, defiant look in her eye.

There she eases herself onto a bar stool and orders a

beer and drinks it down. In her fox-fur and her ostrich leather purse and her ready money. His money.

The Colonel never touched a drop and wouldn't have been seen dead in the café. Now she's spending all his money; she'll take two, maybe three, at the Go-Go and then walk or weave along to the Lapin, and do it all again. Never says a word, gets straight down to business. She is going to drink him dry; she's going to drink him bankrupt.

Just before 12 she's off, floating down the avenue, like she owned the place.

'If I had more like her, I'd retire,' says Dédé.

Siggie and I watched the Colonel's Lady drain her beer, slowly, lovingly. Siggie watched Gretel throw back her head and laugh as Pascal backed a small pair, and won.

He said, 'You know, Christopher, if we leave those bones in the mud, they'll all go!'

* * *

There was in Kissac, for a brief spell, the realization that love was tied to death. Without death, love was unthinkable – and without love, death was unbearable. That's why we had such sympathy with Pascal's father, and the little coffins and the Colonel's Lady; what we felt was love and approval. Only in the agony of love could we show how much we cherished, kept faith, remembered, honoured what was human in us. And without it – we were no more than viper skins on a country road; or dusty junk on the shelves of some country *brocanteur*.

CHAPTER 20

———◆———

THE BIG THINGS – love, death, despair, laughter – came in big servings around here. And there was a rough gaiety in the Midi, that made Thierry uneasy. He knew it was a form of war, aimed at the too-smart bastards from the north, who thought themselves so clever.

It's not an advantage, in Kissac, being from where he's from. But once I saw Thierry fight back – in his way. I saw him take where he came from – call it what you like: the north, Paris, books, brains – and go to war.

On a raw Sunday night in mid-January we were sitting on red plush banquettes, in the Café du Commerce – over in Limoux. The wind off the peaks behind the town had snow on its breath. It was Carnival. Hawkers were flogging sugared almonds, *frites*, saucissons – and masks of the familiar carnival creatures: witches, greybeards, fat-heads, phantoms. Every day, every night, from January to March, teams of dancing revellers with ancient names – the Old Ones, the Arcades, the Miller's Men – followed their bands, *les fanfares*, around the medieval town square, past the dark green, cast-iron fountain, adorned with nymphs showing their breasts.

It all made Thierry restless. He didn't approve, that was

the thing. Even the café – such a warm, good place – fell to pieces under his baffled eye. The shining metal bar stuffed with drinkers; waiters so deft between the tables they could have been running on rails; the big brown coffee machine feeding the small cups, tucked under its warm belly. Too cheap and glitzy – too much shine, steam, cheer. Too much fun.

He was having his usual Thierry effect; the waiters, and the customers, gave him a wide berth. As if dark eyes and powdery stubble, crumbling shirt collar all said: here's bad bad news – an ex-con, a crazy.

He was neither – but he was strange. He got thinner and his handshake stronger, his voice deeper. He'd grip my hand and boom like a foghorn – it was a heartiness I didn't believe in for a moment.

Thierry had just moved – again. To look after yet another farmhouse, this time in the Corbières. And, once again, he'd stored his pathetic goods in Siggie's barn. Once again, Siggie let him do it – for the perverse pleasure of inspecting Thierry's junk, as it lay naked on the concrete floor; the balding grey blankets, the works of Goethe, the latest addition – saddest of all – a flexible metal chest expander, like a silver snake among the knotty cudgels, the dead typewriter, the rusted pots. Siggie shook his head in redoubled disbelief. That any man should keep such stuff! And amazed, at himself – how could he have let this rubbish into his sacred barn, among his beauties from the Black Mountains? What had come over him?

But that was the thing about Thierry – for a helpless man, he got things done.

And he surprised me, as he always did, by settling well

into his new place, making a workroom in the kitchen; several bearded John the Baptist heads of his friend, the genius, stared from the wall. Over the kitchen table, and above the sink, he'd pinned a few unarguable mottoes: 'Art Is Eternal', 'Remember – Always Beauty!'; and he went back to work, translating Dante and Heraclitus.

I asked how he managed for food and he said, 'I eat a lot of tomatoes.' He said it in a way that really didn't leave much room for discussion. He was suddenly a gardener, something he'd never been before. In jacket and tie, he showed me his tomato patch, touching the berries with bitten fingernails, saying briskly how good it was to get out into the country.

Then he asked, delicately, if perhaps he might make use of my *voiture?*

He had this trick of elevating things by tone alone – wine, women and, it had happened, song. No *vins ordinaires* for Thierry; my old Volkswagen Golf was suddenly up there, among the Big Reds of the car world. This tendency was not flattery – in Thierry's hands it was a form of force. One of the ways he got things done – always remembering that Thierry was a helpless man.

He wanted a lift to Limoux. He'd met Helen of Troy, and she lived over the mountains. He'd been trying to thumb a lift on the road between Narbonne and nowhere, sweating gently; in his mac, grey suit, tie, carrying a brief-case. A professional mourner, a debt-collector.

Why should anyone stop?

Edith stopped. She had given him a lift in her mauve Twingo.

Thierry told her he loved music. He meant Mozart.

Edith said she loved music, too; she meant marching bands.

They arranged to meet at the Café du Commerce, on the square.

Aspirin-pale, and tiny, Thierry stroked his bald dome with fine fingers. He owned fewer clothes each time I met him, shedding garments as he moved from one free house to the next. Tonight he was the mortuary assistant, his grey suit and smoky eyes, with this carnival novelty: like a splash of blood on a coffin lid – a dark red silk bow tie.

God knows where he found it. But he told me that artists, before our lousy times, had always 'dressed' – Beethoven, Rimbaud, James Joyce – rebels, yes. Not tramps.

'Greatness', said Thierry, 'has style.'

Or it did – until we got to our shoddy era.

We ordered drinks and the waiter came over, shielding his eyes as if Thierry gave off rays.

He was saying, 'I'll go to my grave, like Dante.'

He wouldn't, of course. He'd go in someone else's hearse, on someone else's money. All the horses would wear black plumes.

Thierry was sipping coffee; then he ordered a Scotch. 'I usually drink malted.' Or 'the big Bordeaux reds'.

He always said so, and you had to admire him because, usually, he drank water.

I drank wine, the plainer, the smaller, the better, when I was with Thierry. It seemed the thing to do. In Limoux it was *blanquette*, the sparkling white of the town. Thierry throbbed with reproach. With wine, with Art: Thierry hit home runs only: it was Dante–Molière–

Shakespeare every time. The big reds of Art – and if they weren't on the menu then forget it!

When I say the Midi made him unhappy, that's wrong. It appalled him.

Take, say, the art of Madame de la Pipe, who strolls along the banks of the Canal du Midi offering unusual sexual services to passing motorists. I like her clothes, her style, her originality; she's not a streetwalker, she's a canal walker!

Thierry does not only *not* approve of Madame de la Pipe – it's worse than that. I pointed her out, walking along in her white beret and her tartan tracksuit and her long red scarf and her white trainers, and Thierry said, 'Where? I don't see anything.'

I've always rather resented his blindness to Madame. If he can't see her – what can he see?

Her solitary trudge beside the milky green waters of the canal, casting an eye at the howling traffic, is great theatre, it is sad and unmissable comedy. I think she's brave; braver than the fishermen who also try their luck beside the canal. They catch more. They go home to proper houses; but 'La Pipe' is a fisher of men: she uses the facilities, such as they are, and if she does not land a client or two she doesn't eat. She's an artiste.

She said to me in our one fragmentary conversation: 'It's for love, monsieur; it's because of the child.'

No one seems sure if there is a child, or a phantom baby. Everyone knows, at least those who see her, that Madame walks to and fro on the towpath in her oversized trainers, her body muffled in jersey and coat, in her outrageous expectation that she can solicit passers-by with the very little she has on offer.

When Thierry thinks of courtesans he thinks of Cleopatra, Carmen, Madame du Pompadour, *les grandes horizontales* of the *belle époque*, the lovers of the Marquis de Sade.

But Thierry fell for a wine-maker from Limoux – and refused to touch a drop of her life's work.

* * *

We'd been sitting for about an hour in the Café du Commerce, when it turned out that Thierry did not have a firm date with Edith.

I said, 'We've come all this way – and you can't be sure of seeing her?'

'Oh yes, we will,' said Thierry.

He'd checked the timetable. It's printed in the newspapers; it's on display in the shop windows. Teams are assigned weeks ahead, and that night it was to be the turn of the *blanquettièrs*. Edith would be marching around the square at about 9. And the processions always started from the Café du Commerce.

The bar was crowded with men in funny hats, they carried saxes, tubas, flutes, and lined the bar, knocking back *pastis*. They were that night's band, *la fanfare* for the *blanquettièrs*. They wore red neckerchiefs and pointy black hats and laughed a lot. It was a carnival joke; they wore deconstructed rural togs. They were hicks and proud of it! Bumpkins dressed as yokels. They made the braying demented sound of a band tuning up, shook spit from their mouthpieces; and scraps of tuba, trumpet, sax flew past our ears like birds trapped in a room.

Let's face it, this band was not the Vienna Philharmonic, they played things like 'My Father's Moustache' and 'The Devil in a Dustbin'. They were young, they laughed a lot, solid blokes having fun. When they weren't being *la fanfare*, they were in the rugby team.

Then the carnival creatures began pushing through the glass doors. Two Apache dancers in striped shirts, a burglar in a mask with a bag of swag, two keystone cops, a hunchback, a baby, several clowns with green hair, kids probably, in those blank white Venetian masks that look like walls with eyes.

In walked a fat little washerwoman with grey hair and cherry cheeks and a blue laundry bag over her shoulder. When she lifted her mask, she was young and she had good brown eyes, tanned skin. Olive and russet were her colours. And she wore blue jeans, so she shared the sloppiness of modern life Thierry deplored. But he didn't mind, he just grinned.

Edith said very little: '*Bonsoir, monsieur,*' to me, and '*Ça va?*' to Thierry, and then she went back to the gorilla.

I hadn't noticed the gorilla till then. He stood some way behind Edith, tapping a plastic orange truncheon in his palm.

Thierry went on grinning. He was a goner, Siggie would have said he was out of order. Aflame with what he called, with childish pleasure at the rhyme, 'the burning yearning'. Thierry was what Hercule called the Hermit, who had *not* tried to sell me his house — a fool for love. Thierry wanted what Madame de la Pipe promised, and Sophie prayed for, and the automaton felt for Claire, and Plusbelle taught Gretel. He was riddled with those desires which, the anonymous writer of the guide to Paris complained, were so weakly represented in French by the 'forms of *aimer*'.

I don't think either of them would have known what to say to this expression of passion in the Café du Commerce. I had never seen him like this before. He sat there, in his burgundy bow tie, grinning like an idiot at a girl dressed up as Widow Twankey.

Thierry hated pantomime. He loathed the red *banquettes*, and the steam and the booze and backslapping of the Café du Commerce; and the fête beyond in the icy square, where stallholders hawked crêpes and sticky *gaufrettes*.

Thierry loved only great women, usually dead women; heroines of literature and art and music; and courtesans, or whores, for Thierry is no prude, he was happy with real greatness, wherever it was found.

But this girl wasn't Helen of Troy – she wasn't Madame O either. She was Edith from the Co-op, and she made plonk.

And even sex has its big reds. It was Thierry, yet again measuring his aspiration against the highest achievements, who once told me he wasn't having as much of it 'as the Marquis de Sade'.

* * *

Rubbing their hands the musicians stepped out into the cold: trumpeters in front, tubas and serpents at the rear. The carnival creatures wheeled out their float: a wooden steam engine with funnel and whistle. The band struck up the slow voodoo wail that is the music of carnival. The keystone cops stepped inside the engine frame and began walking it, like a pantomime horse; the washerwoman and an Apache were leading the steam engine on long reins; the marchers following the float began their strange, snaking, stomping, hand-waving dance, tracing their fingers left and right. There was something Indian about the fingers, or Balinese. But it was local. Babies did it; it was something you were born with, in Limoux.

And the gorilla shook his truncheon at the spectators.

When the procession hit Le Grande Café, all of twenty metres away, they nipped in for another quick one. They do that at every watering hole around the arcades of the square.

Thierry said, 'I'm going to take a closer look. I may march.'

I said he shouldn't. Limoux spends a year preparing for the Carnival, strangers come to watch but they don't join. Thierry gave me that look of his which says he's gone deaf and walked into the night.

The marchers were spilling out of the Grand Café, wiping their mouths, and formed up; the keystone cops climbed back into the steam engine, the washerwoman took the reins, the *fanfare* struck up and the weird swaying walk began again.

It's a small square and a complete circuit, allowing for drinks, takes about twenty minutes. When the marchers stopped in front of the Café du Commerce again, there was Thierry, right behind the gorilla. He'd bought himself a mask, the grinning *senex*, the old fool of the proceedings, and clamped it on and joined the marchers.

I suppose he thought he blended: when you put on a

mask you think you can't be recognized. But Thierry stood out a mile: he's about as tall as Toulouse-Lautrec, his bow tie drooped under the mask and he couldn't do the zombie walk. He didn't have the fingers, the rhythm.

He came back into the café and sat down, very pleased with himself.

Edith came in next. She pulled off her mask, dropped her bundle of washing on the floor, brushed her brown hair out of her brown eyes, and a waiter brought her hot chocolate.

'You shouldn't join,' Edith told Thierry, and blew into her big cup.

Thierry smiled his deaf smile. 'I can do it. I did it.'

'You didn't. You can't,' said Edith.

The gorilla walked into the café then.

Thierry noticed nothing. He began talking about the history of *la fanfare*. How it harked back to very early Europe, to 'real' things: it was magic, it sang of rain, war, worship.

Edith wasn't listening. She was watching the gorilla who had taken off his head and tucked it under his arm like a crash helmet.

It was strange – what I called the 'Thierry effect'. Introduce him into any sort of jollity and he closed down the show. When he joined the *blanquettièrs* the other marchers lost step – the tuba and the sax went to pieces. If you had a parade, Thierry was rain.

I was mulling this over when the gorilla, his head under his arm, stepped up and hit Thierry several times on the head, with his orange truncheon.

'You don't belong here,' the gorilla told Thierry. He

turned to Edith. 'Why do you go on meeting men on the quiet?'

Edith threw her hot chocolate at him then, and if he hadn't lifted his mask to his face he might have been rather badly burnt.

No one else paid any attention. That's Carnival for you.

And then *la fanfare* swallowed their drinks, stumbled into the cold for another circuit of the square, the washerwoman and the gorilla went with them, and it was quiet again. Thierry said nothing but I had the feeling he was replaying the hollow smack of the plastic truncheon on his bald head.

* * *

Next day, Thierry went into Carcassonne and got hold of Sven, a tall Swede who keeps a boat on the Canal du Midi. Next he had a word with Sam the Englishman, who has a boat at Capstang. Then he got M. Belladon, the village carpenter, to use some of the spare wood, kept for making coffins, to build a couple of platforms. These were fixed to the stern of each boat; they looked like big wooden spoons. A thin handle stuck out over the water, ending in a round scoop about a metre wide.

And he searched for a *fanfare*. I heard that he tried Jo-Jo, who has a famous band over in Caunes called *Ton-ton est faim*, or The Hungry Uncle. Jo-Jo dressed like the late President Mitterrand, in red scarf Homburg, and dark blue coat. But Thierry got nowhere. The Uncle is a famous *fanfare*, it has made CDs and they weren't playing for nothing.

There is in Kissac a little *fanfare* called *La Tante*

Gallopante – the Galloping Auntie – which plays when the Cavalcade marches through the village. The Cavalcade is a squadron of male drum-majorettes, dumpy men in pleated tennis dresses, wigs, lipstick, glasses and beards.

They swing past the *boulodrome*, the tennis courts and the municipal camping site, followed by floats, pulled behind tractors and occupied by kids who fire confetti at the spectators on the pavements. The Aunt is a pasty little *fanfare* of no importance or rank, and Thierry's deal meant a public perfomance, and maybe that's why René, who heads the band, said he'd do it.

The Aunt had small forces – two trumpets, four saxes, a small boy who plays the bass drum, which is cleverly attached to a wheel so he can push it ahead of him like one of those machines for painting stripes on the road. Yves, the tuba player, is blind and he is led by his wife, a striking blonde. Yves married the best-looking woman in the area and never set eyes on her, say his friends. Admiringly, ruefully, René, the bandleader, walks backwards, counting time.

René agreed he'd have the Auntie on the humpback bridge over the Canal du Midi, Sunday morning, at dawn.

Then Thierry phoned the gorilla from the public phone box on the road to Narbonne and challenged him to a water joust.

A challenge like that cannot go unanswered. In real life the gorilla was Luis, the eighth man in the Limoux rugby squad.

* * *

I knew where Thierry had got the idea.

There was in the coastal town of Agde, in the summer, the tournament on water. Two big boats took to the river, crewed by a dozen oarsmen in white tunics and tight white pants. On the prows, jutting out over the water, stood the fighters, carrying long wooden lances. The opposing teams of rowers wore sashes of red or blue over their white sailor suits.

A *fanfare* was ready in the stands, at the centre of the watery lists, the midway point where the boats crossed, and the fighters hit. At the heart of the joust, the trumpets sounded, the oars flashed, the boats gathered speed. All the town crowded into the stands – people drank, gambled, and whistled on the reds or the blues, as the boats ran towards each other. High on their platforms over the water, the fighters levelled their lances.

A man dropped when the long lance hit him below the heart, and fell slowly into the river. The *fanfare* howled. It was a bullfight on water. A tourney; pitting knight against knight. Little dinghies pushed off from the bank and pulled the loser out of the drink.

* * *

The bridge across the canal at La Redorte, on Sunday morning, is a long way from the summer jousts on the river in Agde, with hundreds in the stands.

This was the canal at its most soft, flowing like quiet green milk.

It is always something, and somewhere else, the canal. It was a grand impersonator. Some days old men hang fishing lines from its bridges. There is something Japanese in their exquisite stillness. Sometimes smoke slips from the chimneys of the houses on the bank, and there is something Dutch about the sudden arrangement – canal, trees, sky.

In good weather painters sketch its curves, its flat calm flow; its flexible, flowing trees. And the canal effortlessly paints them in return: very quick, just a few licks, a bridge, a cloud or two – and it has its painters to the life. Then, like a good artist, goes on to the next place, and doesn't look back.

Edith stared hard at the arrangements. Seen through her eyes, these did not please. Thierry's effort had been brave, but we were down to basics. Two tatty canal boats, and Sven the Swede saying, 'For God's sake, don't fall anywhere near my propellers.' And Sam the Englishman, saying, 'Keep your pecker up' to Thierry, who spoke no English, and wouldn't have known a pecker if it bit him, and has never known which way is 'up'.

And Edith saying, bitterly, 'I suppose I'm the prize?'

Then she went and locked herself in her Twingo and did her nails.

Thierry wore his red bow tie and his suit, and balanced over the water on his fighting platform; he did not look at all like a knight-at-arms, he was a small, bald fighting moth. Luis wore the green and gold jersey of the Kissac rugby team, and good gym shoes, and planted his big calves on his fighting platform like he'd been doing this all his life.

Their lances hit centre chest and Thierry swayed and fell, surprise on his face, and the Galloping Auntie shrieked. We were all shouting – except for Edith. You can't help getting excited. The *fanfare* plays music to drown by.

Thierry hauled himself aboard, and the boats turned and ran the other way.

Three times Luis knocked Thierry into the water. He had weeds on his head, and his underpants showed through his grey flannels when Sven hauled him out with the boathook.

Three times was the deal. But Thierry spat water and said he'd go on. And Luis knocked him off his perch again and again, and all the time Edith sat in the car and looked the other way, and the Auntie wailed in demented joy.

Four, five, six falls later – Sam stepped in.

'You'll drown, you fool!'

'Yes,' said Thierry, 'I will.'

Blind Yves's wife saved him; she led her husband away because she would not let him watch a man drown. And the *fanfare* packed it in. And you can't have a tourney without a *fanfare*.

And not once did Edith look at Thierry. He had made things impossible for her. Even if she hated Luis, she knew she was saddled with him now.

* * *

On the last night of Carnival we were in Limoux, but this time we chose *Le Grand Café*. The restaurant in the upstairs room looks out onto the square and you can see but not be seen. Luis was swearing to kill Thierry if they ever met again.

All the teams were marching behind their bands, the square was packed, the marchers waving fingers like windswept trees. The last night of Carnival was sacred. At the end of the night, the revellers bring out a man made of straw, dressed in fine clothes. They pay him every respect, he is 'Our Lord Carnival'; then they tie him to a stake in the square and light a fire under him.

Thierry looked pleased. The way he had the night he marched. He was a dangerous man. Sam the Englishman had it half right. If the Galloping Auntie hadn't packed it in, something bad would have happened. Thierry was not necessarily trying to kill himself, but he would have gone on until Luis killed him – or gave up. That's why Luis wanted him so badly now, when it was too late.

All Thierry would say was: 'If someone wins, someone must go under.'

There was a finesse about that.

Thierry got there, to the sharp edge, by using his head, the same head the gorilla had hit him on. He played for keeps.

It made him deadly.

The others couldn't see that. They thought marching and music and masks were theirs and they could do as they liked. Carnival was a game, and *la fanfare* was a bunch of rugby players in smocks, it was all fun.

Thierry believed fun was lies. The Carnival, the water joust, the lances – they were to do with magic, hope, or tears. Life, or the end of a life, blood in the sand, the bull's ears, the lady's favour, the knight's head, death or glory, do or die – that's what the *fanfare* said.

The crowd lit the bonfire beside the fountain. The pretty dark green fountain, where the cast-iron maidens around the water show rich breasts of the sort that once sent Kissac's new doctor so crazy that he exposed himself on the hillside.

Now the Lord of the Carnival was burning. Everyone was excited, the flames lit up their faces. His nose caught fire, and then his straw hair. He danced in his wooden shoes like a hanged man, and the *fanfares* led the masked creatures around the square, the music wailed and thumped.

And the gorilla waved his orange truncheon.

A waiter came over, shuffling sideways, not looking at Thierry. I took the wine list and found a pricey Bordeaux. Thierry was very surprising. I remembered the sardines he grilled over his kitchen fire, at that unforgettable lunch; his bitten nails on the tomato frames; the wearisome mottoes about Art above the kitchen sink; the way he surfaced in the canal, weeds on his bald head.

The waiter went off for the wine, and I wondered if it helped. You called for your Big Reds, but were they ever big enough?

That was the trouble – with Thierry, with life, with death.

CHAPTER 21

———•———

I SUPPOSE WHAT the *fanfare* said – and Thierry knew –
was that love and death went together. No love without
loss; no sense of the sacred without an awareness of our
helpless mortality; but then again – no antidote to death,
but love. What gave love its power – and its sadness – was
its sister shadow, imminent loss.

I saw this in Kissac when the Mayors clashed, and old
and new worlds collided. I saw M. Angelo, the *arriviste*,
the modern man, the new Mayor and bustling socialist, the
technocrat who believed in Marx, and the movies, take on
M. Rivière, the old Mayor, who believed in de Gaulle, and
looked as if he'd stepped out of the movies. M. Angelo
thought he could sail ahead, and not for a moment hear
or acknowledge how old and strange and thronged with
ghosts were the places around him.

How many ghosts there were in Kissac, and the country
of the vanished Cathars. Fighting, killing, war had something to do with it. Where there has been mass-murder,
the ghosts are always more clamorous. And the Albigensian
believers in worlds of absolute light and dark – the Cathars
– were exterminated in a programme run by Church and
State, as thorough as any modern example. It was one of

those solutions called final – but they never are. Because you might, as happened, kill every heretic from Albi to the sea – but you never get rid of the ghosts.

Languedoc was alive with remains of other vanished migrants. Neglect is a fine museum, poverty preserves things money never does, the traces – the neolithic shelters of Bronze-Age man; caves, barrows, and menhirs standing up in the vineyards, astonishing, mad erections raised to powerful gods by vanished peoples for unknown reasons; stone beehive huts, the rocky igloos of early settlement, now tumbles of rubble in the hill; Roman bridges and Gothic towers and Crusader churches. And there was also that ghost of more recent memory, the last War, with crosses to mark a massacre, or a fading photograph behind glass, remembering some boy shot behind a barn, and ugly Soviet-style concrete shrines to the phantom *maquis*, who fought the Germans in the Black Mountains.

M. Rivière, whom the new Mayor wished was a ghost but who was still substantial flesh, would not lie down and die. He was a hero of the Resistance and, on high and holy days, at ceremonies remembering the Wars against Germany, he stood with generals, and mayors, bemedalled and proud, before the memorial column of marble, outside the Lapin.

In the weeks after I moved into my house, a series of brief, bitter battles was fought between old and new Mayors; they split Kissac into opposing camps, and came to be known as the Wars of Religion.

But as it was with those bloody feuds, the name was misleading. Our wars also concerned the Church, and to some degree, God Herself, but they lacked any real religious content and were, like most wars, about hubris, stupidity and ambition.

* * *

Down beyond the defunct railway station, near the parking lot where the travelling Circus of Dreams stretched its greasy plastic groundsheet, and pitched its little top, stood the wine Co-op, and the communal wine cellars. The front half of the Co-op dated from the 1920s, with huge wooden doors, red-tiled roof and a handsome gable. The rear end was an ugly cream hangar rammed into place in the 80s; beyond it stood four steel storage tanks – like metal teeth, or studs.

Kissac, like all the villages around about, was founded on, floated in, and funded by wine. We were also in a classic bind – we made too much, and not all of it good. But wine was all we made.

The Co-op was managed by M. Vargin, a smiling fellow, always happy to help *négociants* with their paper-work.

You bought your wine for a week – *vin ordinaire* – in 10, 11 or 12 degrees of alcohol, and a passable rosé.

You bought fresh wine. What wasn't finished by Friday you threw away.

Other villages tarted up their cellars with plastic vine leaves and painted bottles, but Kissac did not believe in fancy things like bar counters, wine tastings and uniformed staff; our Co-op was a serious place – smelling of old must, with its dark and winey gloom, the cash register with its dull bell; its wooden vats and fading certificates of competence from long-forgotten *concours*.

You would take your wicker-covered jerrycans, holding anything up to 15 litres, or your plastic bottles, down to the co-op once a week, stand them on the iron grille where the dregs sluiced away, and M. Vargin would fill them straight from the barrel, using a plastic hose, much yellowed over the years by the tannin – you fetched your wine the way you filled your car at the village petrol pump. We took a particular pride in this plainness. It seemed truer, more honest.

Until the day Vargin vanished and it was discovered that all the money earmarked for paying VAT went missing about the same time.

And the members of Kissac Co-op, the local *négociants*, were flabbergasted.

Mayor Angelo called a meeting of all interested parties, in the Foyer Municipale. Everyone was shouting. Everything had to be repeated. The *négociants* were bewildered, hurt and angry and the Mayor had to tell them several times that the co-op owed money to the fisc which the Co-op did not have.

Worse and worse. It then turned out that M. Vargin had not fled, as one might have expected, to some other country or vanished entirely – not at all, he had merely relocated, he was living in Perpignan, he had been seen there *en famille*, some of whom were doing rather well; his son had a bicycle shop and his brother had a café.

And no one could tell the farmers how it happened. No one could explain M. Vargin's insouciance, or his move to Perpignan, or his continuing liberty. It looked obvious but it was complicated. The only sure thing was that he was in clover and they were in shit.

And there was only one thing to do and that was to shout.

Mayor Angelo was not very happy, having to stand there and repeat himself and not be heard. It didn't matter – because he kept repeating the same thing:

'The situation is grim; the Co-op is broke.'

Why – one farmer demanded – did no one see it coming?

'It's our own fault,' someone else yelled.

The farmers blamed M. Vargin. They blamed each other. And when they tired of that – they blamed the Mayor.

M. Angelo was struck by the unfairness of it all. The Co-op manager had been appointed under the old regime, if anyone was to blame it was M. Rivière.

But he had an idea. If he could be blamed for mistakes made by a previous council, then perhaps he could use the previous council to advance his own cause.

And M. Angelo, like many French kings and presidents, decided that it was time to start a programme of public works. His supporters, the municipal cop, the baker, the angry butcher, and of course, his party, spread the word – the new Mayor was embarked on a building programme almost Pharaonic in scope and energy.

His aim – to change the very face of Kissac.

Let there be no more talk about the missing VAT money. The time had come to praise famous men.

* * *

M. Rivière was pretty cool when the news reached him; he smoothed back his still dark and gleaming hair. At seventy, the question always intrigued – was it his own, or was it dyed? M. Rivière did not give a damn for these petty challenges, and stepped through the village streets with all his old assurance. He was a handsome man. He looked like Marlene Dietrich's ideal Frenchman, the actor Jean Gabin.

It was very amusing to hear all this talk about the new Mayor filching credit for the building programme – but he didn't believe it would work. Kissac was a small place. Who would forget that every building project now under way had begun when M. Rivière was mayor? The greatest of these – the work which he was proudest of – was the restoration of the old Priory.

It had begun soon after I arrived in the village, and was still going on five years later. Backed by money from Paris, and funds for preserving the patrimony of Cathar country, teams of restorers, stonemasons and tilers replaced the roof and restored the porch, repaired the choir and the organ and the altar and brought the old Priory back to that peak of perfection it had last seen when it sent teams of executioners to hunt down the very Cathars whose history the Mayor was so determined to celebrate.

But that was history and this was tourism, and M. Angelo drew a sharp line between the two. Modernity. Professionalism. The scientific approach. After many years, and many millions of francs, the thousand-year-old church was ready for the next millennium. At night, it was a tower of honey under the floodlights. On each summer night there would be a *son et lumière*. It was automatic, it worked off a switch, it broadcast whether anyone was there or not. The same single little switch worked the church clock, the bells and the fire-extinguishing sprinkler system.

M. Angelo was proud of the new church, so proud you would have thought it was his very own work.

M. Rivière next heard that the Mayor was planning an official opening of the Priory. He simply didn't credit it. His disbelief was based on religious grounds. He was a devout Catholic; he went to Mass every week. But Angelo was a socialist, an atheist and a modernist. He was also openly anti-clerical and quite probably approved the shooting of priests and nuns, as Republicans like his grandfather had done in Spain, during the War against Franco.

'Mayor Angelo is not a believer. He won't be telling everyone that he was the one who got the Priory under way. Unless he's had a sudden Damascus conversion to the joys of our Lord.'

But M. Angelo had ambitions. And he had, above all, a burning desire to get the farmers off his back. The idea seemed fair to him – if M. Rivière could escape the blame for the vanishing VAT money, then he could take the credit for the Priory. He planned a short but vibrant speech from the Priory steps, a new restaurant in the cloisters, a clock museum and wine tastings in the crypt.

He began drafting his speech.

*   *   *

Around this time news began spreading about Sophie, down in her cottage in the woods, living like a hermit, and, by all accounts, wasting away.

Sophie's landlords, Hervé and Marie-Jo, were at their wits' end. Sophie had stopped paying rent. And when Marie-Jo called at the cottage and tried to collect it, Sophie had been very unhelpful. She threatened to cast a spell on Marie-Jo.

Hervé said he'd deal with her. He was from an aristocratic family, he still possessed the ancient right to ride a horse in several of France's most famous cathedrals; he had a square chin and a strong way.

He knocked on the door, asked for his money.

Sophie stared at him with her frozen eyes. She was awaiting 'an angel of the Lord', she told Hervé, and he was not going to show up if her landlord was present.

'And then,' said Hervé, 'she threw what she said was "a ring of invisible light, protective as steel" around herself – and waited until I went away.'

At this point the Mayor decided to do something. He had heard she was starving and he did not want a dead New Zealander spoiling things in the run-up to the Grand Opening. The commune would offer Sophie help.

Hervé warned that giving her gifts was not easy. It was hard to keep God in the sort of conditions she had been accustomed to. She didn't say thanks. And she was very expensive.

It was not so surprising. It was always difficult dealing with saints. Heroic sanctity and blinding faith, unshakeable modesty or grand simplicity never came cheap. And Sophie was not merely saintly – she was divine. The farmers in the woods and the neighbours who met her foraging for mushrooms in the fields gave her carrots and greens, but it was hard, all this constant giving – Sophie's neighbours felt a bit like friends of Gandhi's had done – that it was costing them a packet to keep her in poverty.

Sophie took what they gave, without needing it for a

moment. She needed nothing. She had faith, and even if winter was coming on and her only source of heat was the pine cones she collected and burnt in her fireplace, she was triumphant and happy.

But Kissac had the responsibility for sending her to hospital if she fell ill, and the *Mairie* worried about the cost of supporting the deity on the doorstep.

Mayor Angelo arrived with a practical gift – several pockets of potatoes.

Sophie saw him off the premises. One does not sully one's hands with *pommes de terre* while awaiting the Angel of Revelation.

Whenever Siggie thought of Sophie he shook his head and repeated to himself, 'Oi, yoi, yoi, yoi, yoi!'

Mayor Angelo declared the Priory open from the front steps. He was returning the Priory to the people – from now on Kissaquiennes would be able to visit the old church absolutely free. Everyone clapped.

But ambition got the better of him. He had suggested the Mass of Thanksgiving. He planned to sit in the front pew and take the credit. Instead he had to stand in the porch, where he had made his fine speech, and watch the priest who had come to say the Mass, changing into his vestments in the parking lot. There was no choice. It turned out that after all those years spent taking the church apart, someone had forgotten to replace the sacristy, when they put it together again.

And the Mayor could not for the life of him see what all the fuss was about. But the village did – and the comment was cruelly pointed: one heard it in Mimi's grocery and the bakery and the Lapin:

'First he loses the VAT money. Now he loses the sacristy! Go-ahead he may be. But for the village – or himself? He's a law unto himself. The *Mairie* is being run like an old-style Soviet.'

Madame Cabrol summed it up one day, as I was walking past her bench in the Avenue de la Montagne Noire:

'A church without a sacristy? It's like a house without a kitchen.'

M. Rivière had listened, stunned, to the Mayor's address. He had been robbed, cheated, he could not believe his ears. Now he hit back. He took what seemed like a civilized low-key option, but one calculated to do the widest possible damage to the Mayor's already moth-eaten credibility.

He got up a petition: '*To M. le Maire, from the Concerned Citizens of Kissac. Give us back our Sacristy!*'

He stepped around the village in a dark red cravat and a lot of people signed. And then, marching at the head of a small committee called Concerned Catholics for Kissac, he handed it in to the *Mairie*.

* * *

That was when the War broke out.

The next morning in the bakery, and the Bar à Go-Go, and the pharmacy, and Mimi's grocery, opposite the *Mairie*, people were clutching copies of a letter that had been pushed through every letter box after dark. They fanned their faces with the single pink page with its angry type, they shielded their eyes from the sun with it, they read bits to each other; they waved a hand in that characteristic gesture of trouble brewing, flicking imaginary hot water from their fingers and as they did so they raised their eyebrows, and their voices in a chorus of astonished delighted anticipation: 'Ooh la-la-la-la-la!'

The Mayor's midnight letter began with a big headline: '*En Voila – Assez!*' (Enough's enough!) – and got straight to the point:

> Let me say this: I have not lost the sacristy – because the sacristy shouldn't have been there in the first place. This is the advice of experts: the architects of ancient monuments.
>
> Yes, certain people – like M. Rivière – want the sacristy back. But how will he pay for it? Will he use money the *Mairie* has put by for a crèche, for a retirement home?
>
> Did he lift so much as a little finger when the Co-op manager ran off to Perpignan with – or without – the VAT money?
>
> Who was it who met wine farmers and treasury officials? I even went to Paris and fought to have the debt reduced.
>
> What has M. Rivière done? Formed '*une cabale*'. Plotted and schemed.
>
> If that's not politics, then tell me what is!

The Mayor ended with a solemn oath: 'This is the truth, the whole truth, and nothing but "*toute la verité*".'

The village was split, angry, *en brûlé*.

A few nights later, a second letter dropped through our letter boxes:

From M. Jean Rivière to Monsier le Maire de Kissac

You have done me the honour of crediting me with electoral ambitions, but you've missed the train.

Politics is not my '*métier*'. Yes, I am a Gaullist. But I belong to no political party. I have fought for peace and liberty.

Yes, I support the petition for a new sacristy – but only for the sake of the village I love and where I wish to end my life . . .

When I saw your letter, I thought – the public-address system has broken down! Why else would the Mayor run through the village streets at night, dropping me in it among the inhabitants?

Monsieur le Maire, let me give you some advice – keep your cool!

CHAPTER 22

———————

I THINK SIGGIE had a conscience about Sophie. One day he asked me if I'd visit her. He went into the cellar and fetched a bowl of cherries.

'Tell her – here are some cherries from paradise.'

I drove out to Sophie's place. A young man was with her, dark, and solidly built. The man was Shaun, her son, who had flown in from Christchurch. I thought he had a rather dazed look; this large New Zealander in a small French cottage in a wood. They sat before the fire of pine cones. On the mantelpiece were many portraits of blonde angels with swimming-pool eyes, which mother and son painted. Pretty angels; sugary, sickly angels, like the platoons of painted hairdresser Christs that Hercule bought in job lots.

Shaun was uncommunicative – but he did say he was happy to be in Cathar country, because it was a 'geologically stable' part of the world.

I found Sophie much thinner than I remembered. She told me she'd given up meat, cheese and fish. As I'd rather suspected from Shaun's remark, we were going to talk about Last Things. And we did. We sat on the floor, God and me and the Son of God, and talked about Armageddon.

Soon earthquakes were to sweep the world beginning –
Sophie's eyes gleamed – with New Zealand. How she hated
the place! After the earthquakes came tidal waves. New
Zealand, or what was left of it, and Japan, and countless
islands in the Pacific, would drown: millions would perish!

Only in Languedoc would a community of saints
survive, an inner-world government run by the Divine
Mother.

In a cool, bare cottage mother and son meditated, and
listened to Dire Straits on their Walkmen. I never could
quite connect Sophie's taste in pop with her Godhead. At
that stage the electricity still worked though they hardly
ever used it. Sophie had a sleeping bag for extra warmth
in her bedroom: Shaun slept on the sofa; they had a phone
and a TV; and these sugar-sweet angels with eyes like
blowtorches looked on.

I handed over the cherries and left.

A few weeks later, as the winter came on, bearing
another jar of cherries from Siggie's cellar, I headed for the
little cottage, now huddled in the cold, sodden valley.

Sophie took some time to answer my knock. She took
even longer to recognize me; it turned out that she had
lost one of her contact lenses. It was freezing in the house.

She was thinner still, wearing thick blue eyeshadow,
and she had a crystal taped to her forehead. Her eyelashes
were sticky when she fluttered them. She told me of very
exciting developments on the Angelic front. She sat in the
semi-darkness, wrapped in a large blue blanket. It was
desolate. The phone and the power had been cut. She had
taken to combing the fields for firewood, and late berries,
and mushrooms. She cooked rice in a pot, slung over a

mean fire of pine cones. And she had around forty francs in the world. But everything was wonderful! Around the walls were cardboard boxes – once used for bananas and oranges – got from the *Intermarché* and tied up with string. Sophie was packed and waiting.

I wondered about the boxes. Where was Shaun?

She told me he'd flown home to New Zealand. Sophie wouldn't say why but I had the idea he'd jumped ship. But everything was wonderful! She was infused with the joy that makes martyrs so difficult to deal with. At last, people were beginning to recognize the treasure in their midst. There were frequent gifts. Neighbours chipped in with carrots and green vegetables, lifts to town, jam.

Best of all – her Angel was near. Her time close. And not just any old seraphim, she was getting top wing. It had been 'seen' on the news. Sophie Magdalena talked of her visions as if they were TV game shows, and she'd won all the prizes. She was packed and ready. Golly! when I'd knocked she'd thought, 'He's here!'

She'd had an exciting revelation. She was, said Sophie 'to unite' with the Angel messenger! She fluttered her sticky lashes. The lucky Angel knew nothing about this. Yet. He was working in a position of 'great importance', in America. But it was useless to resist; destiny propelled him into union with the Godhead. Destiny – and a good career move. Angels, she explained, stood lower in the beatific scheme than Ascended Masters; her conjunction with the Angel was doing him a favour – in fact, it meant she was marrying beneath her.

Of course there was no question of a sexual bond – it was to be a '*mariage blanc*'.

She gave her radiant, short-sighted smile and offered me some of my cherries.

* * *

The Mayor sent in the gendarmes, it was an admission of failure but he was past caring. The affair of the missing sacristy was getting to him. The gendarmes knocked and Sophie appeared with her 'Are you the Angel?' look and asked if they had come to take her away? This embarrassed the police – and they left.

A few days before Christmas, I drove out to the cottage on an impulse.

I saw her long before she saw me. The rain and cloud were thick on the track that goes winding out of the wooded valley and up the hill to the main road. Sophie was struggling along under a red brolly.

She blinked when I pulled up: closed one eye, focused – and climbed in.

'This is my second miracle today.'

She had been walking to the village shop in Cuxac-Cabardés for beans and salt. Cuxac was ten miles away – and it would have taken most of the day. Now that she was in the car she changed her mind: she'd rather go to the *Intermarché*, twenty miles away: beans were cheaper there.

I thought, as I swung the car towards Carcassonne and the supermarket, that it's clever of the Great Mother, to run the Cosmos and yet to know, somehow, where beans are on special.

I asked if she needed some money. Sophie thought it over and then accepted graciously. As we drove she told me how fine things were and how lucky she was; her well-being made her laugh breathlessly, shake her head at her good fortune; and the news was spreading; her presence on earth had begun to be appreciated.

'An Ascended Master', said Sophie Magdalena, 'is like the propeller on a plane; you can't see it turning, but it's there driving the machine forward. Just as I am drawing the world towards the light.'

Her first miracle had been the message that morning while meditating – the Angel was on his way!

At the *Intermarché* of the *Three Musketeers* Sophie bought beans, sugar, bread; 'Just enough to tide me over before *he* comes.'

I had never seen her so thin. She had just completed a forty-day fast in preparation for her angelic lover's arrival. In fact, my sudden appearance had made her think, just for a moment – her one good blue eye rested on me with faint disappointment – that her bridegroom had arrived to carry her off.

Where to?, I asked.

She looked at me, radiant, blue-eyed, half blind.

What she told me next made me want to weep.

God is a patriot but She is also just a girl at heart: true miracles are American; they are practical, sexy, desirable, affordable. Where is heaven? Heaven is in California; heaven is a place where you take the miraculous for granted: where divinity comes in doses.

Sophie's miracles were as follows: her stretch marks (Shaun had been a large baby) would melt away, her wrinkles vanish; her breasts revive: she would throw away her contact lenses and become so divinely lovely she'd be mobbed by admirers, in an adoring world.

All this she told me, with her supermarket bag on her lap, and her round plump red brolly slowly dripping a pool of water on the car floor, and rain beating out of a slate-grey sky.

We got back to the cottage and the cold hit me. Sophie seemed relieved when I said I wouldn't stay. The Angel might arrive at any moment.

I'm afraid I lied to the Deity then: I told Sophie that Shaun had asked for one of my books. Would she give me his phone number and his address in New Zealand?

Sophie wrote it out for me. Then she thanked me for being her second miracle of the day and said that in a previous life I had almost certainly been an important American.

I wondered whom she had in mind.

'George Washington,' said Sophie generously, in the way someone who has just hit the jackpot might say, 'Hell, this is my lucky day – take a thousand for yourself!'

Then she smiled brilliantly, squared off her crystal in the middle of her forehead, and closed the door.

Shaun in Christchurch was surprised to hear from me. I said Sophie did not know I was calling. Shaun said she knew everything.

I told him if he didn't act soon, his mother was unlikely to survive the winter. Shaun said he'd send her something, and I gave him my address. The postman had stopped delivering to Sophie ever since she took him for the Angel and made, he said, a series of embarrassing suggestions.

A week late Hervé phoned to say that he got no response to his knock, the curtains were drawn. Sophie was missing; or she might be locked in the cottage, dead. He thought it was time I went to the police.

The same day a parcel, addressed to Sophie Magdalena, arrived from Shaun. I thought it must hold cash and I felt uneasy about opening it. So I went to the police. But I took Siggie with me: he thought he could get by with the occasional bottle of cherries; but he had taken Sophie in, and moved her on – and I reckoned he was in this as deeply as I was. He was the responsible landlord.

We went to the *gendarmerie* in Cuxac-Cabardés, the town Sophie had been walking to the day I met her on the hill: and reported her missing. The *gendarmerie* is new and rather ugly and sits on the edge of a neat housing estate. A tall gendarme and a short gendarme took statements. They knew all about Sophie, they'd called at the Mayor's request to see if she had frozen to death and she had insisted on blessing them. It still rankled.

I gave them Shaun's parcel. And very gingerly they opened it. Inside was a small bottle marked: BACHS FLORAL POTION, NO 5, and Shaun had added: RESCUE REMEDY. There was nothing else. The policemen hurriedly closed the packet and handed it back to me. I think they felt I was having them on. Was this some sort of typical English joke? Wasn't it bad enough that we had produced the wandering madwoman?

'What happens if she dies?' demanded the tall policeman. 'Who cleans up afterwards?'

She was a New Zealander, said the short policeman reproachfully. Surely the Queen of England bore some responsibility?

Next day, alerted by the police, the *pompiers* broke into

Sophie's cottage. Hervé phoned to say they'd found it empty. The neighbours feared she had drowned herself in the lake. There were unconfirmed sightings that she had been seen on the road to Carcassonne. There was talk of searching the woods.

Another letter arrived from Shaun; this one I opened: it held a wad of money.

And I had no way of knowing how to get it to Sophie.

* * *

But then God works in mysterious ways. I can vouch for this – because she sent me a fax. It arrived a few days after her disappearance, and carried the letterhead of the American Consul in Rome:

Hullo Christopher,
I understand that some money was being sent to you from Shaun to help with Ascended Master Work of the Inner World Government. It is needed at the American Embassy in Rome ASAP for The Magdalene. If you feel the impulse to assist with this step – great! If not, well, it will come to us somehow.

Rome, the Eternal City. Nice one that. It distressed Siggie who thought it might have been some Catholic plot, after all. But it made me quite dizzy with admiration. I felt, yes – this is what I call a miracle! God is not dead – she's in the American consulate in the Eternal City.

When the *pompiers* broke into her cottage they found her packed boxes, her Walkman, her purse with fifteen francs, her paintings of angels, her jewellery, even her eye make-up. Sophie wasn't equipped to get to the corner shop; how did she get many hundreds of miles north, to Rome?

A clue is to be found, perhaps, in the note, added to Sophie's fax, by the American Consul.

'Ms Magdalena plans,' the consul writes, 'to stay in Italy to contact an Australian citizen she met on a train . . .'

It may explain how Sophie got herself from Kissac to Rome without passport or money or food or any sense of direction whatsoever. A miracle! She got there with the help of an Angel – an Australian Angel she'd met on a train, and not the American expected, but any angel will do in a crunch.

I parcelled up the money and sent it to Rome.

* * *

I was in two minds about Sophie. I did what one does not do about the Mistress of the Cosmos – I worried about Her. There was the essence of my flawed faith. But the truth was that I had some misgivings about Sophie's role and expectations. It seemed to me sad that God no longer expected to be maintained in a style to which I believed She was accustomed. I had a whole lot of other feelings which, had She been around, I would have passed on, in the interests of preserving the Deity.

I wasn't sorry She'd gone, I went on believing that Sophie had done something quite remarkable. I hoped the money would tide her over. Kissac had grown too small to hold Her. Rome was a fine place to be and I trusted and prayed she'd be happy there.

But I did harbour feelings the Deity will tolerate as little as She does sympathy – doubts.

If you're going to be serious about your divinity – and in a world where science or Hollywood are the other alternatives, or, worse, common sense and the dreary agnosticism of progressive politics, or the crass stupidities of the video world, Sophie's Godhead was more interesting, more plausible, and certainly a lot more fun – then you need to take pretty seriously matters of image, strategy and decorum.

Based on my experience of the Divine Presence, I reluctantly offer the following suggestions:

For a start, God should not wear blue eyeshadow.

She should not wear contact lenses, and if She must – and they are better than seeing God in glasses – then She should take care not to lose them.

She should not go out on a limb, the way Sophie did, and hole up alone in a cottage in the woods, without support. Divinity needs disciples, a team, a kind of holy family, and try though he did, Shaun was no real substitute for an extended clan of close believers.

God wants to keep a clean set of books, and to ensure that donations from believers flow into Her coffers on a regular basis. The meanest saint or American preacher understands this – how much more true for the Creator.

She does not want to depend on the Mayor of her commune for gifts of potatoes.

She does need to speak the local language. The Germans say that God lives in France, and I can confirm it – She was my neighbour in Kissac. And there are other gods, and other paradises.

God needs high standards, quality wonders, immaculate miracles.

She wants, wherever possible, to keep out of her dreams and visions, the contaminating fictions of bad American movies; and bad American magazines – God should not read women's magazines, She should be above that sort of thing – and anyway, they only give Her the wrong ideas. She is Mistress of the Universe and Master of the Inner World Government – not Madame Bovary.

All these things I might have said, given the chance. As it turned out I was not given the chance.

One morning, some two weeks after Sophie had spirited herself to Rome, I had another fax from the American Consul. It was shocking news; Sophie Magdalena was dead. She had left the sheltered accommodation where the Consul had arranged for her to stay and gone out into the streets of Rome. She had met a man, a Nigerian, selling handbags, and moved into his apartment – where she was found dead.

I began to feel I knew the story then; Sophie's expectation of the Angel had always been exceptionally tolerant – after all she was prepared to swap the American shining one, for an Australian on a train – and so, when she met the Nigerian handbag-seller, she would have simply adjusted her expectation once again. For one thing had always been consistent about Sophie, she believed that heaven has a sense of humour, and played catch as catch can with the employees and, to some extent, with the boss – and simply because she was the Omnipotent One did not remove her from heaven's habit of playing tricks on its incumbents.

Or she might have felt sure this time she really did have the Angel – because the name of the black handbag-seller was Christian.

I read the deposition Christian made to the Italian police. It seemed he was pretty well-off for a hawker of handbags, because he owned not one but two flats and offered Sophie the use of one of them. And it was there, some days later, when Christian arrived one morning to find the door locked, and eventually broke in, that Sophie was discovered dead.

A post-mortem was to be performed, but the opinion of the police was that she had died of a heart attack.

It was a strange tale. It got stranger still when someone in Rome tried to tap into Sophie's bank account, in New Zealand. This was silly: she was broke. I knew that among her miracles was the ability to extract money from a cash machine when she had no funds in her account.

It got stranger when Christian applied for New Zealand nationality with identity papers Sophie had given him.

Another thing disturbed me; and it still does. Sophie died a few days after I had published in a British newspaper an account of her life and works, her months as my neighbour and her life in the cottage in the woods – up until the day she suddenly disappeared. I stated my belief that, wherever She was, God was not dead. I felt terrible to be proved wrong.

I sometimes wonder if she had read the piece, written as it was with a certain steely awe. But then I know it's unlikely. I never saw Sophie read anything – except the small esoteric texts of Ascended Masters, which she bought from America for large amounts of money – much to Siggie's distress.

And Siggie? He couldn't believe it. Though he was nicely disrespectful, as usual, about Sophie's passing.

He said – ever practical, 'Marie-Jo and Hervé can forget about collecting their rent.'

But he was cast down – we all were – the season of vipers was well advanced.

CHAPTER 23

———————

THE WEEK AFTER Sophie disappeared, Siggie lost all his clocks and Hercule, the hunchback, went to Israel in search of his Jewish relatives.

Both events were connected in curious ways – both had a peculiar effect on Siggie and had repercussions that have always intrigued me. On paper, at least, he was almost more upset about Hercule's Israeli adventure than the loss of his clocks. He'd always thought his friend's physical disabilities, and his fatal sense of timing, were enough trouble for anyone to handle; tracking down Jewish relations seemed to Siggie the height of folly.

'Maybe he thinks because his brother's a communist he has to be something, too?'

Siggie was almost as much discomforted by the sheer distance Hercule travelled for this folly. A man who had never left the Black Mountains went all the way to Jerusalem! I got the feeling that, for him, there was something of a personal slight in this large movement into the world. Siggie condemned it so violently because it threw into sharp relief his own deeply conservative travelling patterns.

Regular, predictable. I could draw you a map: the villages of the Black Mountains, Albi, Mazamet, Castres and

Carcassonne, and all the *brocanteurs* in between, each Wednesday; on the first Monday of each month, the big dealers' fair, the *déballage* in Beziers; on Sunday mornings the Café du Sport, in Olonzac, for a couple of glasses of dry white wine. The rest of his trips were lightning raids on the houses and cellars of the deceased, or on demolition sites found for him by his scout. None ever took him further from home than a couple of hours; and he was always home by lunchtime, when, again, iron routine required radishes, red wine, lunch, a siesta on the scarlet chaise-longue, a few hours in the clock workshop; and then it was sundowner time, the carafe of red wine, supper of bread and cheese, and the nightly game of billiards.

And so he felt Hercule had shown him up.

When Hercule came back from Israel, and told us that he hadn't found a trace of a single relative, and people were 'aggressive', Siggie could not have been more pleased.

'*What* Jewish relatives? Even if you find them – what will you do with them? And anyway – Jews and Arabs, they're all Semitic. But they hate each other. You don't want to get involved in religion.'

*   *   *

Then his clocks were stolen.

He had been in the hills, picking mushrooms, when burglars had broken into his cellar and taken every clock hanging on the walls around the billiard table. Maybe the thieves had been disturbed, or simply in a rush, because they left behind the pendulums, leaning against the walls like the cast-off limbs of one-legged men, wearing the discarded hats.

They had also broken into the solid steel safe which once belonged to the Duke of Wellington and stood beside the dark red silk chaise longue, where the King took his afternoon siestas.

Siggie's reaction was remarkable. He had no insurance, of course, and he refused to go to the police because he never dealt with men in uniform or officials of any sort. He blamed gypsies for the theft, and for days after the robbery he would jump into his car each time a suspicious vehicle passed his front door, and follow it into the mountains, memorizing the number.

He had discovered tyre tracks in the soft soil, across the road from his front door, and felt sure they were left by the thieves. He made a plaster-of-Paris cast of the tyres and kept it on the table, beside the naked torso of the teenager, the Wolfgang donation – and he would show the cast to guests from time to time, and reel off the car numbers he'd memorized.

But neither car tracks nor registration numbers were really anything to be taken seriously, because Siggie also believed that the gypsies who had stolen his clocks were in the pay of the Mafia, which was controlled from Rome, by the Catholic Church, and the Pope.

'Even as we speak, my clocks are chiming in the Vatican apartments of some Cardinal!'

Those clocks, like Hercule, had strayed too far; they'd travelled, and travel was trouble.

He had other clocks, but his cherished night-time collection was gone, and he began to think of protecting what remained. He changed his attitude to the Mayor; he started peace talks.

He approached M. Angelo with a suggestion: 'How would it be if I put my clocks on display, in the Priory? Give me a room and I'll make your clock museum. If you'll insure my clocks, I'll loan them to the *Mairie* for five years.'

M. Angelo needed allies, and, above all, he needed a useful diversion – under fire for 'losing' the sacristy; he'd ordered it to be put back but that would take time. The Clock Museum would be very welcome.

* * *

Humph-Humph, the print dealer, helped Siggie to set up, and equip, the new Clock Museum, to transport the old station clocks, chronometers, exquisite little carriage clocks, the great groaning naked mechanical clangers once used in church spires, and grandfather clocks which had waited for years in Siggie's barn.

Humph-Humph had been a colonial administrator in West Africa, where his nickname was suggested by the sounds he made, according to the old Africa hands, in the grip of passion. He had spiky black hair and the look of an amiable hedgehog. His special field was the works of Daumier but his own taste was for Steinlen's soldiers, cats and kids, and especially propaganda posters of the First World War; honest mustachioed warriors for France; machine-gun nests, trenches and barbed wire.

Humph-Humph brought his father along every day and while they worked he stood the old man in a corner, rather like a grandfather clock. The old man never protested though sometimes he fell asleep on his feet and snored gently.

'I love my father,' Humph told Siggie, 'but he has kept me from women. Because of him, I never married . . .'

On the other hand, his reputation as a lover was legendary, but, as so often with legendary exploits, very hard to square with the man himself. Anyway women, or the lack of them, were a problem – and his old dad.

On the day of the *déballage* in Beziers, Humph left the old chap at home. Maybe he got careless, maybe he simply tired of having his dad in the corner – who knows. But it cost him dearly.

Humph didn't show up at the museum for a week. When he came back he didn't offer any apologies, he was still hopping mad. On the only day he'd left his dad at home, the old boy had pulled the ultimate fast one.

'He waited till my back was turned. Then he went ahead and dropped dead.'

Humph accepted a glass of *pastis*. Seven days had passed since he got home to find Papa had 'passed the casserole', and he was still very upset. Just how upset became clear when he offered Siggie two dozen oak cupboard doors.

It was a significant gesture. At the *déballage*, he spotted this job-lot. Doors, customarily, he didn't do. But Siggie did. At a guess – *à vue de nez* – he reckoned they'd fetch two to three times the price he'd paid. Siggie could have them at cost.

Siggie appreciated the offer. He saw how desolate Humph was.

'Eighty-five, your papa,' the King of the Clocks nodded approvingly, 'and still sinking his litre of wine every day.'

To show further solidarity he told Humph about his great good news from the clock robbery. The gypsies had broken into his safe – but if they thought they would find money they were mistaken. The safe was empty but for a black and white photograph of an orang-utan, lifting two derisory fingers.

Siggie handed the photograph to Humph-Humph with a bark of laughter.

He knew how Humph felt. He too was bereaved. The clocks were almost certainly on their way to Rome by now. And he tried to amuse his friend with a fine impersonation of the robbers – when they first saw the semi-naked jazz trio on the podium; they'd even stolen his posters of the young Ronald Reagan.

Humph-Humph was too caught up in his own loss to care about Siggie's Roman theories. The ruin his dad had made of his love life! He'd never liked a woman in the house. What sort of life was it – with his venerable guardian angel forever insulting any female he brought home?

Now he was left alone.

Siggie said he would always remember the colour of the old man's nose. A lovely purple, said Siggie, touching his own broad Prussian nose with a respectful finger. Magnificent. Like a pope's.

To help him over his grief, the King offered to let Humph look at the antique stereoscope he'd found at Loud Lilly's. Built of polished cherrywood, made in Lille in 1910, it came complete with a thousand glass slides of women reclining on leopard-skin rugs, wearing only Egyptian head-dresses, being tickled with ostrich feathers. In 3D.

But Humph's mood would not lift. He sat back fingering what Siggie at first took to be a stopwatch, strung by a leather thong around his neck. Every so often the little machine emitted a sharp high ping.

Now the King could identify any timepiece in moments but he had never seen anything like this. Yet its ring reminded him of something. He did not feel he could ask straight out; it smacked of business and to show how well he understood Humph's loss, and his kindness in offering him the cupboard doors, he turned the conversation to the trade in human bones.

A whole new possibility had opened up, as it were, in his own backyard. He was trying to work an angle and Humph was best at angles. Would he take a look?

They walked up along the Avenue de la Montagne Noire and turned up rue des Corps Saints that climbed the hill behind the village. It was about 6 in the evening with few people about. In a quiet street redolent with apples because a greengrocer stored his fruit there, they came upon a couple of large mechanical diggers which earlier that day had been gouging out the earth in the field above the village florist shop.

The machines had cut a bank about two metres high. Protruding from the bank were human bones. Fingers and knee-bones.

'So little time we have,' said the King of the Clocks. 'Then this. Even then, they pile the next lot on top of us.'

But Humph was still smarting about his dad.

'I told him I'd be back at the usual time from the *déballage* in Beziers. I bought some very pretty terracotta. But he wouldn't wait. He ate the lunch *I left* him, mind you. Then he died. And left *me* to do the washing up.'

The instrument around his neck chimed again and

Siggie knew suddenly what he was reminded of; it was like the ping of a microwave at the end of its cooking cycle. Humph-Humph instinctively stroked it, as one might a St Christopher medal or some devotional scapular. It seemed to give him comfort.

Siggie pointed out several pear-shaped indentations in the soft sand walls the diggers had cut. Every day another skull went missing. Somebody had an eye for a windfall. These things were going begging and the waste was scandalous. It was a perfect opportunity, for the right man.

Now here was his problem. There were dealers, discotheques, phrenologists, surgeons – who paid top dollar for human bones. The market at La Grande Ronde, in Toulouse, had a couple of traders in skeletons. Anywhere else and he'd have helped himself.

'But I live here.'

'I get your point,' said Humph-Humph.

His neighbours were very likely related to these bones, and it would not look good if Siggie turned up with his mushrooming knife and a plastic bag from the *supermarché*.

He had tried to persuade Ria to let him make a midnight raid. After all, what good did it do to let the stuff go to waste?

'The neighbours are taking them. Why shouldn't I?'

But she had laughed in his face and threatened that if he brought so much as a single human bone into her house she would leave him immediately. And report the matter to the *mairie*.

Ria always recalled, rather bitterly, that when her parents died in Holland Siggie had objected to the funeral costs in Amsterdam. Why could she not bring them down to Kissac? A friend, dealing in lead pipes and eighteenth-century nails, sent a truck down to Languedoc weekly; he'd take her parents as a part-load, and they could be buried in the garden – for nothing. They had a big garden.

'I never talk to him about burials,' said Ria. 'He is a monster-child. My Mammi and Pappi – next to our swimming pool!'

'Whole skulls are there for the taking,' said Siggie.

Siggie and Humph-Humph sat side by side in the jaws of the yellow mechanical digger, trailing their feet in the soil of the new parking lot. Humph toyed with a femur. Siggie scuffed with his toe at a bleached knee-bone. He couldn't touch the bones, but he grieved at the waste. Perhaps Humph might like to pass by some night?

He'd had his old man cremated, said Humph bitterly. But the guys who ran the ovens were all crooks. He'd removed his father's gold teeth.

Siggie was impressed. He had heard how they ripped off people at the crematorium.

'Then I thought – I may as well do the pacemaker, too.'

Of course, that was what it was! Siggie knew now what Humph wore on the thong around his neck. But he had to ask himself how Humph had liberated the machine? And the answer confronting him was so radical, he couldn't say anything and waggled his head and opened and closed his bright eyes rapidly to show Humph he was speechless with admiration.

There was a further reason for his silence: honour among dealers. You might ask *where* a man had come by an object; but you never asked *how* he had done so.

Later, talking to Ria about it, he used the pacemaker to swing a point. If she thought a visit to the bones in the parking lot at midnight was bad – imagine what it took to compete with Humph-Humph?

Ria told him the idea of competing was the most disgusting thing she had heard and only someone who had spent his life in the slums of Kalingrad would think of it.

Then she wondered exactly what Humph really sounded like. And Siggie turned on the microwave and they listened to the ping at the end of the cycle, and Ria shrieked softly to think of Humph going round the place ringing like that.

Siggie and Humph finished the Clock Museum, and they made a beautiful room, full of shining faces, early chronometers, clocks in gilded cases; exquisite balletic workings under glass bells, chiming bells, movable moons and suns, cuckoos – a time-factory spanning some 200 years.

And the Mayor, good as his word, insured the clocks, fixed an efficient burglar alarm system on the outside wall, and offered Siggie free tickets, whenever friends wished to inspect the museum. The security precautions were impressive and as Siggie said 'for nothing'; a stout door and coded lock and heavy insurance. Presumably the Vatican would respect the sanctity of the Abbey. There was even staff – a superior young woman who drove a glistening Cabriolet and showed tourists the clock room.

* * *

The raid on his clocks, the war of religion, the gathering clouds over Kissac, the curious signs and symptoms of unease, all added to the feeling that, as Siggie said about my house, 'it got darker, as you went lower.'

So they float before me, ghosts and lovers and villains. Tomàs vanished after his last bout of pickle-making. I didn't see him for months. But early one morning Tomàs stood in the street outside my door.

'Were have you been, Tomàs?'

'Inside.'

'What, all winter?'

'All winter.'

He was white as a tuber, and his undyed hair was smooth and soft and shapeless, the grey-white colour of last night's ash. Even his tattooed ladies lacked that tensile, pneumatic quality I'd come to associate with them.

* * *

And Lizzie from Lézignan?

Catastrophe. It has been, she says, the strengthening pound. This has resulted in the growing confidence of the British abroad. It has been so bad for Lizzie; she's actually made more money from her paintings than from the big oak bed, the fox-hunting scenes and the Horlicks.

If this goes on she may have to contemplate the very worst fate of all, she may have to leave France and Go Home.

Perhaps, she wondered aloud, she might apply for some kind of grant? In Britain? Perhaps the National Lottery would give her a grant?

I said it was a wonderful idea.

* * *

And Madame de la Pipe?

Soon after Pascal's father failed to kill himself, for the last time, his wife was driving into Carcassonne and saw Madame plying her trade by the canal. Thinking this was some poor woman walking home, she stopped, rolled down her window, and called to her.

Madame de la Pipe came running, but when she got a bit closer and saw it was a woman in the car she shook her head and uttered the immortal words:

'I'm sorry, madame. But I do it with men . . . only.'

* * *

And Gretel? Shapely and languorous she mooned about; she would not lift a finger to help her mother pick the cherries or cook or clean the house. Love made her inert; she did nothing – she went to the Lapin Fou and gazed into the face of her lover.

When Pascal was posted to Martinique, Gretel asked if she could go with him, and finish her exams overseas.

Ria refused; Gretel was still in school, she was too young; but Siggie wouldn't take sides and Gretel got her way.

'It's her own fault,' Ria told Siggie.

'No. It's our fault – for letting her do it,' he said.

Siggie was left with Plusbelle. She was drinking heavily now and if you didn't offer her something she tended to butt you; Ria's visitors who rented the apartments complained she was gatecrashing their barbecues in the garden. She was a boor as well as a drunk.

Ria began muttering about the horse butcher. Gretel had got them into this – and now she'd swanned off to a place in the sun, leaving them to cope with Plusbelle.

Siggie moved her to a patch of land by the bend in the river where the road into the Black Mountains leaves the village and climbs for Citou, where the sweet onions are best. A picnic spot when the sun shines. Plusbelle has been put out to grass.

Gretel writes to her mother that she is coming to terms with Martinique. She doesn't do much washing of clothes; but they have help in the house. She can't cook very well. But she is studying for her 'bac'. She and Pascal are happy, and it is very warm, all the time. She never asks about the donkey.

On some nights, Plusbelle lifts her head to the hills and brays in her melancholy fashion. For those who loved her are elsewhere.

The village knows that patch of fields down by the river, where Plusbelle cries. The Colonel used to drag his wife there after dark, too far away from the houses for anyone to hear her cries as he systematically beat her.

Cries in the dark, cries of love or pain.

Sometimes one can't tell the difference.

* * *

Humph-Humph hadn't yet finished with his father.

One day when Siggie called he found Humph-Humph rather slow to answer his knock. And when he did so, he looked very sheepish and Siggie saw, reflected in the gilt mirror behind Humph, a girl, hiding, and from the shape of her silhouette he saw she was pregnant.

'I got married,' said Humph. 'That's why I haven't been around.'

He and the woman had been playing hide-and-seek,

said the King, and did not invite him in. He was astonished, he told Ria. After all, Humph's place with its shelves of posters and forests of rolled prints and the accumulated junk which he and his dad had assembled over decades made ideal hiding places. But the girl was too big in the belly to conceal herself easily and Humph had been wearing his pacemaker around his neck which meant that every so often, no matter how well he was hidden, the pacemaker tinkled. What was the point of hiding if you wanted to be found?

'*Au contraire*,' said Ria, 'what's the point of hiding – if you *don't* want to be found. They make love, Siggie,' she explained patiently, 'because it's better than death. Sometimes we love those who die.'

'Or hate,' said Siggie.

Then the council workmen laid tarmac on the new parking lot and the bones beneath were buried for good.

* * *

When Siggie packed Plusbelle off to the river, and his clocks off to the museum; and Gretel went to Martinique, and Sophie went to Rome and Lizzie fell on hard times, Hercule decided he was going to China. Research suggested his family might have been Jewish merchants in Hong Kong.

Siggie, whose field of exploration was so circumscribed, astounded me when he decided to go along.

'I can't let Hercule go alone.'

And he went; on the Trans-Siberian Express: ten days on a train from Russia to China, and all the way they drank beer and played cards.

'Chinese people,' said Siggie, 'were shocked when Hercule asked them, "Are there any synagogues?" '

Hercule found no Jewish relatives, but he did meet a giant, in the market in Beijing.

'Hercule photographed this huge porter. The guy lifted Hercule off his feet, in one hand. And I really thought he'd kill him. I said, "Give him your camera." And Hercule did – and the man crushed it in his other hand, so that was OK.'

They had a good time. He began saying to me, 'Christopher, you don't travel enough. Come with me next time, I'll show you around.'

I could see why he liked China – the stories were there. Once upon a time, in China, a hunchback and the handsome woodcutter's son went to market where they met a giant . . .'

It was the French form.

* * *

I also have to record that the Clock Museum failed.

The museum was barely ready when the King resigned from his own creation and now never goes near the place. He paid a price for dealing in the adult world, where Rumpelstiltskin is a junk-bond dealer; the woodcutter's idiot son never gets the princess, and everyone over four foot is a killjoy. The Mayor reneged on a promise of free tickets; and the King was damned if he'd pay to see his own clocks.

He pretends now he doesn't care but clearly the injustice stings. The grown-ups have no idea how to treat his toys. They neither play with them nor show them off decently.

When he learnt that the sniffy mademoiselle in the fancy Cabriolet had cut visiting time in the clock chamber to three minutes he was furious. Then, just as suddenly, he was philosophical. After all, what does one expect from *les fonctionnaires?*

So he has reverted to older, surer methods. He has replaced his lost clocks with a new collection, twice as good. But this time he has housed them in the attic. The pale-faced referees of his nightly billiards are back, sporting silk toppers and straw boaters. The old company hangs, unchanged, above his table among film posters of the young Ronald Reagan and Simone Signoret.

Between the clocks he has hung crucifixes of all shapes and sizes; from graves and churches; mother-of-pearl, ivory, silver and ebony, brass and stone. It's cheaper than insurance – he buys them in job lots from Loud Lilly's Emporium of Junk – as effective as garlic against vampires, or silver bullets against werewolves. If ever the Vatican sends in the gypsies again, the King will be ready.

He must have made at least one visit to the parking lot, because a skull wearing an English bobby's helmet appeared above the billiard table, along with pendulum sentries who watched his nightly games in his new billiard room.

* * *

The King came over to my place, towards sunset, and we sat on the terrace, with its swimming-pool tiles which Tomàs swore came from the old chapel, in Citou, and Siggie swore came from his cellar floor – I prefer Tomàs's version. Ahead of us ran the humped dark Corbières, a smoky smudge below the higher white cloudiness of the Pyrenees. In the evening light they turn blue-black and lie like sleeping whales. From the market gardens below the old fortified wall, where my house sat, high above the municipal wash-house, floated the Neapolitan voices of the Italians among the tomato frames of the gardens.

It came down to happiness; a feeling of being somewhere entirely foreign but not alien at all; the best sort of home, filled with magical strangers with stories to tell. Not so much a country but an affair of the heart. Filled with the French form.

I thought about Siggie's words: 'it got darker as you went lower' – and not just in my house. And there were serpents in paradise; even so, the blood worked in the veins. Everywhere there was a rough and magic life; desperate, at times, certainly not nice and, at least – not since the Northern forces, in the Croisade des Albigois, annihilated the Cathars, the culture and even the tongue of this country, Langue d'Oc – never refined. A place of gods and ghosts.

The old medieval cemetery is under the tarmac of the parking lot; the 'new' graveyard, beyond the station-yard where the Circus of Dreams pitches its little top, is very full and places must be booked. Even then, stays are of limited duration. I'd be happy to rent space – to have my bones mingle with those of the people of Kissac – if I could be sure Siggie would not be along, itching to get his hands on the funerary furnishings, with an eye to the traders in bones, at La Grande Ronde in Toulouse.

We drank red wine on the terrace as the light faded and the bells in the Priory chimed; ten minutes late – they always were. Siggie had quite recovered from his loss. He had cast a spell and changed his fortunes.

Wasn't he worried, I wondered, about another raid?

He wasn't. His crucifixes were ready to repel burglars. His bony English Bobby was watching. Besides, gypsies were great respectors of death. With insurance like that, if the thieves ever came back to the scene of the crime, he would be ready for them.

He was suddenly very cheerful; he always was when he'd snatched a prize from the grave. He even began celebrating a very good year for business: good customers had taken all his clocks – even if, unfortunately, they'd forgotten to send a cheque.